UNIONS AND RIGHT·TO·WORK LAWS

the global evidence of their impact on employment

UNIONS AND RIGHT·TO·WORK LAWS

the global evidence of their impact on employment

edited by FAZIL MIHLAR

Copyright © 1997 by The Fraser Institute. All rights reserved. No part of this book may be reproduced in any manner whatsoever without written permission except in the case of brief quotations embodied in critical articles and reviews.

The authors of this book have worked independently and opinions expressed by them are, therefore, their own, and do not necessarily reflect the opinions of the members or the trustees of The Fraser Institute.

Printed in Canada.

Canadian Cataloguing in Publication Data

Main entry under title:
Unions and right-to-work laws

   Includes bibliographical references.
   ISBN 0-88975-179-X

   1. Open and closed shop--Law and legislation.   2. Right to labor.   3. Union security--Law and legislation.   I. Mihlar, Fazil, 1966- II. Fraser Institute (Vancouver, B.C.)

HD4903.U54 1997   344.01'8892   C97-910687-7

Contents

*Foreword: Closed-Shop Provisions Violate the
Charters of Rights and Freedoms*
Roger J. Bedard   xv

Introduction
Fazil Mihlar and Michael Walker   1

Canada's Labour Laws: An Overview
Dennis R. Maki   19

*Unionization and Economic Performance: Evidence on
Productivity, Profits, Investment, and Growth*
Barry T. Hirsch   35

Right-to-Work Laws: Evidence from the United States
James T. Bennett   71

*Economic Development and the Right to Work: Evidence
from Idaho and other Right-to-Work States*
David Kendrick   91

*The Process of Labour Market Reform
in the United Kingdom*
John T. Addison and W. Stanley Siebert   105

*Economic Impact of Labour Reform: Evidence from
the United Kingdom*
Charles Hanson   137

*Free to Work: The Liberalization of New Zealand's
Labour Markets*
Wolfgang Kasper   149

Critique of Alberta's Right-to-Work Study
Fazil Mihlar   215

About the Authors

JOHN T. ADDISON is currently the John M. Olin Visiting Professor of Labor Economics and Public Policy at the Center for the Study of American Business at Washington University in St. Louis, and professor of Economics at the University of South Carolina. He was educated at the London School of Economics and Political Science (B.Sc., M.Sc., Ph.D.). A labour economist, Addison has published widely in the major economics and specialist labor journals, including the *American Economic Review, Economic Journal, Review of Economics and Statistics, Journal of Labor Economics,* and *Industrial and Labor Relations Review*. He is the author of a number of labor texts and co-editor with W. S. Siebert of *Labor Markets in Europe: Issues of Harmonization and Regulation* (The Dryden Press/Harcourt Brace, 1997). He is the co-author with John Burton of the Fraser Institute monograph *Trade Unions and Society: Some Lessons of the British Experience* (1984). Professor Addison's current research interests include labor market re-regulation in Europe under the social charter/chapter initiatives, formal analysis of employment mandates, unemployment duration, and the effects of German works councils on firm performance.

JAMES T. BENNETT is an Eminent Scholar at George Mason University in Fairfax, Virginia and holds the William P. Snavely Chair of Political Economy and Public Policy in the Department of Economics. He is also an adjunct scholar at the Heritage Foundation and a member of the Mont Pelerin Society and the Philadelphia Society. He received his Ph.D. from Case Western Reserve University in 1970, specializing in research related to public policy issues, the economics of government and bureaucracy, labour unions and health charities. He is the founder and editor of the Journal of Labour Research and has published more than 60 articles in professional journals such as the American Economic Review, Review of Economics and Statistics, Policy

Review, *Public Choice,* and *Cato Journal.* His books include *The Political Economy of Federal Government Growth* (1980), *Better Government at Half the Price* (1981), *Deregulating Labour Relations* (1981), *Underground Government: The Off-Budget Public Sector* (1983), *Destroying Democracy: How Government Funds Partisan Politics* (1986), *Unfair Competition: The Profits of Nonprofits* (1988), *Health Research Charities: Image and Reality* (1990), *Health Research Charities II: The Politics of Fear* (1991), *Official Lies: How Western Media Misleads Us* (1992), and *Unhealthy Charities: Hazardous to Your Health and Wealth* (1994).

ROGER J. BEDARD is a solicitor and president of Bedard & Associates, a legal firm specializing in employee relations. Mr. Bedard has helped over 400 companies build positive relations, mostly in union-free environments. He has represented employers in hundreds of cases before various labour courts. Over the past twenty years, he has published a dozen books on the practice of constructive labour relations.

CHARLES HANSON was lecturer and senior lecturer in the department of Economics at the University of Newcastle upon Tyne, U.K., and remains associated with the Department. As well as books on closed-shops and profit sharing, he has written *Taming the Trade Unions* published by Macmillan/Adam Smith Institute. He has also published numerous articles and papers on trade unions, workings of the labour market and management. Dr. Hanson's work has been published by the Institute for Economic Affairs, the Adam Smith Institute and the Cato Institute. He was an employment advisor to the Institute of Directors from 1983 to 1996 and, as such, contributed to the United Kingdom's program of labour market reforms during the 1980s.

BARRY HIRSCH received his Ph.D. in 1977 from the University of Virginia and is now professor of Economics at the Florida State University. His research has focused on the determination of wages and employment in labour markets and on the role of labour unions. He is author of *Labor Unions and the Economic Performance of Firms,* co-author with John Addison of *The Economic Analysis of Unions: New Approaches and Evidence,* and co-author with David Macpherson of an annual source book, *Union Membership and Earnings Data Book: Compilation from the Current Popu-*

lation Survey, published by the Bureau of National Affairs. Professor Hirsch also publishes regularly in leading journals dealing with labour economics and industrial relations. Recent work includes the study of wages and unions in regulated and deregulated markets (airlines, trucking, and the postal service); unions and the effects upon incentive from workers' compensation; unions and the distribution of wages and skills; and the determination of wages in health care labour markets. Professor Hirsch serves on the editorial boards of Industrial Relations, the Journal of Labor Research, and the Southern Economic Journal.

WOLFGANG KASPER is professor of Economics at the School of Economics and Management, Australian Defence Force Academy, University of New South Wales, in Canberra, Australia. After studies in Germany and elsewhere in Europe, he earned a Ph.D. at The Kiel Institute of World Economics. He also worked for the German Council of Economic Advisors, The Kiel Institute, The Harvard Development Advisory Service (at the Malaysian Treasury), the Australian National University, the Reserve Bank of Australia and Organisation of Economic Cooperation and Development. A frequent visitor to New Zealand, he wrote a study arguing for freer immigration into New Zealand. His research interest cover economic prosperity, liberalization, international trade, factor flows and institutional economics. He is a member of the Mont Pèlerin Society and serves on the advisory councils of the Centre for Independent Studies (an Australian-New Zealand free-market think tank), and Melbourne University's Institute for Applied Economic and Social Research.

DAVID KENDRICK is the program director for the National Institute for Labour Relations Research (NILRB), based in Springfield, Virginia. The NILRB is a non-profit organization which supports research of the various social and economic inequities of compulsory unionism. Mr. Kendrick has served as legal information director for the National Right to Work Legal Defense Foundation. In this capacity, he communicated to American workers that, due to the United States Supreme Court's Beck decision, they could not be forced to pay union dues for union political activities with which they disagreed. As well, he has worked as the editor of Religious Freedom Alert, an organization committed to exposing government violations of religious freedom at federal, state, and county levels. He is a 1983 graduate of Wofford College in Spartanburg, South Carolina with a B.A. in English.

DENNIS R. MAKI is a professor in the department of Economics at Simon Fraser University. He completed his undergraduate studies at the University of Minnesota in 1964, received a Ph.D. in economics from Iowa State University in 1967, and joined Simon Fraser University in 1967. In addition to his teaching, he worked for the Economic Council of Canada in 1970. Professor Maki's research interests are primarily in the area of labour economics with specific emphasis in recent years on the macroeconomic effects of trade unions. Most of his research deals with the empirical testing of theoretical models. His publications include papers on the effects of unemployment insurance on reported unemployment rates, the costs of strikes and the effects of variations in these costs on observed strike activity, the effect of labour unions on productivity and profitability. He has also published on such disparate topics as agriculture in Pakistan and immigration policy in Canada.

FAZIL MIHLAR is a senior policy analyst at The Fraser Institute and coordinator of the Institute's Centre for Economy in Government and the Survey of Senior Investment Managers in Canada. He received a B.A. in Economics from Simon Fraser University, and an M.A. in Public Administration from Carleton University. He also received a Diploma in Marketing from the Chartered Institute of Marketing in London, England. He is the author of several reports on the economic performance of provincial and federal governments, and has written on a number of subjects including labour market policy and regulation policy. His columns have appeared in various newspapers including *The Globe and Mail*, *The Financial Post* and *The Vancouver Sun*. Before joining the Institute, Mr. Mihlar worked at the Small Business Consulting Group at Simon Fraser University as a Business Consultant.

W. STANLEY SIEBERT is professor of Labour Economics at the University of Birmingham. He received his B.A. from the University of Cape Town and his M.Sc. and Ph.D. from the University of London. He is co-author with Sol Polachek of *The Economics of Earnings* (Cambridge University Press, 1993) and co-editor with John Addison of *Labor Markets in Europe: Issues of Harmonization and Regulation* (The Dryden Press/Harcourt Brace, 1997). His current research uses personnel records from the United Kingdom and continental European firms to investigate the hypothesis that labour market mandates reduce the job opportunities of unskilled workers.

MICHAEL WALKER is the executive director of The Fraser Institute. Born in Newfoundland in 1945, he received his B.A. (summa) from St. Francis Xavier University in 1966 and completed the work for his Ph.D. in Economics at the University of Western Ontario in 1969. Dr. Walker writes regularly for daily newspapers and financial periodicals. His articles have also appeared in technical journals in Canada, the United States and Europe; these include *The American Economic Review*, the *Canadian Journal of Economics*, *Canadian Public Policy*, *Health Affairs*, and the *Canadian Tax Journal*. He has written or edited 40 books on economic matters.

Unions and Right-to-Work Laws
The Global Evidence of Their Impact on Employment

Foreword
Closed-Shop Provisions Violate Canadian and Provincial Charters of Rights and Freedoms

ROGER J. BEDARD

Canada and Australia are now the only two developed countries that have not yet outlawed the closed-shop and mandatory union dues. Every province in Canada has laws that authorize closed-shop unions and/or mandatory union dues and, under all provincial labour codes, exclusive representation means that workers are not free to decide as individuals whether or not to be represented by a union; nor can competing unions offer representative services to minorities.

In this Foreword, I shall first describe briefly the 17 interrelated cases that we are currently arguing before the Superior Court, Hull Division. We are contending that the "freedom of association" of section 2(d) of our Charter of Rights and Freedoms includes the freedom not to be forced to join a union, and that the practice of private union "taxers" of collecting mandatory union dues are a violation of the rights of Canadian citizens. Second, I shall describe the way in which 101 countries around the world have outlawed closed-shop provisions altogether through legislation, court decisions, or international agreements. Finally, I shall raise a few questions about the silence of Canadian academics and journalists about the flagrant abuses of the closed-shop and of compulsory union dues.

Closed-shop and Charters of Rights and Freedoms

The Theriault and other interrelated cases

With respect to the legal aspects of closed-shop and Rand formula practices, the legal contention in the 17 cases pending before Superior Court, Hull Division, is very specific and quite straight forward. Closed-shop provisions and the Rand formula violate the rights of employees regimented in unions against their will and "taxed" privately by the unions. The cases presented argue that these practices are blatant violations of the rights guaranteed to all Canadian citizens by the federal and provincial charters of rights and freedom.

Section 2(d) of the Canadian Charter of Rights and Freedoms guarantees freedom of association as a "Fundamental Freedom." Further, the Quebec Charter of Rights and Freedom provides the following basic rights:

> Sec. 10: Every person has a right to full and equal recognition and exercise of his human rights and freedom without distinction, exclusion, or preference.

> Sec. 13: No one may in a judicial act stipulate a clause involving discrimination. Such a clause is deemed without effect.

It is important to recognize that the "freedom of association" of section 2(d) includes the freedom from compulsion to join a particular union on pain of losing one's job. It is also important to recognize that the closed-shop involves the "discrimination, distinction, exclusion, [or] preference" prohibited by the Quebec Charter of Rights and Freedom. There have been several decisions in which the Canadian courts have clearly considered the freedom of the individual more important than collective rights.

Case law around the world

The evidence from around the world also suggests that freedom of association should be construed to include the freedom not to join a union; courts of law from many countries have issued decisions to this effect.

United States   As early as 1947, the Congress of the United States adopted the Taft-Hartley Act. Section 14(b) of this Act reads:

> Nothing in this Act shall be construed as authorizing the execution or application of agreements requiring membership in labor organization as a condition of employment in any State or Territory in which such execution or application is prohibited by state or territorial Law.

The Supreme Court of the United States declared the Taft-Hartley Act constitutional in 1949, when it heard *Lincoln Federated Union v. Northwestern I and M*; and in *AFL v. American Sash Door Company*. Since the 1940s, 21 states have adopted right-to-work laws and these are still in force today. These states are now among the most prosperous in the United States and have some of the lowest rates of unemployment in the country.

Since 1949, hundreds of court decisions under the Taft-Hartley Act have confirmed that the freedom of association includes freedom from coercion to join a union and the freedom to pay or not to pay union dues, even in states that have not enacted right-to-work laws.

Great Britain   The British Parliament, when it adopted the Trade Disputes Act of 1906, included a provision for closed-shop unions. Seventy years later the closed-shop union was challenged in the famous case of Young, James, and Webster *v.* British Rail. In 1976, Young, James, and Webster, employees of British Rail, cancelled their membership in the Trades Union Congress and refused to pay union dues. They were promptly dismissed by British Rail and a court battle ensued. Five years later, in August 1981, the European Court in Strasbourg issued a judgment in which it ordered British Rail to reinstate the three claimants in their jobs and to pay them £145,000 in compensation for the damage they had suffered.

This decision was a first step towards eliminating closed-shop union provisions in Great Britain. Employment Acts adopted by the British Parliament in 1982, 1988 and 1990 gradually outlawed the provision of closed-shop and mandatory union dues in Great Britain.

Section 1 (1) of the Employment Act of 1990 states:

1 (1) It is unlawful to refuse a person employment:
  (a) because he is or is not a member of a trade union or
  (b) because he is unwilling to accept a requirement
    (i) to take steps to become or to remain or not to become a member of a trade union;
    (ii) to make payments or suffer deductions in the event of his not being a member of a trade union.

Switzerland Section 356(1)(a) of the Code of Obligations adopted in 1911 and further amended in 1956 reads:

The provisions of a collective agreement or of a private agreement that coerce employers or laborers to join an association are null and void.

Belgium The closed-shop was outlawed in Belgium by a law adopted on May 24, 1921 and still in force. It reads:

Sec. 1: The freedom of association is guaranteed. No employee will be forced to join a union nor hindered from joining a union.

France Statute No. 56-416 enacted on April 27, 1956 reads:

1. No employer shall consider the fact that a candidate is a member or is not a member of a union nor that the candidate takes part or takes no part in the union in decisions pertaining to hiring, assignment of work, social benefits, disciplinary action nor dismissal.
2. Closed-shop provisions to coerce an employer to hire or maintain in employment only union members are null and void.

Japan Neither the Labor Relations Act of Japan of 1946 nor any labour law adopted since by the Diete has authorized the closed-shop (International Labor Office 1980). The freedom to join a union is guaranteed by section 28 of the Constitution of Japan—1946 (Blaustein and Franz 1993: 15–22). Since 1946, the Japanese courts have consistently ruled that the freedom of association under section 28 includes the freedom from coercion to join a trade union.

New Zealand Section 99.1 of the Industrial Relations Act of New Zealand reads:

> 99.1 Nothing in any award or any collective agreement or in any other agreement between one or more workers and an employer or employers or a union of employers or an organization of employers shall require a person:
> (a) to become or remain a member of any union ...

Eire The sections of the Constitution adopted by Ireland in 1937 that deal with freedom of association read:

> Sec. 40.3 The State guarantees in its laws to respect and, as far as practicable, by the laws to defend and vindicate the personal right of the citizens.

> Sec. 40.6 1° The State guarantees liberty for the exercise of the following rights subject to public order and morality:
> (iii) the right of citizens to form associations and unions.

International charters

South American Convention on Human Rights This convention (also called the Pact of San Jose, Costa Rica) was signed by Mexico, the countries of Central America, South America and states in the Caribbean—30 countries overall. Section 8.3 reads:

> 8.3 No one may be compelled to belong to a trade union.

African Charter on Human and People Rights The African Charter on Human and People Rights was signed by 49 African countries in Liberia on July 20, 1979.

> Sec. 10(1): Every individual shall have the right to free association provided that he abides by the law.

> Sec. 10(2): No one may be compelled to join an association.

Defending individual freedom in Canada

Canadian institutions, including universities, the mass media and business groups have not been forward in defending the rights of workers to decide whether they will or will not join a union.

Over several hundred years, universities have been major centres for the development of sound thought and effective action.

"Knowledge is power" wrote Bacon in the sixteenth century. Indeed, in the most dynamic countries of the world, universities have been on the frontlines in defending individual freedom.

Canada has approximately 50 universities but, in the past five decades, not many of our Canadian institutions of higher learning have published meaningful books, brochures or papers about the destructive impact of the closed-shop and the Rand formula. Why have most universities in Canada been so silent about the flagrant abuses of the closed-shop and of compulsory union dues?

Canadian mass media have long been thought of as a bulwark in the defense of individual rights and freedoms for Canadians. Surprisingly, when it comes to mandatory unions, this is not the case. One does not see television programs, or hear radio programs dealing with the 4,000,000 Canadian employees who are forced into trade unions by closed-shop and Rand-formula provisions. Newspapers and magazines do not print stories about the fate of millions of Canadian employees who are privately "taxed" for hundreds of millions of dollars each year through compulsory union dues. Why has the mass media in Canada generally been silent about the infringement of the basic freedoms of individuals by closed-shop and mandatory union dues?

In most of the free-market societies of the world, employers' associations have defended the individual's right to the freedom of association. During the 1940s and 1950s, the United States Chamber of Commerce and the National Manufacturers Association of the United States were among the most active and the most persuasive supporters of the Right-to-Work. In Canada, employers' associations have indulged in the rhetoric of free market and its virtues, have accepted without protest the closed-shop and mandatory union dues. How does one explain the fact that not a single employers' association in Canada—none whatsoever—have challenged these abusive practices in Court over the past four decades?

Conclusion

We may hope that this dismal picture that I have depicted will be turned around in the not-too-distant future. There are several cases pending before the Courts, which will question the justification for the existence for closed-shop unions. We are hopeful that the courts will put individual freedoms before collective interests.

Some institutions of higher learning are reconsidering the freedom of individual Canadians in the scale of values. Canadian media like the *Financial Post* are performing again the job for which they were created—to defend the freedom of the individual. And employers' associations like the Merit Constructors Associations are also vigorously defending the concept of freedom of association.

References

Blaustein, A.P., and G.H. Flanz (1993). *Constitutions of the Countries of the World: Japan* (vol. 9). Dobbs Ferry, NY: Oceana Publications.

International Labour Office (1980). *Labour Market Information for Decision-Making: The Case of Japan.* Geneva: ILO

Introduction

FAZIL MIHLAR AND MICHAEL WALKER

The tragedy of high unemployment

Jobs, or the lack of jobs, are once again a serious item on the political agendas of the federal and provincial governments. There are 1.5 million people unemployed in Canada, about 10 percent of the workforce (Statistics Canada 1996c: 15). This translates into a significant loss of potential output and also imposes a major burden on taxpayers due to increased social welfare expenditures. Moreover, many of the unemployed have been out of work for extended periods of time, with the result that their skills depreciate, their morale drops, and they experience a variety of psychological problems (see Shackleton 1996). Of increasing concern is the stubbornly high unemployment rate (16.3 percent)[1] among Canadian youth, which can cause disaffection and alienation from the rest of society and, eventually, a plethora of social problems ranging from crime to drug abuse.[2]

While there has been increasing focus on the problem of unemployment, the solution has been elusive. Since this book deals with solutions, it will be useful first to consider more directly the economic analysis of the labour market.

Notes will be found on pages 14–15.

Economics of the labour market

In principle, the analysis of the labour market is no different from the analysis of the market for any other good or service. All things being equal, the demand for labour by employers falls as the real cost of labour rises. As the per-unit cost of labour input rises, firms will substitute relatively cheaper capital for relatively expensive labour as part of their cost minimization strategy. Meanwhile, the supply of labour rises as the after-tax rate of return to labour rises. For a given tax rate, a higher real wage means that the price of leisure has increased (i.e., if one chooses to stay at home, more income is lost), which induces households to supply more labour input. Equilibrium in the labour market can only be established when the real wage rate equalizes the demand and supply of labour (Dornbusch, Fischer and Sparks 1989: 451–85, ch. 14). As long as there are mechanisms in place that restrict the adjustment of real wages, unemployment will persist.

Given this standard understanding of how the labour market works, it is possible to analyze the effects of government intervention in the market for labour on such variables as the wage rate, the level of labour input employed, and the unemployment rate. For example, minimum wage laws, which set the wage rate above the equilibrium wage rate, will tend to create an excess supply of labour as the higher-than-market wage rate mandated by the law will increase the supply of labour. However, firms will not want to hire as many workers because it will be relatively more costly to do so. Faced with higher labour costs, firms will substitute capital for labour input and employment will fall. Meanwhile, workers who are less productive and who would have been willing to work at the market wage will be unable to find employment as the value of what they produce is below the mandated minimum wage (see, e.g., Stigler 1946; Neumark and Wascher 1995). Closed-shop union provisions that weaken the bargaining position of employers may enable unionized workers to raise the wage rate above equilibrium, inducing a fall in employment analogous to that caused by the minimum wage law (Addison and Burton 1984).

Economic theory of unemployment

Many hypotheses have been put forth to explain why the unemployment rate in Canada is persistently higher than that in the United States. Several authors have concluded that Canada's generous employment insurance system is a source of high unemployment, arguing that some workers simply choose to remain unemployed because of the incentives facing them (pay rates, employment insurance, welfare benefits, and other government regulations: see Grubel, Maki, and Sax 1975; Grubel and Walker 1978). Other authors reject the explanation (Ashenfelter and Card 1986). The overwhelming evidence gathered over the years, however, appears to indicate that the policies of the typical welfare state (e.g. [un]employment insurance, welfare, etc.) have contributed to high unemployment rates. The analysis contained in this book, however, focuses on union behaviour, high real wages, and the rigidity in the labour market as a source of the unemployment problem.

The theory of real wage unemployment emphasizes the importance of real wages and real productivity as the primary factors in determining business investment.[3] In other words, it emphasizes the importance of real wage costs and profitability as determinants of investment and employment levels. In a small open economy like that in Canada, if the increase in real wages is greater than the increase in real output per hour, profit margins will diminish. This will result in a higher number of bankruptcies, reduced investment, and higher unemployment.

The empirical evidence suggests that this theory is close to reality given that labour income is about 85 percent of net domestic income (Statistics Canada 1996a: 60). Labour costs account for about 65 percent of GDP in the Canadian manufacturing sector. In Canada, between 1978 and 1991 real wages increased at a relatively faster pace than real output in manufacturing.[4] In some cases, this phenomenon has induced firms to invest in labour-saving technologies that reduce employment growth.[5] The evidence clearly demonstrates that Canadian firms have automated their operations: between 1975 and 1991, productivity growth was dominated by capital, with a consequent increase in unemployment levels (see Galarneau and Maynard 1995). In other cases, this disequilibrium can lead to less investment in physical capital and to plant closures and higher levels of unemployment (see Daly and MacCharles 1986; Hirsch 1997).

If the goal of labour market policy is to ensure that the labour market clears and that workers are able to find employment suitable to their skills and productivity the free interaction of the demand for labour and the supply of labour is essential. It is only through such a free and undistorted labour market that employment can be created. Hence, the optimal labour market policy is one that introduces the least rigidity into the labour market (OECD 1994). In short, it is a policy that keeps the labour market as flexible as possible so that employers and employees can respond to the changes that inevitably occur as society progresses.

The impact of union behaviour on labour markets

According to contract theory, labour contracts are negotiated and settled so that wages are neither too high or too low. Employers are aware that they need to pay a wage rate that will attract the quantity and quality of personnel they need to get the highest level of profits. At the same time, employees and their union representatives know how much firms can afford to pay so as to remain competitive and adopt technologies to keep desired employment levels. At times, when these contracts have been drawn up, high-wage situations arise when the expected rise in output prices fails to materialize or costs escalate at a higher rate than was anticipated. Unemployment could be the unfortunate result of this disequilibrium, but would not be the result of the unions' exercising their power but of unforseen circumstances. Unemployment persists, according to contract theory, because it takes time for old contracts to expire and new ones to be set.[6]

Contract theory, however, cannot forecast how rapidly excessively high wages should be adjusted downward. Real wages in the Canadian manufacturing sector have not declined drastically since 1981, in spite of unemployment rates averaging around 10 percent over the last 10 years. Why did competitive pressures not lower wages when contracts were being renegotiated? If we are to give a meaningful answer to this question, it is important to evaluate critically the assumption behind the theory. The assumption that unions would demand wages that assured the continued success of the firm and sustains jobs needs to be addressed in light of what neoclassical theory tells us. Since wage rates influence the number of jobs available in every industry and firm, union representatives face a trade-off between higher wages and fewer jobs and union members (Grubel and Bonnici 1986).

Union leaders generally do not care very much about the effects of their wage demands on employment levels in their respective industries as long as they do not face an absolute decline in workplaces and membership. In fact, the loyalties of union representatives are to current members of the union or "insiders."[7] Since high wages that lead to a reduction in employment growth adversely affect only potential members or "outsiders," who have no influence on union elections and policies, union leaders need not be concerned about employment growth in the industry as a whole. The demand for wage increases lead firms to use more labour-saving capital, leading to less employment growth.

Several logical and relevant questions arise from the preceding analysis. Why do unemployed workers not undercut the employed union workers by accepting relatively lower wages corresponding to productivity growth? Why do entrepreneurs not start new enterprises that will compete with unionized high-wage firms by employing non-union workers at relatively lower wages?

Depending on how favourable the labour code is to union activities, unions can prevent potential competition to their unionized firms or industries by threats of unionization or boycotts. This kind of threat can raise the cost of entry and business operation for new firms interested in hiring the unemployed at a relatively lower wage rate. Thus, entrepreneurs find that it is not worth the effort. In short, insiders have the necessary power to stop outsiders from threatening their secure position (Grubel and Bonnici 1986). For example, in British Columbia the provincial labour code allows unions to prevent the entry of new firms and the hiring of non-union labour. These provisions include a ban on the use of replacement workers, allowing secondary picketing, and provisions that make it easier to unionize a workplace. Additionally, a "Fair Wage Law" similar to the federal government's "prevailing wage" dictum prevents low-wage contractors from bidding for government work—a significant fraction of the total (Mihlar 1996).

The threat of unionization affects not only the entry of new firms, it also curbs wage reductions among workers in the non-union sector. Employers operating in the non-union sector face the threat of unionization if it is perceived that there is too wide a gap in wages between them and the unionized sector. It is in their interest to avoid the costs of unionization and its consequent rigidities that may cripple their business operation.

The problem: monopoly unions and rigid labour markets

All Canadian provinces have various provisions in their labour codes that provide unions with exclusive representation. Under exclusive representation, all individuals who wish to work in a particular industry must belong to a designated union. Closed-shop unions and the Rand formula thus represent a violation of a fundamental individual freedom: the freedom of association (Hayek 1960). However, the Supreme Court of Canada in *Lavigne v. Ontario Public Service Employees Union* argued, in effect, that collective rights of workers are more important than individual rights of particular workers. Therefore, it appears that the Rand-formula clauses are safe from a constitutional challenge.

There are, however, several economic reasons for opposing exclusive representation. By entrenching monopoly privileges restricting who can work in a particular industry or firm, closed-shop and Rand-formula provisions introduce more rigidities into the labour market. Given that unions have monopoly power, they can secure a larger portion of the economic rents that are induced by new capital investments. Moreover, productivity growth, investment growth, employment growth and profitability is much lower in unionized firms compared to non-unionized firms (Becker and Olson 1986; Maki and Meredith 1986; Long 1993; Addison and Wagner 1993; Laporta and Jenkins 1996; Hirsch 1997). Work by Professor Leo Troy, an expert on the economics of trade unions, shows that in recent decades the trend in many industrialized countries has been toward less unionized work forces (Troy 1995). This, in part, is a reflection of the fact that dynamic and innovative economies of the late twentieth-century require flexible work places in order to adapt to rapidly changing circumstances.

Flexible labour markets: a necessary condition for job creation

Canada's small, open, economy is dependent on trade, with an export-to-GDP ratio of about 38 percent (IMF 1995), and Canada cannot insulate itself from global changes. Canadian industries face heavy competition for investment capital and human resources, which are increasingly mobile as transportation and communication costs drop. Labour market regulations that are more costly than those adopted by our trading partners, particularly the United States, will induce firms to move their business out of Canada. The risk is that foreign and Canadian investors will invest in more "business friendly" jurisdictions. This lack of investment will lead to reduced levels of economic and employment growth and a lower standard of living.

Empirical evidence from around the world suggests that those nations that have the most flexible[8] labour markets are able to benefit more from technological change, have the best job creation record, and experience the fastest economic growth (OECD 1994). The contrast between the recent unemployment experiences of the United States and the European Union is indicative of the benefits that result from flexible labour markets. The United States, with what is arguably one of the world's most flexible labour markets, has in recent years experienced one of the fastest economic growth rates of all industrialized countries, and it continues to have one of the lowest unemployment rates, currently about 5.4 percent.[9] According to a recent study by the McKinsey Global Institute, American labour productivity ranks first in the world and continues to grow rapidly.[10] In contrast, most nations in the European Union, with their relatively rigid work practices and strong labour unions, have continued to experience very sluggish economic growth, and have had dismal employment growth rates (0.3 percent per year) for the past 35 years (OECD 1994). Canada appears to share this European predicament of rigid labour markets and high unemployment rates. Economist Charles Hanson in his paper in this volume captures the European experience quite succinctly: "What can we learn from the European Union? —that unduly high wages and work benefits coupled with an excess of regulation can severely damage the labour market and create mass unemployment."

Productivity growth is also abysmal in the European Union compared to that of the United States. Given the importance that productivity plays in the economic growth process (Solow 1957; Jorgenson, Gollop and Fraumeni 1987; Lipsey 1996), it seems clear that the United States is better positioned for the future than the European Union. While flexible labour markets alone cannot account for all these differences, they play an integral role in the creation of wealth and employment. Hence, if Canada is to avoid the persistently high unemployment rates that plague the European Union, it must adopt a flexible labour market policy.

Potential solution: Right-to-Work laws

What is a Right-to-Work law? The right to work means that any person can get a job with any willing employer without having to join, or pay union dues to, an exclusive bargaining agent or union. Under the federal and provincial labour codes, however, individual workers in Canada are not free to decide whether to be represented by a union. Once a union receives certification, exclusive representation provisions mean that it faces no competition from other unions that might otherwise offer alternative membership to workers. Meanwhile, union security clauses ensure that individuals are not free to opt out of union membership or the payment of dues.

Right-to-work laws help constrain excessive wage demands by unions and keep wage increases in line with productivity growth. They also ensure competition for the right of representation and place a bound of "reasonableness" on the posturing of union representative during contract negotiations. Thus, if Canadian Airlines workers could have opted to quit the Canadian Auto Workers Union but remain employed, Basil Hargrove, president of the union, could not have forbidden them to vote on contract offers from their employer. If wage levels are in line with productivity levels, there will be less inducement for firms to invest in labour-saving technologies.[11] Consequently, there will be increased potential for job growth.

Synopsis of the evidence on Right-to-Work laws

The so-called British Disease was imported into Canada and remains with us today. While Canada is still plagued with the disease, Britain reformed its labour legislation and is now enjoying the benefits of having introduced Right-to-Work laws. The research evidence gathered by the authors in this volume indicates that jurisdictions with Right-to-Work laws have outperformed jurisdictions without such laws by a significant margin. Following is a synopsis of the evidence.

- In the United States, between 1947 and 1992, manufacturing employment increased by 148 percent in states with Right-to-Work laws. Over the same period, growth in manufacturing jobs was almost zero in states without Right-to-Work laws.

- On average, manufacturing employment increases by one-third when one steps over the border from a state without Right-to-Work laws to a state with Right-to-Work laws.

- Between 1986 and 1993, in the Pacific Northwest of the United States, states with Right-to-Work laws—Nevada, Idaho, Utah, and Wyoming—saw their average manufacturing job growth rise by 26 percent, while states without Right-to-Work laws—Washington, Oregon, Montana and Colorado—saw an average growth rate of 7 percent.

- Among the 20 states ranked as having the best climate for business, according to a major survey 19 of them are states with Right-to-Work laws.

- Surveys show that half of all companies in the United States wanting to relocate will not consider a state without Right-to-Work laws.

- Six years prior to the enactment of the Right-to-Work law, Idaho saw its manufacturing employment decline by 2.1 percent. In contrast, after the law was passed, between 1987 and 1995 Idaho's manufacturing employment grew by 36.2 percent.

- While the number of construction jobs in non-Right-to-Work states increased by 5.5 percent between 1986 and 1994, construction jobs in Idaho increased by 105 percent.

- While manufacturing productivity in Idaho grew by almost 5 percent between 1987 and 1992, in the neighbouring non-Right-to-Work state of Montana manufacturing productivity declined by 4.4 percent.

- In the case of New Zealand, after the enactment of Right-to-Work laws in 1991, the unemployment rate fell from 10.0 percent in September 1991 to 5.9 percent in March 1996.

- Between 1984 and 1991, annual labour productivity growth was 1.1 percent in New Zealand. Between 1991 and 1995, productivity has increased by 1.8 percent on an annual basis.

- In New Zealand, GDP grew by 15 percent in the three years after it enacted Right-to-Work laws in 1991. This is as much as the economy grew in the whole decade between 1974 and 1984.

- Working days lost due to strike activity in New Zealand have declined from 99,032 in 1991 to 23,770 by 1993.
- Firms in Britain that rid themselves of the closed shop have higher levels of growth in productivity.
- While Britain also saw its corporate profitability improve, profits continued to be lower in unionized workplaces.
- After major labour reforms, Britain's unemployment rate has declined from 11.2 percent in 1983 to 6.9 percent in November 1996.
- In Britain, there were 2,125 work stoppages in 1979. Since labour reforms were introduced, the number of work stoppages has declined to 205 in 1994.

Purpose of this book

The Fraser Institute's role is to inform the public about the role of competitive markets—including a competitive market for labour—in providing for the well-being of Canadians. Governments have provided legal sanctions that allow union monopolies to flourish in the Canadian economy. As is evident from labour legislation across the country, the detrimental impact of these monopolies on investment and job creation has not been understood by policy makers and politicians.

New Zealand, the United Kingdom and 21 jurisdictions in the United States have provided workers with choice. Each of these countries or states have reformed their labour laws in different ways, but each shares the common thread of bringing flexibility to their respective labour markets by liberalizing their labour laws. This book presents nine essays that explain the role of Right-to-Work laws and examine their impact on investment, employment, productivity, and standard of living.

Contributions

In his Foreword, ROGER BEDARD examined the legal issues surrounding federal and provincial codes that dictate closed-shop and mandatory union dues. The Canadian Charter of Rights and Freedoms safeguards some basic rights such as the freedom to join or not join an association. Mr. Bedard explained that closed-shop provisions are inconsistent with the freedom of association. Moreover, compulsory union dues—the so-called Rand formula—violate the free use of one's earnings, which includes the freedom to refuse to pay a tribute to private "taxers." He pointed out that closed-shop provisions and compulsory union dues have been outlawed completely in over 100 countries around the world. Canada and Australia are among the last two industrialized nations that have not outlawed closed-shop provisions and mandatory union dues. He remains optimistic, however, that changes will occur in Canada through legal challenges under the Canadian Charter of Rights and Freedoms.

Professor DENNIS MAKI's essay reviews the current status of federal and provincial laws relating to union security clauses in collective agreements, including legislation regarding the ability of unions to expel and discipline members, the duty of fair representation, admission to union membership, and the duty of fair referral. He concludes that there are several remedies other than Right-to-Work legislation that can overcome the adverse effects of closed-shop provisions or the Rand formula. These remedies include restrictions on the ability of unions to expel members for failure to honour picket lines or to dismiss members who are expelled from membership.

Do unions advance or hinder the economic performance of firms and the competitiveness of the economy. The answer to this question has significant implications for public policy and the design of labour law. Specifically, the answer to this question provides us with a rationale for either strengthening or weakening labour legislation governing bargaining rights and union organizing. Professor BARRY HIRSCH evaluates the theory and evidence on the relationship of unionization to productivity, profitability, investment, and employment growth. The evidence gathered by him from the United States and elsewhere indicates that, on balance, unions tend not to increase productivity and to reduce profitability and investment in physical capital and in research and development. Most importantly, unionization tends to lower the rate of employment growth.

American unions have vociferously opposed right-to work laws by claiming that these laws are a "right to work for less." In other words, they claim employees are better off in states that do not have Right-to-Work laws. Professor JAMES BENNETT examines this claim by comparing the cost of living in states that have right-to work laws and those that do not, and finds that workers in states with Right-to-Work laws are better off economically.

DAVID KENDRICK analyzes the economic impact of Right-to-Work laws by examining the economic success of Idaho since it enacted Right-to-Work legislation in 1986. His research finds that Idaho has benefitted from this legislationand that it has been among the leaders in job and income growth in the United States since the Right-to-Work law was passed.

Professor WOLFGANG KASPER starts with an examination of New Zealand's system of centralized wage fixing and arbitration. He then explains the mechanics of the new Employment Contracts Act (ECA), New Zealand's version of Right-to-Work legislation. The ECA turned a centralized industrial relations structure into a decentralized market structure. Professor Kasper analyzes the impact of the ECA on investment, job creation, productivity and level of strike activity, and his evidence suggests that in New Zealand employment has grown by over 10 percent, productivity has increased, and strike activity is down substantially since the ECA was introduced. He concludes that the ECA along with other reforms has created a "Kiwi job-creation machine."

Professors JOHN ADDISON and STANLEY SIEBERT start their essay by describing the process by which the labour market in the United Kingdom was reformed and the impact of the reform upon the level of unionization and, more particularly, upon the closed shop. They go on to analyze the contrasting approaches of the Labour party and the Conservative party to reform of labour law. finally, they marshal the evidence of the economic impact of these reforms, evidence showing that Britain benefited from the reforms of the labour market enacted by Margaret Thatcher.

Professor CHARLES HANSON examines the economic impact of labour reforms in the United Kingdom. In 1979 the British economy was suffering from the "British Disease", the main symptoms of which were low productivity and low levels of job growth. Professor Hanson argues that the British disease has been cured and that Britain has the most flexible labour market in western Europe. His paper outlines the main features of the

Thatcher government's radical program of labour market reform and explains how it has benefitted the British economy. He draws some general conclusions—such as the need to reduce rigidity in labour markets—that are relevant for Canada and other countries contemplating labour market reforms.

The Joint Review Committee's Right-to-Work Study, set-up by the Alberta Economic Development Authority (AEDA) to examine the issue of the right to work and its potential impact upon Alberta did not recommend the implementation of Right-to-Work laws in Alberta. The Committee concluded that Alberta already has a competitive economic regime. FAZIL MIHLAR argues that, while Alberta's economic regime is competitive when compared with other Canadian jurisdictions, it is not competitive when compared with American states and other countries. His paper assesses the findings of the Committee's report, provides a critique of the AEDA's conclusions based on the available research evidence, and explains why the AEDA's conclusions were unfounded.

Policy conclusions

The puzzling phenomenon of the growing divergence between Canadian and American unemployment rates since the 1970s can be explained in part by Canada's higher rate of unionization,[12] and the consequent increase in Canadian real wages above productivity growth. In addition, a generous employment insurance program has added to the unemployment rate by inducing changes in behaviour such as increased readiness to quit, prolonged job search, and the expansion of seasonal industries (Henderson 1997). In general terms, the redistributive policies of the welfare state, including Canada's, have precluded the necessary adjustment in labour markets and have led to persistently high unemployment rates (Krugman 1994). Presently, the United States has an unemployment rate that is about 4 percent lower than the Canadian rate. The evidence supports the view that union behaviour and excessive real wages have, in part, helped to create the divergence in unemployment levels between Canada and the United States. It is important, therefore, that we restore competitive labour markets and eliminate closed-shop and Rand-formula provisions in our provincial and federal labour codes.

The Fraser Institute welcomes the contributions in this book, which shed much needed light on this important public policy issue. Since the authors have worked independently, however, their conclusions and work do not necessarily reflect the views of The Fraser Institute or of its trustees and members.

Notes

1 Statistics Canada 1996b: B-7. Youth is defined as including individuals in the demographic group 15 to 24 years of age.
2 It is important to recognize, however, that not all social pathologies can be attributed to unemployment. There are various other factors (e.g., poor education and the decline of religion, marriage, and community) that have an impact. We should refrain, therefore, from assuming that individuals are mere victims of economic hardship and incapable of looking after themselves or their families. For an exposition of the multiple causes of crime, see Fagan 1995.
3 For detailed discussion on the issue of real wage unemployment, see Daly and MacCharles 1986.
4 International Monetary Fund 1996: 180; Bureau of Labor Statistics [US] 1996: 9–11. Compensation should include payroll and employment taxes. It is important to include these costs since they reduce the net contribution of workers to the economic viability of the firms that employ them.
5 Since 1992, however, Canadian manufacturing productivity has outpaced wage increases. During the years of high real wages relative to productivity growth, firms invested heavily in capital equipment. Given these large investments in capital, firms will need time to adjust to the new circumstance. Therefore, the continuing high unemployment is consistent with the theory of real wage unemployment. In short, this recent change in productivity does not invalidate the theory of real wage unemployment as an explanation for Canada's high unemployment rate.
6 Taken from Grubel and Bonnici 1986.
7 For a detailed explanation of the insider-outsider theory, see Lindbeck and Snower 1985, 1986.
8 The notion of "flexibility" refers not only to flexible wages, but also the flexibility for firms to change their capital-labour mix due to changing market conditions.
9 Cited in Economic Indicators, *The Economist* (Dec. 21), 1996: 142.

10 Cited in Economic Focus: America's Power Plants, *The Economist* (June 8–14), 1996: 82.
11 It is important recognize, however, that the existence of competitive labour will not retard technological innovation and productivity growth. Entrepreneurs will always be looking for new opportunities to fill a market niche, and many will succeed by introducing upgraded products, using new labour-saving technology, and underpricing their competitors. As they expand their market share, they will have to hire new employees by paying them higher wages. It is through this incremental process that incomes can be raised.
12 Between 1970 and 1994, Canada's unionization rate increased from 33.6 percent to 37.5 percent of the labour force. In contrast, the United States has seen a steep decline in unionization from 29.6 percent to 15.5 percent of the labour force during the same period.

References

Addison, John T., and John Burton (1984). *Trade Unions and Society: Some Lessons of the British Experience*. Vancouver, BC: The Fraser Institute.

Addison, John T., and Joachim Wagner (1993). U.S. Unionism and R&D Investment: Evidence from a Simple Cross-Country Test. *Journal of Labour Research*, 15, 2 (Spring): 191–97.

Ashenfelter, O., and D. Card (1986). Why have Unemployment Rates in Canada and the United States Diverged? *Economica*, 53: S171–S195.

Becker, Brian, and Craig Olson (1986). Unionization and Shareholder Interest. *Industrial and Labour Review*, 42: 246–61.

Bureau of Labour Statistics (1996). *International Comparison of Manufacturing Productivity and Unit Labor Cost Trend, 1995*. Washington, DC: United States Department of Labor.

Daly, D.J., and D.C. MacCharles (1986). *On Real Wage Unemployment*. Focus No. 18. Vancouver, BC: The Fraser Institute.

Dornbusch, R., S. Fischer, and G. Sparks (1989). *Macroeconomics*. 3rd Canadian ed. Toronto, ON: McGraw-Hill Ryerson.

Economic Focus: America's Power Plants (1996). *The Economist* (June 8–14): 82.

Economic Indicators (1996). *The Economist* (December 21): 142.

Fagan, Patrick F. (1995). *The Real Root Causes of Violent Crime: The Breakdown of Marriage, Family and Community*. Backgrounder (March). Washington: The Heritage Foundation.

Galarneau, Diane, and Jean-Pierre Maynard (1995). *Measuring productivity*. Perspectives, Catalogue 75-001E. Ottawa: Statistics Canada.

Grubel, Herbert G., and Josef Bonnici (1986). *Why is Canada's Unemployment Rate So High*. Focus No. 19. Vancouver, BC: The Fraser Institute.

Grubel, Herbert G., Dennis Maki, and Shelley Sax (1975). Real and Insurance-Induced Unemployment in Canada. *Canadian Journal of Economics*, 8, 2 (May): 174–92.

Grubel, Herbert G., and Michael Walker, eds. (1978). *Unemployment Insurance: Global Evidence of its Effects on Unemployment*. Vancouver: The Fraser Institute.

Hayek, F.A. (1960). *The Constitution of Liberty*. London: Routledge and Kegan Paul.

Henderson, David R. (1997). Canada's High Unemployment Rate Is No Mystery. *The Globe and Mail* (February 11): A-21.

Hirsch, Barry T. (1997). Unionization and Economic Performance: Evidence on Productivity, Profits, Investment, and Growth. *Public Policy Sources*, No. 3. Vancouver, BC: The Fraser Institute.

International Monetary Fund (IMF) (1995). *International Financial Statistics Yearbook*. Washington, DC: International Monetary Fund.

——— (1996). *World Economic Outlook* (October). Washington, DC: International Monetary Fund.

Jorgenson, Dale W., Frank M. Gollop, and Barbara M. Fraumeni (1987). *Productivity and U.S. Economic Growth*. Cambridge, MA: Harvard University Press.

Krugman, Paul (1994). Past and Prospective Causes of High Unemployment. *Economic Review, Fourth Quarter, Federal Reserve Bank of Kansas City*: 23–43.

Laporta, Pasquale, and Alexander W. Jenkins (1996). Unionization and Profitability in the Canadian Manufacturing Sector. *Relations Industrielles*, 51, 4: 756–76.

Lindbeck, A., and D.J. Snower (1985). Explanations of Unemployment. *Oxford Review of Economic Policy* 1, 2: 34–69.

——— (1986). Wage Setting, Unemployment and Insider-Outsider Relations. *American Economic Review* 76, 2: 235–39.

Lipsey, Richard G. (1996). *Economic Growth, Technological Change, and Canadian Economic Policy*. Toronto, ON: C.D. Howe Institute.

Long, Richard (1993). The Effect of Unionization on Employment Growth of Canadian Companies. *Industrial and Labour Relations Review* 46, 4 (July): 691–703.

Maki, Dennis, and L.N. Meredith (1986). The Effects of Unions on Profitability: The Canadian Evidence. *Relations Industrielles* 41: 55–67.

Mihlar, Fazil (1996). *A New Labour Regime for British Columbia: Towards Job Creation*. Vancouver, BC: The Fraser Institute.

Neumark, David, and William Wascher (1995). The Effects of New Jersey's Minimum Wage Increase on Fast Food Employment. Unpublished manuscript.

Organisation for Economic Cooperation and Development (1994). *OECD Jobs Study: Part 1*. Paris: OECD.

Shackleton, J.R. (1996). Unemployment and Labour Markets in the 1990s. *Economic Affairs* 16, 2 (Spring): 4–7.

Solow, Robert M. (1957). Technical Change and the Aggregate Production Function. *Review of Economics and Statistics* 39 (August): 312–20.

Statistics Canada (1996a). *National Economic and Financial Accounts: Quarterly Estimates*. Catalogue no. 13-001-XPB.

Statistics Canada (1996b). *The Labour Force*. Catalogue no. 71-001-XPB (May).

Statistics Canada (1996c). *Canadian Economic Observer: Statistical Summary*. Catalogue no. 11-010-XPB (July).

Stigler, George (1946). The Economics of Minimum Wage Legislation. *American Economic Review* 36 (June): 358–65.

Troy, Leo (1995). *Canadian Unionism: The Meaning, and the Measure, the Reality and the Myth*. Vancouver, BC: The Fraser Institute.

Canada's Labour Laws
An Overview

DENNIS R. MAKI

This paper is primarily concerned with the current status of federal and provincial labour laws relating directly to forms of union security clauses in collective agreements. It goes beyond this central concern for two reasons. First, the impact of any union security clause depends directly upon labour laws relating to other matters such as (1) the ability of trade unions to discipline or expel members, (2) the duty of fair representation, and (3) admission to membership. An example will help illustrate this point. Consider that the primary difference between a Rand-formula shop[1] and a union shop is that under the former the covered non-members may ignore union directives, such as not crossing a picket line, with impunity. However, if the power of the union to discipline members for similar infractions is severely limited by legislation, the impact of the two different security clauses may be identical.

The second reason for going beyond the limited central focus on security clauses is that a number of other forms of legislative

---

Notes will be found on pages 31–33.

clause may be functional substitutes for security clauses. As an example, assume, as does most of the literature dealing with the effects of unions on various macroeconomic variables such as wages, productivity and profits,[2] that the main source of union power is membership. In this case, in a hypothetical growing economy where the unionized sector is growing as rapidly as the rest of the economy, security clauses guaranteeing a union shop will ensure that membership density ratios and hence union power will not be diminished by economic growth. In the presence of Right-to-Work laws, other clauses in labour codes that make organizing easier—such as "automatic" recognition on the basis of membership cards without a required supervised vote—may serve as alternative means of maintaining or increasing membership densities.[3] For example one of the advantages of a union shop over a Rand-formula shop is that the former increases union control over potential strikebreakers. However, legislation in many jurisdictions forbidding the hiring of strikebreakers does this directly.[4]

General considerations

Before looking at legislative provisions relating to specific topics, there are three general points that apply to all. First, many other types of legislation can serve as substitutes for security clauses. In any bargaining situation, the union faces some outcomes that they prefer to other outcomes. Generally, reducing the price-of-labour elasticity of demand for the workers they represent will aid in achieving a more preferred outcome. This can take the form of reducing the price elasticity of demand for the product or service produced, reducing the elasticity of substitution between the workers they represent and other inputs, or affecting the elasticity of supply of other inputs. Thus, union power is increased by the following partial substitutes for security clauses: tariff barriers or other impediments to trade that reduce competition for the goods or services produced by unionized workers; regulations pertaining to immigration of persons who are to some extent complementary or substitute inputs, minimum wage laws; child labour laws; regulations related to unemployment insurance, pensions, public assistance, occupational health and safety; environmental protection and human rights legislation. The main point is that there are complex interactions not only among different labour code provisions but also between labour code provisions and labour standards legislation, social security legislation and other law.

Second, when discussing any area of Canadian labour legislation, we must recognize that jurisdiction is primarily provincial (only about 10 percent of workers fall under federal jurisdiction) and that there is diversity in legislative provisions across jurisdictions. Further, given the polarity in the positions of the leading political parties in many provinces, a change of government often leads to substantial changes in provincial labour codes, producing diversity in legislation over time within a jurisdiction.[5] Changes in labour codes are often associated with changes in labour standards or other related legislation, exacerbating the effects of the interactions discussed in the previous paragraph.

Finally, there is considerable evidence that small differences in legislative provisions can have large effects.[6] One implication of this is that every jurisdiction has legislation that differs somewhat from all others, making tabular presentation of clauses very difficult and rendering generalizations regarding similarities inaccurate for many purposes.[7] In what follows, such generalizations should thus be regarded as useful only for the purposes of this chapter.

Union security legislation

In Canada, the principle of exclusive jurisdiction holds. That is, a union must represent all workers in the bargaining unit.[8] The weakest form of union security is the check-off, where the employer collects union dues from workers and remits them to the union. Check-off provisions may apply only to union members who voluntarily sign a form authorizing the employer to do this, or a stronger version may bind the employer to collect dues from all union members, without authorization by individual workers. The strongest version of the check-off makes it mandatory for the employer to collect union dues or the equivalent from all workers in the bargaining unit whether they are union members or not. This is commonly called a Rand-Formula clause in Canada and an agency shop in the United States.

The union shop requires that all workers must join the union within a stipulated period of time after becoming employed in the bargaining unit. There are several variations of the union shop, including those with a "grandfather" clause where only workers hired after a specific date—perhaps the date when the current union was certified as the bargaining agent—are required to join the union as a condition of employment. Another variant is the maintenance of membership clause, where no worker is required to join the union, but any worker who voluntarily joins is required to remain a member (sometimes for a stipulated minimum period). A combination of the grandfather and maintenance of membership clauses is commonly referred to as a modified union shop.

The strongest form of union security is the closed shop, where workers must be union members before they can be hired into the bargaining unit. The closed shop is most prevalent where workers have a weak attachment to a given employer (despite strong attachment to the industry); e.g., construction and longshoring. Kumar (1988: 600) reports that, outside the construction industry, 1.4 percent of employees covered under agreements involving 500 or more employees were in closed shops in January 1988. The same statistic for March 1980 was 3.2 percent. The economic impact of the closed shop depends upon the extent to which it coincides with a closed union, discussed below in the sections dealing with the duty of fair representation and admission to membership.

There is also preferential hiring, which can occur under either a closed or a union shop, where the employer agrees to hire union members as long as they are available but, if none are available, the employer is free any hire anyone. The effect of this provision is to encourage union membership and discourage the employment of non-union workers (see Opie and Bates 1995: 497).

All of the above forms of union security are legal in every jurisdiction in Canada,[9] although Alberta recently considered Right-to-Work legislation outlawing at least some of the stronger variants of union security (see Koch 1995; Serres 1995). One difference across jurisdictions relates to whether strong forms of union security must be bargained for, or whether they are available to the union as a matter of right under the law. Regarding the check-off, for example, in Alberta, British Columbia, New Brunswick, Nova Scotia and Prince Edward Island, the employer must collect dues from employees and remit them to the union only when the employee voluntarily authorizes the deduction. Newfoundland, Ontario and the federal jurisdiction incorporate the Rand formula at the request of the union with no need for bargaining. Quebec and Manitoba make the Rand formula mandatory under legislation, even without a request from the union. Saskatchewan requires the modified union shop together with the Rand formula at the request of the union, without any need for bargaining.[10]

The landmark case dealing with the Rand Formula following passage of the Canadian Charter of Rights and Freedoms in 1982 is *Lavigne v. Ontario Public Service Employees Union*.[11] Lavigne argued that since the union used dues money for non-bargaining purposes, such as supporting a political party and abortion rights campaigns, the Rand Formula violated the statements in the Charter of Rights regarding freedom of association. The Supreme Court of Canada ruled that Rand-Formula clauses were safe from attack on constitutional grounds (see Carter 1992).

The apparent assumption of the legislators who enact laws making the Rand Formula a matter of right for the union and of the courts that enforce such laws, is that union members all gain from collective bargaining, and if some persons need not pay for these gains, they become "free-riders." In reality, to the extent that individual bargaining allows for a distribution of wages (and other conditions of employment) in the absence of unions, even if unions negotiate average benefits that are greater than average benefits would have been in the absence of unionization, some persons at the upper end of the distribution of ability and benefits may actually lose when collective bargaining forces all workers to receive the same average benefit. Forcing these workers to pay union dues and assessments adds insult to injury.

Although all jurisdictions allow and, in some cases, mandate strong forms of union security, most have laws that reduce the possibility of abuse of such power by the union.[12] These laws provide for legislative control over the procedure of admission to, or expulsion from, membership, or over the union's power to compel an employer to fire an employee who has been denied membership in, or been expelled from, the union. Normally, legislative control is exerted over how union security clauses are enforced. The usual enforcement mechanism is either through grievance arbitration, or via complaints of unfair labour practice to the relevant labour relations board, or ultimately through the courts. Hence a reasonably complete understanding of the actual impact of any given legislation in this area requires examination of a large number of cases and becomes very complex. The following section conveys the flavour of the issues involved.

Expulsion and discharge

It is accepted in all jurisdictions that it is incumbent on the employer to dismiss any employee (excepting anyone granted religious exemption) who refuses to join a union or remain a union member, in contravention of a union security clause in a contract in force. It is less clear that the same action is required of the employer in cases when the union either refuses to accept the employee as a member, or expels the employee from membership. Ever since the Orenda decision[13] in 1958, there has been a question of the extent to which the employer is required (or entitled) to examine whether the reasons why the union requests discharge of an employee are in accord with the union's constitution and by-laws.

Further, statutes can prohibit (1) having an employee discharged because they have been expelled from a union, or (2) the union from expelling a member except for specified causes. There is considerable variation among jurisdictions in legislation governing union discipline of members. Prince Edward Island and Ontario[14] do not regulate expulsion directly but do regulate whether expulsion can lead to discharge. All other jurisdictions require that discipline be reasonable (i.e., the punishment should fit the crime), fair and nondiscriminatory. Alberta and Nova Scotia prohibit discrimination in matters of membership against "persons," while the federal legislation refers to "employees."[15] New Brunswick limits the nondiscrimination clause in matters of membership to cases where membership is required by a security clause in the collective agreement. Alberta regulates the disciplinary process (e.g., charges must be made in writing, members have right to counsel), and British Columbia and Saskatchewan guarantee the right to natural justice. Saskatchewan legislation also notes that any employee who is denied membership will still be deemed to be a member if he pays all dues and assessments required of members, with the result that unions cannot force an employer to dismiss an expelled member, except for nonpayment of dues and assessments.

From 1986–1992, the British Columbia Labour Code prohibited discipline that was unreasonable or unfair, and prohibited requiring termination of an expelled employee unless the expulsion was due to failure to pay dues or assessments, or activity against the union that was contrary to the Code. The revisions to the

Code by the NDP government in 1992 removed these provisions, thereby increasing the power of unions to discipline members.

Under Manitoba legislation and current British Columbia legislation, the only expulsions prohibited are those that are done in a discriminatory manner, or involve refusing to take part in an illegal strike. Newfoundland allows workers who have been "unfairly" expelled to file a complaint with the Board. The Quebec Labour Code is silent on the question of discipline and expulsion. The court cases of interest regarding expulsion and discharge primarily involve circumstances where the discipline was a result of failing to honour a picket line.

International Woodworkers of America v. Moose Jaw Sash and Door Company[16] is often cited to illustrate the importance of labour code language. The union asked the employer to dismiss three employees: two had been refused admission and one had been expelled; all three had refused to honour a legal picket line. The Saskatchewan Act in force at the time allowed dismissal only for non-payment of dues or for "activities against the union." The ruling held that failing to honour a legal picket line was most surely an "activity against the union" and that dismissal was justified. The Act was subsequently changed so that the greatest penalty the union can impose for failing to honour a legal picket line is a fine.

This raises the question of how large a fine a union can impose, and what they can do to collect it. At the federal level, the Trade Unions Act[17] explicitly states that unions have no access to civil courts to enforce the payment of fines. Saskatchewan is the only jurisdiction to have an explicit clause regarding collection of fines from members by unions.[18] The legislation allows unions access to the civil courts to collect fines for members having worked for the struck employer during a legal strike, with the amount of the fine limited to the net earnings of the worker during the strike. In *Alcorn v. Grain Services Union*,[19] it was made clear that the union cannot fine members of the bargaining unit who are not also members of the union.

In other jurisdictions, collection of fines by unions is apparently covered only by common law. The landmark case is *International Association of Machinists v. Perks*,[20] where the Newfoundland Supreme Court ruled that the courts have no jurisdiction to order payment of a fine assessed against a member by a union for failure to honour a picket line.

Duty of fair representation

The issue of fair representation is basically the result of the potential conflict between collective interests and individual rights, and usually arises because the union has considerable discretion regarding whether to take a grievance to arbitration. It can also arise because unions inevitably must select certain issues to emphasize during bargaining, and some members in the unit will not agree with the choice made (e.g., older workers may feel pensions are an important issue while younger workers may not). The duty of fair representation is important because the extent to which a union can treat members differently from covered non-members in an open-shop bargaining unit can be a powerful incentive for membership. If, for example, covered non-members have no access to grievance machinery or no say in the selection of bargaining issues they may well voluntarily elect to become members.

The concept of the duty of fair representation comes from the United States, where the Supreme Court held in 1944 that there is a statutory duty to represent all workers in the bargaining unit, making discrimination against African-Americans a violation.[21] In Canada, all jurisdictions except Nova Scotia, New Brunswick and Prince Edward Island include duty of fair representation clauses in their labour codes. Further, in *Canadian Merchant Service Guild v. Gagnon* in 1984,[22] the Supreme Court of Canada held that the duty of fair representation exists under common law, even with no statutory provision. It is implicit in the concept of exclusive jurisdiction.

The main difference between the common law guarantee and provincial legislation lies in access to remedy. Under common law, the case must be taken to the courts while, under provincial labour codes, it can be taken to the labour board, often a simpler and cheaper remedy. However, there is considerable variation among provinces in the nature of the guarantee provided. Six jurisdictions[23] note that a union cannot act in a manner which is "arbitrary, discriminatory or in bad faith," while Alberta and Newfoundland only proscribe situations where the union acted in bad faith. British Columbia requires that an employee make a *prima facie* case (not mere undocumented allegations) before the board will consider the case.

While the common law duty of fair representation applies to both access to grievance machinery and selection of issues for negotiation, most provincial statutes refer only to grievance representation. Only British Columbia and Ontario directly refer to the conduct of bargaining. These two jurisdictions, plus the Canada Labour Code, note the duty extends to referral of workers to employers under a closed shop.[24]

The content of labour codes regarding fair representation is important, despite the common law guarantees, because the courts have very limited remedial power. Employee A has a complaint against employer B, and union C refuses to process a grievance. A sues C for violation of the duty of fair representation, and all the court can do is award damages from C to A. The employer is unaffected and the employee does not get the benefit (e.g., a promotion) originally desired. Labour boards have much wider access to remedies; they can, for instance, order arbitration of the original issue, provide the workers with counsel if it is felt the union will not do so adequately, or order the union to compensate the workers for that part of any loss that is due to the union's action or inaction.

The duty of fair representation in the negotiation of collective agreements is obviously a complicated issue. There will always be minority versus majority positions within any group of covered employees, and the fact that unions have control only over bargaining positions, not the eventual settlement, complicates matters. This consideration leads to a distinction between cases where the issue is the actual provisions negotiated for the collective agreement and cases where the issue is the process of negotiation.

Regarding actual provisions, discrimination on the basis of race, colour or gender would generally be held to violate fair representation. Discrimination against casual, probationary, or part-time workers is often held not to violate the duty of fair representation. For example, in a 1994 case,[25] the Canada Labour Relations Board held that a collective agreement provision denying casual workers just-cause protection is not a violation of the labour code. Since it is likely that casual, probationary, and part-time workers have less commitment to the union than do other workers, and are therefore less likely to be union members in an open shop situation, under this interpretation current legislation allows unions to discriminate against covered non-members.

Regarding the process of negotiation, the main issues that arise relate to voting: which issues should be voted upon, and who is eligible to vote. Strike votes are mandatory in most jurisdictions, for example, but are not required in the federal jurisdiction or in Ontario. In Nova Scotia, a strike may not be declared unless a vote is taken and "the majority of the employees concerned vote in favour" (Labour Canada 1994: 39). In other jurisdictions, a majority of the employees voting is sufficient. There are similar differences among jurisdictions about the need for ratification votes. Regarding the question of who is eligible to vote, there is one case[26] where the British Columbia Board suggested there are circumstances where a union may deny non-members the right to vote without violating the duty of fair representation.

In summary, Carrothers, Palmer, and Rayner (1986: 78-9) note that in the United States "by 1950 the doctrine [of the duty of fair representation] had been well established," but that it "started effectively in Canada in the early seventies and is steadily being adopted across the country." There is obviously still much that could be done to strengthen the concept.

Admission to membership and duty of fair referral

This section deals with the question of whether a closed shop can also be a closed union. To the extent that a union can control the supply of workers, they may restrict supply to keep wages higher than they would otherwise be. A union that can control supply does not need to control wages. Since Canada allows the closed shop (illegal in the United States since 1947), it is of interest to examine the state of legislation regarding "closed unions."

Historically, unions have been viewed as private organizations, free to make up their own rules regarding admission to membership. More recently, the trend has been to prevent unions from excluding persons from membership for arbitrary or discriminatory reasons. The effects of any trend determining who unions must accept as members are not trivial. Consider an unregulated market for union services where all actors are perfectly informed, and for simplicity there exists a single "union" offering services. Given a Johnson-Miezkowski (1970) world, where union workers gain at the expense of non-union workers, or even a world where some workers can gain at the expense of capital-owners if they unionize, but others cannot do so. The workers who have something to gain from unionization will attempt to join the union and will be accepted as members, while other workers would not join (and would not be accepted, if they wished to join). If you introduce a cost of providing union services into this scenario, a situation results where there are persons wishing to join whom the union would not want to accept. Forcing unions to accept workers who will dilute union power is one means available to public policy to reduce the power of unions.

Most labour relations legislation in Canada notes that employees have the right to join unions (see MacNeil, Lynk and Englemann 1995: 8-4), but this has been interpreted to mean that employers cannot hinder employees from joining, not that unions must accept applicants. Presumably, suitably explicit language can force unions to accept certain applicants, or even focus organizing activities in certain areas. A "duty to attempt to organize" upon *bona fide* request is a fascinating concept.

Current legislation varies considerably by jurisdiction. With some risk of over simplifying differences in language, the Canada Labour Code and legislation in Newfoundland prohibit discriminatory membership rules for employees, while Alberta and Nova Scotia have a similar prohibition applied to "persons." Saskatchewan legislation states that no employee shall unreasonably be denied access to membership, while British Columbia legislation prohibits discriminatory membership rules for "persons." New Brunswick legislation protects the right to membership only for persons who are required by the terms of the collective agreement to be members of the union. Ontario and Prince Edward Island do not directly regulate admission to a union,[27] and Manitoba and Quebec have no provisions regarding admission to membership.

Enforcement of these legislative provisions is another matter. As an example of how "small things matter," in *Andrews* v. *Health Employees Union, Local 180*,[28] the Board held that the union's refusal to admit to membership a volunteer worker who had crossed the picket line during a legal strike was "unfair and unreasonable," and the Industrial Relations Act in force at the time required that union decisions on admission be fair and reasonable. When the NDP government revised the Industrial Relations Act into the Labour Relations Code in 1992, the "fair and reasonable" clause was omitted, and it is at least possible that if the case were considered today the outcome would be different. In a 1995 case,[29] the Saskatchewan board ruled that temporary workers who were members of the bargaining unit and who had been denied the opportunity to pay initiation fees and join the union had been denied the opportunity to exercise their rights under the act, largely on the basis of the argument that there was no rational basis for refusing entry. As a final example, when a union has a closed shop, it has generally been held able to refuse new members while existing members are unemployed. If the union does not have a closed shop, refusal to accept members while current members are unemployed creates, in effect, a closed shop where there is not one under the collective agreement, and this has been held to be neither fair nor reasonable.[30] Briefly citing three cases does not establish a complete picture of how Labour Boards have interpreted admission to membership clauses,[31] but does suggest that carefully worded clauses might be enforceable.

The duty of fair referral becomes potentially important in closed-shop situations since, if a union refuses to refer a member to employment through the hiring hall, this is equivalent to either dismissal or refusal to admit under a union shop arrangement. A less severe penalty can take the form of not referring a member to employment in as timely a manner as equal treatment would demand. Further, since not all jobs are equally attractive, another opportunity for discrimination exists. The Canada Labour Code requires unions to develop, post, and follow written rules, which they use in making referrals to employment.[32] The Board has the right to review these rules to ensure that they are not unfair or discriminatory, but the union is free to develop its own rules.

British Columbia and Ontario have legislative provisions dealing with the operation of hiring halls, which prohibit referral practices which are discriminatory or in bad faith. Other provinces appear to have no provisions directly regulating referral, and MacNeil, Lynk, and Englemann (1995: 7–37) note that "To date, there are no cases in which it has been claimed that there is a common law duty of fair referral." There have been a number of cases where Boards have found that unions have violated their own constitutions in their referral practices, leading to remedies, but there have been other cases in which being in violation of their own constitutions and by-laws was not sufficient grounds for ordering remedies.[33] Overall, there appears to be considerable scope for extending duty of fair referral legislation, both geographically in scope of coverage.

Conclusions

If one is concerned about the adverse effects of strong union security clauses but does not wish to mount a frontal assault through Right-to-Work legislation—especially in view of the apparent futility of doing so—there are a number of other legislative provisions that can reduce these adverse effects. Restrictions on the ability of unions to expel members for stated infractions such as failure to honour a picket line, restrictions on the ability of unions to have workers expelled from membership dismissed, strengthened legislation enforcing the duty of fair representation and the duty of fair referral, and more forceful admission-to-membership clauses have all proven feasible alternatives in some jurisdictions in recent history. Other legislative measures described in the paper could achieve the same ends that Right-to-Work legislation attempts to attain.

Notes

1. Named after Justice Ivan C. Rand of the Supreme Court of Canada who arbitrated the "Rand Formula" as a solution to a dispute between the Ford Motor Company and the United Auto Workers in 1945.
2. See Freeman and Medoff 1984 for a survey of several studies; in the Canadian context, see Gunderson and Riddell 1993.
3. One implication of this consideration is that it is somewhat shortsighted to ascribe all of the differences in economic performance between Right-to-Work states and other states in the United States to clauses banning strong forms of union security. Even if the differences are due to legislation, the Labour Codes in these groups of states differ with respect to other clauses as well.
4. See Geddes 1995 regarding a recent proposal at the federal level to ban strikebreakers.
5. See Standberg 1996 for a general statement. Eaton 1996 notes that the Tories in Ontario changed the Labour Code within a month of taking office in 1995. An election is now required for certification, whereas a "card count" had been sufficient since the 1940s. See also Scotland 1995 regarding changes in the Ontario Labour Code in late 1995. A final point is that Labour Codes are subject to frequent minor adjustments; see Gauvin and Brennan, various dates.

32   *Unions and Right-to-Work Laws*

6 See Riddell 1993 and especially Weiler 1983 for support for this proposition. For an opposing view, see Robinson 1995.
7 Labour Canada 1994 presents a large format outline that quotes relevant sections of legislation to avoid giving an impression of spurious homogeneity of clauses among jurisdictions.
8 Note that legislation governing bargaining unit determination thus becomes very relevant to a number of questions. This is not covered in this chapter.
9 But see below for some critical differences among jurisdictions on fine points of legislation.
10 Much of this information is taken from MacNeil, Lynk, and Englemann 1995: 4-4-4-7. References to the relevant sections of the Acts are contained there.
11 (1991), 81 Dominion Law Reports (4th) 545, (1991) 2 Supreme Court Reports 211.
12 Except for this note, this paper will not discuss exemption from membership on religious grounds. Alberta, British Columbia, Manitoba, Ontario, Saskatchewan and the federal jurisdiction provide for such an exemption, with most legislation having clauses providing that a sum equivalent to union dues will be paid to a charity. Rigorous tests are applied to ensure that the request for exemption is based on religious, as opposed to philosophical, economic, ethical, or political grounds.
13 International Association of Machinists v. Orenda Engines Ltd. (1958), 8 Labour Arbitration Reports 116 (Laskin). The ruling in this case held that employers can require unions to explain the circumstances of the case leading to a request for dismissal, so that the employer can be satisfied that dismissal is appropriate under the union's constitution and bylaws and will be protected against a charge of having conspired with the union to violate the worker's rights.
14 Except for a revision to the Ontario Labour Relations Act in 1993 relating to union officials in the construction industry.
15 The difference in language may reflect the belief that the federal government only has jurisdiction in an employment context. But, because the Canada Labour Code provides no protection to persons who are not employees, a union can refuse membership to, or expell from membership, a person who is not currently employed. This makes a big difference in closed shops or union shops.
16 (1980), 81 Canada Labour Law Cases, paragraph 16,071 (Canada Labour Relations Board).
17 Revised Statutes of Canada, 1985, c. T-14.
18 Revised Statutes of Saskatchewan, c. 47, s. 18. The clause was added in 1994.
19 (1995) Saskatchewan Labour Relations Board Reports no. 26.

20 (1986) 62 Newfoundland and Prince Edward Island Reports 69, 87 Canada Labour Law Cases paragraph 14,007 (Newfoundland Supreme Court).
21 See cases cited in MacNeil, Lynk and Englemann 1995: 7-2.
22 (1984), 9 Dominion Law Reports (4th) 641, (1984) 1 Supreme Court Reports 509.
23 British Columbia, Manitoba, Ontario, Quebec, Saskatchewan and the federal jurisdiction.
24 Fair referral legislation is considered below.
25 Canada Post Corporation v. Canadian Union of Postal Workers (LeBrun), (1994), 94 di 67.
26 Esco Ltd. v. Canadian Association of Industrial, Mechanical and Allied Workers, Local 1, (1977) 2 Canada Labour Relations Board Reports 564 (BC).
27 But note the provisions regarding discharge previously discussed.
28 (1988), 88 Canadian Labour Law Cases, paragraph 16,023 (BC Industrial Relations Council).
29 Stewart v. Saskatchewan Brewers' Bottle and Keg Workers, Local No. 340, (1995), Saskatchewan Labour Relations Board Decisions No. 33.
30 Baker v. International Brotherhood of Electrical Workers, Local 70, (1986), 86 Canadian Labour Law Cases, paragraph 16,055 (British Columbia Labour Relations Board).
31 See MacNeil, Lynk, and Englemann 1995, ch. 8, for more cases.
32 Revised Statutes of Canada, 1985, c. L-2, s. 69.
33 See MacNeil, Lynk, and Englemann 1985: 7-37, 7-42, for examples.

References

Carrothers, A.W.R., E.E. Palmer, and W.B. Rayner (1986). *Collective Bargaining Law In Canada*. 2nd ed. Toronto: Butterworths.
Carter, Donald (1992). Canadian Industrial Relations after Lavigne. In Canadian Industrial Relations Association, *The Industrial Relations System: Future Trends and Developments* (Proceedings of the 29th Conference of CIRA): 215–225.
Eaton, Jonathan (1996). Bill 7 May Transform Ontario Labour Relations. *Toronto Star* (February 26): c2.
Freeman, Richard, and James Medoff (1984). *What Do Unions Do?* New York: Basic Books.
Gauvin, Michel, and Jeffrey Brennan (various dates). Changes in Canada Labour Law [regular feature]. *Relations Industrielles*.

Geddes, John (1995). Lobbyists Work Overtime to Halt New Scab Laws. *Financial Post* 89, 5 (February 4): 12.

Gunderson, Morley, and W. Craig Riddell (1993). *Labour Market Economics*. 3rd ed. Toronto: McGraw-Hill.

Johnson, Harry G., and Peter Mieskowski (1970). The Effects of Unionization on the Distribution of Income: A General Equilibrium Approach. *Quarterly Journal of Economics* 84 (November): 539-47.

Koch, George (1995). Lumps for Labour: An NCC Off-shoot Takes on Forced Unionism. *Alberta Report* 22, 14 (March 20): 19.

Kumar, Pradeep, Mary Lou Coates, and David Arrowsmith (1988). *The Current Industrial Relations Scene in Canada, 1988*. Kingston, ON: Industrial Relations Centre, Queen's University.

Labour Canada (1994). *Industrial Relations Legislation in Canada, 1993/94*. Ottawa: Canada Communications Group/Publishing.

MacNeil, Michael, Michael Lynk, and Peter Englemann (1995). *Trade Union Law in Canada*. Aurora, ON: Canada Law Book.

Opie, Theo Anne, and Lauren Bates (1995). *Canadian Master Labour Guide*. 9th ed. North York, ON: Commerce Clearing House Canadian Ltd.

Riddell, W. Craig (1993). Unionization in Canada and the United States: A Tale of Two Countries. In D. Card and R.B. Freeman (eds.), *Small Differences That Matter: Labor Markets and Income Maintenance in Canada and the United States* (Chicago: University of Chicago Press): 109–47.

Robinson, Chris (1995). Union Incidence in the Public and Private Sectors. *Canadian Journal of Economics* 28, 4b (November): 1056–76.

Scotland, Randall (1995). Chrysler, CAW Team Up to Request Bill 40 Repeal. *Financial Post* 89, 39 (September 30): 9.

Serres, Christopher (1995). A Bombshell for Organized Labour: Alberta's Unions Battle for Survival against Right-to-Work Legislation. *Alberta Report* 22, 38 (September 4): 14.

Standberg, Diane (1996). Labor Code Should Not Become a Target. *Langley Times* (March 16).

Weiler, Paul (1983). Promises to Keep. *Harvard Law Review* 96 (June): 1769–1829.

Unionization and Economic Performance
Evidence on Productivity, Profits, Investment, and Growth

BARRY T. HIRSCH

Central to policy debate regarding labour law reform and the appropriate role for labour unions in an economy is the effect of unionization on economic performance. There exists widespread support for a legal framework that permits the exercise of a collective voice representing workers. The impact of unions on economic performance, however, bears heavily on the degree to which public policy should facilitate union organizing and bargaining power. There has been extensive study in recent years, particularly in the United States, of the relationship of unionization to productivity, profitability, investment, and employment growth. The broad pattern that emerges from these studies is that unions significantly increase compensation for their members but do not increase productivity sufficiently to offset the cost increases from higher compensation. As a result, unions are associated with lower profitability, decreased investment in

---

Notes will be found on pages 64–65

physical capital and research and development (R&D), and lower rates of employment and sales growth. As long as unionized companies operate in a competitive environment, weak economic performance in union firms relative to nonunion firms and sectors implies a continuing decline in membership, in the absence of changes in labour law favourable to union organizing. Yet the deleterious effects of unions on economic performance undermine rather than buttress the case for governmental regulations and policies that promote union strength.

This chapter examines the evidence on unions and economic performance. It presents, first, a simple economic framework for interpreting union effects on performance and examines briefly the difficult issue of measurement. It then examines the empirical evidence: studies of union effects on productivity, profits, investment, and growth. Emphasis is on outcomes in the United States, where this topic has been studied most extensively, although results from Canada, Britain, and elsewhere are briefly mentioned. Following a summary of the empirical evidence, the paper explores implications for public policy and labour law.

A framework for analysis

A useful starting point in our assessment of unions and performance is the framework popularized by Freeman and Medoff (1979, 1984), who contrast the "monopoly" and "collective-voice" faces of unionism. Standard economic analysis emphasizes the monopoly face. Unions are viewed as distorting labour (and product) market outcomes by increasing wages above competitive levels. Unions distort relative factor prices and factor usage (producing a deadweight welfare loss), cause losses in output through strikes, and lower productivity by union work rules and reduced management discretion. More recently, economists have emphasized unions' role in taxing returns on tangible and intangible capital, and examined empirically union effects on profitability, investment, and growth. It is this latter literature that is emphasized in what follows. In both the "old" and "new" literatures, union bargaining power or ability to extract gains for its members is determined primarily by the degree of competition or, more specifically, the economic constraints facing both the employer and union.

The other, not necessarily incompatible, face of unions is what Freeman and Medoff refer to as "collective voice/institutional response." This view emphasizes the *potential* role that collective bargaining have in improving the functioning of internal labour markets. Specifically, legally protected unions may more effectively allow workers to express their preferences and exercise "collective voice" in the shaping of internal industrial relations policies. Union bargaining may be more effective than individual bargaining in overcoming workplace public-goods problems and attendant free-rider problems. As the workers' agent, unions facilitate the exercise of the workers' right to free speech, acquire information, monitor employer behaviour, and formalize the workplace governance structure in a way that better represents average workers, as opposed to workers who are more skilled and therefore more mobile or hired on contract from the outside the plant. In some settings, the exercise of collective voice should be associated with higher workplace productivity, an outcome dependent not only on effective collective voice but also on a constructive "institutional response" and a cooperative labour-relations environment. The "monopoly" and "collective-voice" faces of unionism operate side-by-side, with the importance of each being very much determined by the legal and economic environment in which unions and firms operate. For these reasons, an assessment of unions' effects on economic performance hinges on empirical evidence.

Let us begin with an analysis of unions' effects on performance when collective bargaining is introduced into what is otherwise a competitive environment. In the long run, profitability among firms in industries characterized by relatively easy entry of firms (e.g., perfect competition or monopolistic competition) tend toward a "normal" rate of return or zero economic profits (i.e., the opportunity costs of resources are just covered). Consider first a single unionized firm in what is otherwise a competitive industry with nonunion firms. The bargaining power of a union organized at a single firm (or more generally, a small portion of the industry) is severely limited unless it can help create value as well as tax returns. A union wage premium—that is, higher compensation for a union worker than an otherwise identical worker in a nonunion firm—must be offset by a productivity increase in order that costs do not increase and profits decrease. Note that in a competitive setting cost increases cannot be passed forward to consumers in the form of higher prices. So, in the absence of a productivity offset, unions should have little bargaining strength in a highly competitive industry. Substantial union wage increases in a competitive setting will lower profitability, investment, employment, output, and, consequently, union membership.

The situation changes somewhat as we allow a relatively large proportion of an industry to be unionized. In this situation, union wage increases (in the absence of increases in productivity) increase costs among many firms in the industry, so that no individual union firm is at a severe competitive disadvantage. In this case, costs can be more easily passed forward to consumers through price increases. But such a situation is difficult to sustain in the very long run, as long as entry and expansion of nonunion companies is relatively easy or the products produced are tradeable in the world market. In short, it is difficult for a union to acquire and sustain bargaining power and membership in a competitive, open-economy setting, in the absence of positive effects upon productivity that offset increases in compensation.

Unions have considerably greater ability to organize and to acquire and maintain wage gains and membership in less competitive economic settings. Such settings include oligopolistic industries in which entry is difficult owing to economies of scale or limited international competition, or regulated industries in which entry and rate competition is legally restricted. An example of the former includes the American motor vehicle industry prior to the influx of European and Japanese imports (and, more recently, of foreign-owned nonunion assembly plants in the United States). Examples of the latter include the American motor carrier and airline industries prior to deregulation, as well as the current United States Postal Service (Hirsch 1993; Hirsch and Macpherson forthcoming; Hirsch and Macpherson 1996; Hirsch, Wachter, and Gillula 1997).

If there is no offsetting productivity effect, a crucial question becomes the source from which union wage gains derive. Were it entirely a tax on monopoly profits, union rent-seeking might be relatively benign. But in most economic settings, monopoly profits are relatively small or short-lived. What appear to be abnormally high profits often represent the reward to firms for developing new products or for introducing cost-reducing production processes, or simply the quasi-rents that represent the normal returns to prior investment in long-lived physical and R&D capital. These profits serve an important economic role, providing incentive for investment and attracting resources into those economic activities most highly valued. To the extent that unions tax the quasi-rents from long-lived capital, union wage increases can be viewed as a tax on capital that lowers the net rate of return on investment. In response, union firms reduce investment in physical and innovative capital, leading to slower growth in sales and employment and a shrinkage of the union sector (see Baldwin 1983; Grout 1984; Hirsch and Prasad 1995; Addison and Chilton 1996).

Although greatly over-simplified, the discussion above provides a reasonable framework for viewing the effect of unions on economic performance. Ultimately, empirical evidence is required to assess the relative importance of the monopoly and collective-voice faces of unionism. It is worth noting two points at the outset, however. First, the effects of unions upon productivity and other aspects of performance may differ substantially across industries, time, and countries. This is hardly surprising given that both the collective-voice and monopoly activities of unions depend crucially on the labour relations and economic environment in which management and labour operate. Second, union effects are typically measured by differences in performance between union and nonunion firms or sectors. Such differences do not measure the effects of unions on aggregate or economy-wide economic performance as long as resources are free to move across sectors. For example, evidence presented below indicates that union companies in the United States have performed poorly relative to nonunion companies. To the extent that output and resources can shift between sectors, poor union performance has led to a shift of production and employment away from unionized industries, firms, and plants and into the nonunion sector. Overall effects on economy-wide performance have been relatively minor. Most visible, of course, has been the rather precipitous decline in private sector unionism.

What has been true for the United States since the 1980s, however, largely reflects the high degree of competitiveness in the American economy, with the increasing importance of trade, deregulation of important industries, technological change that has reduced the use of production labour, relatively flexible labour market norms, and an economic and legal environment not overly amenable to union organizing and bargaining. The recent experience in the United States was not always the case, nor need it represent the current experience in other countries. The important point here is that the role of unions in society and the effects of unions upon performance are very much driven by the competitiveness of the environment in which firms and unions must operate. An obvious policy implication is that those concerned with economic performance should focus on policies affecting economic competitiveness and resource mobility in general and not only on the structure of labour law in which unions operate.

Measurement

The measurement of union effects on economic performance is not straightforward. Union effects on economic performance must be estimated using imperfect data and statistical models and techniques that permit alternative interpretations of the evidence. Because of these limitations, one must carefully assess both individual studies and the cumulative evidence before drawing strong inferences regarding unions' causal impact on economic performance.

Most studies utilize cross-sectional data (at single or multiple points in time), measuring differences in outcomes (e.g., productivity) across firms or industries with different levels of union density (i.e., the proportion of unionized workers in the sample being considered). Estimates are based on regression analysis, which controls or accounts for other measurable determinants of performance. The key question is whether, after accounting for other determinants, one can conclude that the estimated difference in performance associated with differences in union density truly represents the causal effect of unions.

There are (at least) three important reasons why one must exhibit caution in drawing inferences from such statistical analysis. First, there are numerous other factors correlated with performance besides unionization. If one fails to control for an important productivity determinant *and* that factor is correlated with union density, then one obtains a biased estimate of the causal effect of unionism on performance. For example, older plants tend to have lower productivity, and union density is higher in older plants. If a study were to estimate the union impact on productivity among plants, the inability to measure and control for plant age (or its correlates, such as age of capital) would mean that part of the effect of plant age on productivity would be included in the (biased) estimate of the effect of unions upon productivity.

A second reason for caution is that unionization is not distributed randomly across firms or industries or may be determined simultaneously with the performance variable under study; that is, causality may run from performance to unionization as well from unionism to performance. For example, unions may be most likely to organize and survive in firms that are most profitable and, in this case, standard estimates of union effects on profitability (which are almost universally negative) tend to understate the deleterious effects of unions on profits, since unions form where profits (prior to the union tax) tend to be higher.

A third reason for caution in making inferences is that even where one has obtained reliable estimates of union effects for the population being studied (e.g., a particular industry, time period, or country), it is not clear to what extent these results can be generalized outside that population. For example, the most reliable estimates of the effects of unions upon productivity are based on specific industries (e.g., cement, sawmills) where output is homogeneous and can be measured in physical units rather than by value added. Yet, it is not clear to what extent the results in, say, the western sawmill industry can be generalized to the economy as a whole. Indeed, the economic framework outlined previously suggests strongly that union effects should differ across time, establishment, industry, and country.[1]

A number of studies combine cross-sectional and longitudinal (i.e., time-series) analysis, typically examining changes in performance over time owing to levels in union density or changes in union status. Recent studies, for example, have examined changes in firm market value (measured by stock price changes), investment, or employment following the announcement of union representation elections. A limited number of studies have examined changes in productivity or other performance measures following unionization of a plant. The advantage of longitudinal analysis is that each individual firm (or plant) forms the basis for comparison—that is, a firm's performance once unionized is compared to that same firm prior to unionization. In this way, unmeasured, firm-specific, attributes that are fixed over time are controlled for in estimating the causal effect of unionization. Despite this considerable advantage, longitudinal analysis can have severe shortcomings since it assumes that changes in union status are not determined by changes in the performance measure under examination, and the period of change under study must correspond closely to the period over which a union impact occurs. For example, "events" studies examining the effect of certification elections on a firm's market value must be careful to compare market value from a period prior to the expectation of a union election with a period in which the full effects of the election on value have been anticipated (i.e., reflected in the stock price).

Evidence on effects of unions on economic performance is analyzed below. Because of inherent evidential and methodological limitations of individual studies, strong conclusions are drawn only where there exists a study of unusually high quality, where there exists a clear correspondence between theory and evidence, or where there are a relatively large number of studies providing similar results.

Evidence: unions' effects on productivity, profits, investment, and growth

Productivity and productivity growth

Critical to the assessment of labour unions, performance, and labour law is an understanding of unions' effects on productivity.[2] If collective bargaining in the workplace were systematically to increase productivity and to do so to such an extent that it fully offset compensation increases, then a strong argument could be made for policies that facilitate union organizing. A pathbreaking empirical study by Brown and Medoff (1978), followed by a body of evidence summarized in Freeman and Medoff's widely read *What Do Unions Do?* (1984), made what at the time appeared to be a persuasive case that collective bargaining in the United States is, on average, associated with substantial improvements in productivity. Productivity increases, it was argued, are effected through the exercise of collective voice coupled with an appropriate institutional response from management. According to this view, unions lower turnover and establish in workplaces more efficient governance structures that are characterized by public goods, complementarities in production, and long-term contractual relations.

The thesis that unions significantly increase productivity has not held up well. Subsequent studies were as likely to find that unions had negative as opposed to positive effects upon productivity. A large enhancement of productivity because of unionization is inconsistent with evidence on profitability and employment. And, increasingly, attention has focused on the dynamic effect of unionization and the apparently negative effects of unions on growth in productivity, sales, and employment.

A typical union productivity study estimates Cobb-Douglas or (rather less restrictive) translog production functions in which measured outputs are related to inputs. To fix the discussion, below is a variant of the Cobb-Douglas production function developed by Brown and Medoff (1978):

$$Q = AK^\alpha (L_n + cL_u)^{1-\alpha} \qquad (1)$$

where Q is output, K is capital, L_u and L_n are union and nonunion labour respectively, A is a constant of proportionality, and α and $1-\alpha$ are the output elasticities with respect to capital and labour. The parameter c reflects productivity differences between union and nonunion labour. If $c > 1$, then union labour is more productive, in line with the collective-voice model; if $c < 1$, then union labour is less productive, in line with conventional arguments concerning the deleterious impact of such things as union work rules and constraints on merit-based wage dispersion. Manipulation of equation (1) yields the estimating equation:

$$\ln(Q/L) \approx \ln A + \alpha \ln(K/L) + (1-\alpha)(c-1)P \qquad (2)$$

where P represents proportion unionized L_u/L) in a firm or industry or the presence or absence of a union at the plant or firm level (a zero/one categorical variable). Equation (2) assumes constant returns to scale, an assumption relaxed by including a $\ln L$ variable as a measure of establishment size. The coefficient on P measures the logarithmic productivity differential of unionized establishments. If it is assumed that the unions' effect upon productivity solely reflects the differential efficiency of labour inputs, the effect of union labour upon productivity is calculated by dividing the coefficient on P by $(1-\alpha)$.

Limitations attach to the production function test. As Brown and Medoff note, the use of value added as an output measure confounds price and quantity effects, since part of the measured union productivity differential may result from higher prices in the unionized sector. Not surprisingly, estimated effects of unions upon productivity tend to be lower when price adjustments are made (e.g., Allen 1986b; Mitchell and Stone 1992) and are rarely large in studies where Q is measured explicitly in physical units. Union firms can more easily pass through higher costs when they operate in product markets sheltered from nonunion and foreign competition. Use of value-added, therefore, is most likely to confound price and output effects in aggregate analyses relating industry value-added to industry union density. It is less of a concern in firm-level analyses that measure firms' union status and industry union density (Clark 1984; Hirsch 1991a). Not surprisingly, these studies find small, generally negative, effects of unions upon productivity.

One issue discussed in this literature concerns the fact that firms facing higher wages must be more productive if they are to survive in the very long run. Hence, the unions' effect upon productivity is not being measured across a representative sample of firms since union firms failing to increase productivity and survive are least likely to be observed. Measurement of union productivity differentials from among a sample of surviving firms may therefore overstate the effect of unions upon the productivity of a representative firm. In fact, union firms are less likely to fail than nonunion firms, although this is because such firms are older and larger and not due to their union status. Once one controls for age and size, union status appears to have surprisingly little effect on firm failure rates, although unionization is associated with slower employment growth (Freeman and Kleiner 1994; Dunne and Macpherson 1994). The suggestion here is that unions will push firms to the brink of failure but will not shove them over the cliff.

The (rightfully) influential Brown and Medoff (1978) paper is the unavoidable starting point for any summary of the evidence about the effect of unions upon productivity. The assertion that unions in general raise productivity rests almost exclusively on the results of their study. Using aggregate two-digit manufacturing industry data cross-classified by state groups for 1972, Brown and Medoff obtain coefficients on union density of from .22 to .24, implying values (obtained by dividing the union coefficient by $1 - \alpha$) for $c - 1$ of from .30 to .31. In short, they conclude that unions increase total factor productivity by more than 20 percent.

The potential measurement problems previously discussed apply with some force to the Brown-Medoff study. Despite the care with which their paper is executed, subsequent research has proven their results to be neither plausible nor consistent with other evidence. As argued by Addison and Hirsch (1989), parameter estimates from Brown and Medoff would most likely imply an increase in profitability associated with unionism, contrary to the rather unambiguous evidence of lower firm and industry profitability resulting from unionization. Wessels (1985) casts further doubt on the plausibility of high estimates of productivity increases due to unionization by showing that it is difficult to reconcile the productivity and wage evidence in Brown and Medoff with evidence on employment. Offsetting increases in productivity due to unionization and relative labour costs should imply substantial decreases in union employment (holding output constant) as firms shift toward labour-saving capital. Yet unions appear to have little effect on capital-labour ratios (Clark 1984).[3]

There are surprisingly few manufacturing-wide or economy-wide productivity studies and, except for Brown and Medoff, none reports consistent evidence of a overall positive effect of unions upon productivity.[4] Clark (1984) provides one of the better broad-based studies. He uses data for 902 manufacturing lines-of-business from 1970 to 1980 to estimate, among other things, value-added (and sales) productivity equations. He obtains marginally significant coefficients on the union variable of from −.02 to −.03, in sharp contrast to the results in Brown and Medoff. The Clark study has the advantage of a large sample size over multiple years, business-specific information on union coverage, and a detailed set of control variables (although the union coefficient is little affected by inclusion of the latter). In Clark's separate two-digit industry regressions, positive effects by unions upon productivity are found only for textiles, furniture, and petroleum. A similar study was conducted by Hirsch (1991a), who used data on over 600 publicly traded manufacturing-sector firms for the years 1968 to 1980. (Union coverage data for 1977 was collected from these companies by the author.) Hirsch finds a strong negative relationship between union coverage and firm productivity when including only firm-level control variables, but the union effect drops sharply after including detailed industry controls. Moreover, the results prove fragile when subjected to econometric probing. Hirsch interprets his results as providing no evidence for a positive economy-wide effect of unions upon productivity, and weak evidence for a negative effect. As in the Clark study, Hirsch finds considerable variability in the union to productivity relationship across industries. Based on the extant evidence to date, a reasonable conclusion is that the average effect of unions upon productivity is small and, if anything, more likely to be negative than positive.[5]

Results from productivity studies based on firms within a single industry produce a rather varied picture. The primary advantage of industry-specific studies is that many of the econometric problems inherent in studies across a whole economy or the whole manufacturing sector are avoided. Output can be measured in physical units rather than value added, information on firm-level union status is more readily available, and more flexible functional forms can be reliably estimated. From a methodological perspective, among the best analyses are Clark's studies of the cement industry (Clark 1980a, 1980b), Allen's analysis of the construction industry (Allen 1986a, 1986b), and Mitchell and Stone's (1992) analysis of western sawmills. These studies are notable for the use of physical output measures, for allowing production-function parameters to vary between union and nonunion plants, in controlling for firm effects through the study of plants changing from nonunion to union status, in introducing a supervisory labour input measure, and in separating union effects on value-added into its price and output components (not all of the studies do each of these things). Each of the studies provides a wide array of evidence. Clark finds positive, albeit small, effects of unions upon productivity among cement plants. Allen (1986b) finds positive union effects in large office building construction and negative effects in school construction. Similarly, Allen (1986a) finds positive and negative union effects upon productivity, respectively, in privately and publicly owned hospitals and nursing homes. Mitchell and Stone find negative effects of unions upon output in sawmills, following appropriate adjustments for product quality and raw material usage. Although methodological advantages of the industry-specific studies are achieved at the price of a loss in generality, they do increase our understanding of how unions affect the workplace.

Despite substantial diversity in the literature about union productivity, several systematic patterns are revealed (Addison and Hirsch 1989). First, effects upon productivity tend to be largest in industries where the union wage premium is most pronounced. This pattern is what critics of the production function test predict—that union density coefficients in fact reflect a wage rather than a productivity effect. These results also support a "shock effect" interpretation of unionization, whereby management must respond to an increase in labour costs by organizing more efficiently, reducing slack, and increasing measured productivity. Second, positive effects by unions upon productivity are typically largest where competitive pressure exists and these positive effects are largely restricted to the private, for-profit, sectors. Notably absent are positive effects of unions upon productivity in public school construction, public libraries, government bureaus, schools, law enforcement (Byrne, Dezhbakhsh, and King 1996), and hospitals.[6]

This interpretation of the productivity studies has an interesting twist: the evidence suggests that a relatively competitive, cost-conscious economic environment is a necessary condition for a positive effect of unions upon productivity, and that the managerial response should be stronger, the larger the union wage premium or the greater the pressure on profits. Yet it is precisely in such competitive environments that there should be relatively little managerial slack and the least scope for union organizing and wage gains. Therefore, the possibility of a sizable effect by unions upon productivity across the whole economy appears rather limited.

Discussion up to this point has been restricted to studies of the United States. Evidence for other countries is far more limited. British studies, although few in number, show a negative relationship between union density and productivity levels (for a summary, see Booth 1995). Evidence for Canada from Maki (1983), based on an aggregate manufacturing time-series data for the period from 1926 to 1978, suggests initially positive union "shock" effects on productivity, although slower productivity growth due to unionization offsets the positive effects within 5 to 8 years. German evidence is particularly difficult to sort out owing to the widespread presence both of unions with national or centralized bargaining and of mandatory works councils in union and (sometimes) in nonunion settings (for a survey, see Addison, Schnabel, and Wagner 1995). Brunello (1992) finds that unions, except those working for small suppliers facing competitive pressure, tend to have negative effects on productivity (and profits) in Japan. Although international evidence is limited, that which exists is broadly supportive of our interpretation of the American evidence.

Productivity growth

Far less attention has been given to the effects of unions upon productivity *growth*. As shown by Maki (1983), Hirsch and Link (1984), and others, unions' effects on productivity levels and growth need not be the same. For example, unionization initially could be associated with higher levels of productivity owing to the effect of "shock" or "collective voice," while at the same time retarding the rate of productivity growth. Of course, in the long run low rates of productivity growth among union firms will lower productivity levels. By productivity growth, we mean the increase in value-added after controlling for changes in factor inputs; Hence, studies examine union effects on growth after controlling for union-nonunion differences in the accumulation of tangible and intangible capital and other measurable factors of production. As emphasized subsequently, it is unions' effects upon investment and capital accumulation that most affect the sales and employment growth of unionized firms relative to nonunionized firms.

Hirsch (1991a) provides the most comprehensive treatment of unions' effects on productivity growth, based on a sample of 531 firms and covering the period from 1968 to 1980. Following an accounting for company size and firm-level changes in labour, physical capital, and R&D, union firms are found to have substantially slower productivity growth than nonunion firms. Accounting for industry sales growth, energy usage, and trade, however, cuts the estimate of the union effect by more than half. Addition of industry dummies cuts the estimate further, while the remaining effect proves fragile when subjected to econometric probes regarding the error structure. In short, union firms clearly display substantially slower productivity growth than do nonunion firms, but most (if not all) of this difference is associated with effects attributable to industry differences, since union firms are located in industries or sectors with slow growth. As with the evidence on productivity, it is concluded that there exists no strong evidence that unions have a *causal* effect on productivity growth.

Maki (1973), using aggregate Canadian data, concludes that the shock effects of unionization initially increase productivity levels but that unionism is associated with slower productivity growth. Interestingly, British evidence for differences in productivity growth between unionized and nonunionized firms (Nickell, Wadhwani, and Wall 1992, Gregg, Machin, and Metcalf 1993) suggest that unions have either a negative effect or no effect on productivity growth during the early years of their analysis but positive effects during the 1980s. The interpretation of these studies is that a sharp recession during the period 1979 to 1981 and antiunion legislation during the Thatcher period shocked inefficient union plants into operating more efficiently—that is, more rapid productivity growth was precipitated by competitive pressures operating upon a legacy of burdensome union work rules and substantial inefficiency.

Despite the furor and contentiousness surrounding the effects of labour unions on productivity and productivity growth, the most comprehensive studies tend to find little causal effect due to unions. Four points surrounding this conclusion are worth emphasizing. First, a small overall impact does not mean that unions do not matter but, rather, that the net outcome of the positive and negative effects of unions on productivity roughly offset each other. Second, economy-wide studies measure the average effects of unions. Not surprisingly, there appears to be considerable diversity in outcomes across firms and industries, consistent with the considerable emphasis given to the importance of the economic and labour-relations environments. Third, the absence of a large positive effect upon productivity implies that union compensation gains are not offset, implying lower profitability and (typically) lower investment. That is, the important point to bring away from the productivity evidence is the absence of a large positive effect due to unions. Finally, studies of productivity and productivity growth control for differences in factor-input usage and growth. As will be seen subsequently, unionization is associated with significantly lower rates of investment and accumulation of physical and innovative capital. It is primarily through this route, rather than by direct effects on productivity, that we obtain slower growth in sales and employment in the union sectors of the economy and a concomitant decline in union membership.

Profitability

Union wage gains lower firm profitability unless offset by productivity enhancements in the workplace or higher prices in the product market. The evidence on productivity reviewed above indicates that unionization does not typically offset compensation increases. A rise in the price of the product sufficient to prevent a loss in profitability is possible only in a regulated industry where firms are "guaranteed" a competitive rate of return. In more competitive settings, where unionized firms compete with nonunion domestic companies and traded goods, there is little if any possibility of passing along increased cost via a rise in prices. Lower profitability will be reflected in decreased current earnings and measured rates of return on capital, and in a lower market valuation of the firm's assets. *Ex-ante* returns on *equity* (risk-adjusted) should not differ between union and nonunion companies, since stock prices adjust to reflect expected earnings (Hirsch and Morgan 1994).

Profit-maximizing responses by firms to cost differentials should limit the magnitude of differences in profitability between union and nonunion companies in the very long run. Differences in profits will be mitigated through the movement of resources out of union into nonunion sectors—that is, investment in and by union operations will decrease until post-tax (i.e., post-union) rates of return are equivalent to nonunion rates of return or, stated alternatively, union coverage will be restricted to economic sectors realizing above-normal, pre-union rates of returns. Because the quasi-rents accruing to long-lived capital may provide a principal source for union gains and complete long-run adjustments occur slowly, however, we are likely to observe differences in profitability as these adjustments take place.

Empirical evidence shows unambiguously that unionization leads to lower profitability, although studies differ to some degree in their conclusions regarding the magnitude and source of union gains.[7] Lower profits are found using alternative measures of profitability. Studies using aggregate industry data typically employ as their dependent variable the industry price-cost margin (PCM) defined by (Total Revenue − Variable Costs) / Total Revenue—and typically measured by (Value Added − Payroll − Advertising) / Shipments. Line-of-business studies and some firm-level studies have used accounting profit-rate measures: the rate of return on sales, measured by earnings divided by sales, and the rate of return on capital, measured by earnings divided by the value of the capital stock.

Firm-level analyses of publicly traded firms (e.g., Salinger 1984; Hirsch 1991a, 1991b) have used market-value measures of profitability, a common measure being Tobin's q, defined as a firm's market value divided by the replacement cost of assets. Finally, there have been several "events" studies in which changes in market value attributable to votes for union representation or to unanticipated changes in collective bargaining agreements have been examined (e.g., Ruback and Zimmerman 1984; Bronars and Deere 1990; Abowd 1989; Olson and Becker 1990; Becker and Olson 1992).

The conclusion that unionization is associated with lower profitability is not only invariant to the profit measure used but also holds for studies using industries, firms, or lines-of-business as the unit of observation. The conclusion also holds regardless of the time period under study and, although there is diversity in results, most studies obtain estimates suggesting that unionized firms have profits that are 10 percent to 20 percent lower than the profits of nonunion firms.

Economists are understandably sceptical that large profit differentials could survive in a competitive economy, notwithstanding the sizable profit differences between unionized firms and nonunionized firms found in the empirical literature. Yet there are two potentially important econometric biases causing effects of unionization to be understated. First, profit functions are estimated only for *surviving* firms, since those for which the effects of unionization are most deleterious may be less likely to remain in the sample. Second, unions are more likely to be organized where potential profits are higher; hence, the negative effect of unions on profits may be underestimated in empirical work where union density is treated as exogenous. In fact, those studies that attempt to account for the simultaneous determination of union status and profitability obtain larger estimates of unions' effects upon profits (see Voos and Mishel 1986; Hirsch 1991a). That being said, the exact magnitude of the estimated profit differential between unionized firms and nonunionized firms can be sensitive to specification. Omission of factors positively correlated with union coverage and negatively correlated with profitability will cause an overstatement of the union profit effect.

More recently, attention has turned to the sources from which unions appropriate rents (see Addison and Hirsch 1989). Influential early studies concluded that unions reduce profits primarily in highly concentrated industries and that monopoly power provides the primary source for union compensation gains (e.g., Salinger 1984; Karier 1985). But that conclusion has not survived further analysis. Clark (1984) obtained the (surprising) finding that unions reduce profits only among businesses with low market shares. Hirsch and Connolly (1987) examine this issue directly. They find no evidence from their study of product markets or of labour markets to support the hypothesis that profits associated with industry concentration provide a source for union rents. Rather, they argue that returns from a firm's market share, R&D capital, and weak foreign competition are more likely sources for union gains. Hirsch (1990), using a data-set with a firm-specific union coverage measure, even more clearly rejects the hypothesis that concentration-related profits provide a source for union rents. Note that these studies do not conclude that monopoly rents are not a source for union bargaining power and wage gains. Rather, they find that profits accruing from product-market concentration do not provide such a major source, in part because of the rather tenuous relationship between profitability and concentration (e.g., Ravenscraft 1983). There is no suggestion that unions cannot and do not capture rents; they clearly do so, as can be seen from the close relationship between the unions' wage gains and regulatory rents in the trucking industry, the airlines, and the United States Postal Service.

What recent studies of profitability do suggest is that many of the gains by unions come from what would otherwise be normal returns to long-lived investments. This has important implications for the effects of labour unions on investment behaviour and long-term growth, as seen in subsequent sections. For example, Hirsch (1991a) strongly rejects the hypothesis that monopoly profits associated with industry concentration provide a primary source for union gains. He provides evidence suggesting that unions capture current earnings associated with limited foreign competition, both current and future earnings associated with disequilibrium or growing demand in the firm and industry (sales growth), future earnings emanating from R&D capital, and current and future quasi-rents emanating from long-lived physical capital (for related evidence, see Cavanaugh 1996).

The poor profit performance of unionized companies during the 1970s may provide an important explanation for the marked decline in union membership during the 1980s. As noted by Linneman, Wachter, and Carter (1990) and others, employment declines have been concentrated in the unionized sectors of the economy; nonunion employment has expanded even in highly unionized industries. Although important, shifts in industry demand are an insufficient explanation for the marked decline in private sector unionism. The evidence presented here supports the thesis that declines in union membership and coverage in no small part have been a response to the continuing poor profit performance of unionized companies throughout this period. The conclusion that large profitability differences between unionized and nonunionized firms help to explain declining unionization is complementary to the conclusion reached by Freeman (1988), Linneman, Wachter, and Carter (1990), and others that high union wage premiums have accelerated unionism's decline.

Evidence from Britain strongly suggests that union recognition and the closed shop have a negative effect upon profitablility (e.g., Machin and Stewart 1990; see Booth 1995 for a summary). That being said, most of the firm-level studies lack good measures of profitability and instead rely on a subjective managerial evaluation of profit performance. Given that British unions raise wages but do not appear to improve productivity, it would be surprising if the evidence relating unions to profitability indicated anything other than a negative relationship. A recent study by Machin and Stewart (1996), however, finds that the effects of unions upon profits are only half as large in 1990 as in 1984, and that negative effects are most pronounced in the relatively small number of establishments with both a closed shop and restrictions on managerial freedom owing to union work rules.

Union rent seeking and investment in R&D and physical capital

The area of theoretical and empirical research that has received the most attention in recent years has been the impact of unionization on investments in tangible and intangible capital. The theoretical origins for this literature can be seen in articles by Baldwin (1983) and Grout (1984); the earliest empirical article in this literature is by Connolly, Hirsch, and Hirschey (1986). Recent rent-seeking models focus on the fact that unions capture some share of the quasi-rents that make up the normal return to investment in long-lived capital and R&D. In response, firms rationally reduce their investment in vulnerable tangible and intangible capital until returns on investment are equalized across the union (taxed) and nonunion (non-taxed) sectors. Contraction of the union sector, it is argued, has resulted in part from the long-run response by firms to such rent seeking.

The union tax or rent-seeking framework stands in marked contrast to the traditional economic model of unions. In the standard model, the union's monopoly power in the labour market is viewed as changing relative factor prices through its ability to raise union compensation above competitive levels. In response to a higher wage, union firms move up and along their labour-demand curve by decreasing employment, hiring higher-quality workers, and increasing the ratio of capital to labour. Total investment in innovative activity and labour-saving capital can increase or decrease owing to substitution and scale effects that work in opposing directions.

The traditional model is inadequate for at least two reasons. First, settlements off the labour-demand curve, with lower wages and greater employment than would obtain in the on-the-demand-curve model, are preferred by both the union and management. If settlements are not on the labour-demand curve, the effect of unions on factor mix cannot be predicted in straightforward fashion (see Farber 1986 for a review). A second shortcoming is the traditional model's characterization of union wage increases as an independent increase in the cost of labour relative to capital. In the rent-seeking framework, union wage premiums are viewed as levying a tax on firm earnings, much of which is composed of the returns to capital. The union tax in this view is an outcome made possible both by union power in the labour market and the presence of the firm's quasi-rents. Stated alternatively, wage increases to unions are in part a tax on capital and need not lead firms to shift their factor mix away from labour and toward capital (Hirsch and Prasad 1995; Addison and Chilton 1996).

Union rent-seeking may reduce investment not only in physical capital but also in R&D and other forms of innovative activity. The stock of knowledge and improvements in processes and products emanating from R&D are likely to be relatively long-lived and firm specific. To the extent that returns from innovative activity are appropriable, firms will respond to union power by reducing these investments. Collective-bargaining coverage within a company is most likely to reduce investment in product innovations and relatively factor-neutral process innovations, while having ambiguous effects on innovations in labour-saving processes. Expenditures in R&D also tend to signal—or be statistically prior to—investments in physical capital. Therefore, firms reducing long-range plans for physical capital investment in response to unions' rent-seeking behaviour are likely to reduce investment in R&D.

Patents applied for, or granted, are a measure of innovative output emanating from a company's R&D stock. Patent activity is likely to exhibit a relationship with union coverage in a company largely similar to that exhibited by R&D inputs. Unionized companies, however, may be more likely to patent, given their stock of innovation capital, as a means of reducing union rent appropriation (Connolly, Hirsch, and Hirschey 1986). Although the patent application process is often costly and revealing of trade secrets, patents offer the opportunity for firms to license product and process innovations, and transform what might otherwise be firm-specific innovative capital into general capital, and lessen a union's ability to appropriate the quasi-rents from that capital.[8]

Hirsch (1991a) provides a comprehensive empirical analysis of union effects on investment, both in physical and intangible capital. He is also distinguishes between the "direct" and "indirect" effects of unions on investment. The direct effect, as discussed above, stems from the union tax on the returns to long-lived and relation-specific capital, leading firms to cut back on investment so as to equate the marginal post-tax rate of return with the marginal financing cost. The indirect effect of unions on investment arises from the higher financing costs owing to reduced profits (and, thus, internal funding of investment) among union firms.

Using data for the period from 1968 to 1980 on approximately 500 publicly traded American manufacturing firms and a model with detailed firm and industry controls, including profitability, Hirsch estimates the effect upon investment for a typical unionized firm compared to a nonunion firm. Other things being equal, it is found that the typical unionized firm has 6 percent lower capital investment than its observationally equivalent nonunion counterpart. Allowing for the profit effect increases the estimate to about 13 percent; that is, about half of the overall impact of unions is an indirect effect. Hirsch repeats the exercise for intangible capital (annual investments in R&D), and his findings imply that the average unionized firm has 15 percent lower R&D, holding constant profitability and the other determinants. Allowing for the indirect effects induced by lower profitability only modestly raises the estimate. These deleterious union effects on capital investment have been confirmed in subsequent studies with

American data (e.g., Hirsch 1992; Becker and Olson 1992; Bronars and Deere 1993; Bronars, Deere, and Tracy 1994; Cavanaugh 1996). A recent study by Fallick and Hassett (1996) examines changes in firms' capital investment in response to a positive outcome in a certification election. They find a substantial reduction, likening the effects of a vote for certification to the effects of a 30 percentage point increase in the corporate income tax.

International evidence on unions and investment is rather limited. In studies examining the effects of unions upon investment in Canada, Betts and Odgers conclude, consistent with the American evidence, that unions significantly reduce investment in physical capital and R&D (Odgers and Betts, forthcoming; Betts and Odgers 1997). Although their use of aggregated industry data (rather than firm data) make it difficult to distinguish between union and industry effects, Betts and Odgers make a convincing case that they have measured a true effect of unions. Evidence from Britain is rather more limited and results are anything but clear. Machin and Wadhwani (1991) conclude that unions have a positive but insignificant impact on investment in micro-electronic equipment during the early 1980s. Denny and Nickell (1992) in a study based on aggregate industry data conclude that unions decrease capital investment. In a particularly careful study examining the effects of unions on R&D in Britain, Menezes-Filho and van Reenen (1996) conclude that while unionized establishments invest less in R&D, in the United Kingdom this is primarily an effect of the industry location and not of unions. They subject firm-level data from the United States (provided by Hirsch) to the same battery of econometric tests to which they subject the British data. They conclude that, unlike the British evidence, the American evidence of a deleterious effect of unionization on R&D investment is robust. Whereas the union tax model applies well to the United States, the authors speculate that British unions have fewer deleterious effects on research and development than do American unions owing to more explicit bargaining over employment levels and a preference for longer contracts.

Employment growth

The effects of unions upon growth in employment has received less attention than their effects upon productivity, profits, and investment. It would be surprising were decreased profits and lower rates of investment not accompanied by slower employment growth and this is precisely what the evidence indicates. Dunne and Macpherson (1994) utilize longitudinal plant-level data to show that there are more employment contractions, fewer expansions, and fewer plant "births" in more highly unionized industries. They find that unions have no effect upon plant "deaths," even after controlling for plant size (larger plants are less likely to fail but more likely to be unionized). Linneman, Wachter, and Carter (1990) show that much of what is represented as a "de-industrialization" of America is in fact *de-unionization*. Using Current Population Survey data for the 1980s, they show that within narrowly defined manufacturing industries, most displayed increases in nonunion employment while at the same time witnessing substantial decreases in union employment. Moreover, the rate of decline in union employment is directly related to the magnitude of the union wage premium. In one of the few studies to examine firm-level employment growth directly, Leonard (1992) finds that unionized California companies grew at significantly slower rates than did nonunion companies. And in a recent study using longitudinal plant-level data, LaLonde, Marschke, and Troske (1996) show that employment (and output) decrease following a vote in favour of union certification.

Studies for Canada and Britain reinforce findings from the United States. Long (1993) utilizes data from a survey of 510 Canadian business establishments in the manufacturing and non-manufacturing sectors. Union establishments (i.e., establishments with employees covered by collective bargaining agreements) had considerably slower employment growth between 1980 and 1985, although in manufacturing roughly half of the slower growth resulted not from unionization *per se* but from location in industries showing slower growth (industry effects were not important in the non-manufacturing sector). After accounting for industry controls, firm size, and firm age, union establishments in the manufacturing sector grew 3.7 percent per year more slowly than nonunion establishments; in non-manufacturing sectors, union establishments grew 3.9 percent per year more slowly than nonunion establishments. British evidence is similar. Blanchflower, Millward, and Oswald (1991) provide evidence that unionized plants have slower employment growth. Blanchflower and Burgess (1996) show that destruction of jobs (i.e., permanent job loss) and net job loss have been higher among union than nonunion establishments, although differences have declined over time.

Interpretation and implications for policy
Knowledge about how unions affect economic performance is a prerequisite for intelligent debate about the appropriate role for labour law and for understanding the transformation taking place in the workplace and in relations between labour and management. For example, Weiler (1990) and others have argued that changes in National Labor Relations Board's interpretation of American labour law, the increased number of unfair labour practices filed and certified, and strategies adopted by management to avoid union organizing have seriously eroded workers' right to organize. Implicit (and sometimes explicit) in this analysis is the belief that the effects of unions in the workplace are largely benign. An alternative interpretation (see Flanagan 1987; Freeman and Kleiner 1990) is that increased resistance to unions by management and the increase in labour litigation reflect profit-maximizing on the part of the employers and are due in no small part to high wage premiums gained by unions rather than to changes in labour law or in their interpretation and enforcement.

The evidence evaluated in this paper lends credence to the latter interpretation. Despite the very real benefits of collective voice for workers, the positive effects of unions have been overshadowed by union rent-seeking behaviour. Productivity is not higher, on average, in union workplaces. The failure of collective bargaining to enhance productivity significantly results in substantially lower profitability among unionized companies. Because unions appropriate not only a portion of monopoly-related profits but also the quasi-rents that make up the normal return to long-lived capital, unionized companies reduce investment in vulnerable forms of physical and innovative capital. Investment is further reduced since lower profits reduce the size of the internal pool from which investments are partly financed. Slower growth in capital is mirrored by slower growth in sales and employment (and, thus, union membership). The relatively poor performance of union companies gives credence to the proposition that the restructuring in industrial relations and increased resistance to union organizing have been predictable responses on the part of businesses to increased domestic and foreign competition. In the absence of a narrowing in the performance differences between unionized and nonunionized companies, modifications in labour law that substantially enhance union organizing and bargaining strength are likely to reduce economic competitiveness.

Although the evidence indicates clearly that collective bargaining has led to a poor performance in unionized sectors of the economy relative to nonunionized sectors, it is far more difficult to draw inferences about the effects of unions upon economy-wide performance. In fact, a highly competitive economy limits the costs unions can impose since resources flow to those sectors where they obtain the highest return. For example, lower capital investment or employment among unionized firms is in part offset by higher usage elsewhere in the economy. If resources could flow costlessly to alternative uses and if social rates of return were equivalent in nonunion sectors, unions would have little effect on economy-wide efficiency. Increases in unions' power and rent-seeking would simply cause the relative size of the union sector to shrink. However, because unions have some degree of monopoly bargaining power, because the shifting of resources from union to nonunion environments occurs slowly, and because social rates of return differ across investment paths, union distortions at the firm level necessarily translate into some degree of inefficiency economy-wide.

Policy implications derive from the fact that an economy's competitiveness limits unions' bargaining power and the economy-wide costs of unionism. Changes in labour law that severely restrict the rights and ability of unions to organize limit not only the monopoly power of unions but also reduce the benefits provided by a union's collective voice. If an economy or particular sector of an economy is sufficiently competitive, unionism's monopoly face is constrained. At the same time unions, if they are to prosper, must provide economic value added through an enhancement of worker voice and an improved labour relations environment. Those concerned about the economic costs associated with unions should lose sight neither of the potential benefits associated with the provision of an effective collective voice for workers nor the importance of policies that allow a high degree of domestic and international competition. Private sector unions that do not provide net benefits will not flourish in a competitive environment. The dramatic decline in private sector unionism in the United States as well as less rapid declines in Canada and Britain, can be interpreted in this light.

It is important to note that the arguments above have rather less force in the public sector or in publicly financed private sectors (e.g., health care in Canada). Here, competitive pressures play a far weaker role in limiting the unions' monopoly power. In the absence of competitive limitations on union power, labour law in such sectors must be designed not only to facilitate the exercise of collective voice, but also to limit unions' monopoly power.

Ultimately, an evaluation of labour law and employment policies requires that we compare the current system to viable alternatives. In the United States, the decline in private sector unionism to approximately 10 percent of wage and salary employees (Hirsch and Macpherson 1997) has taken place within a labour relations system that all sides agree is overly contentious and marked by tremendous conflict. Indeed, there is no small degree of support both from labour and from management that the current legal structure surrounding collective bargaining, which dates back to the National Labor Relations Act of 1935, is outmoded and in many ways inappropriate to the workplace of the 1990s. At the same time, nonunion labour relations has become overly litigious and, not surprisingly, subject to detailed regulation (e.g., laws against discrimination on the basis of age and disability, regulations governing workplace safety, and rules about pensions and benefits). Workers want both an effective collective voice in the workplace and a cooperative relationship with employers.[9] Yet this combination of collective voice and cooperation has not been realized in many, if not most, union and nonunion workplaces.

There may be no feasible political route to move from the current labour relations environment to one envisioned either by organized labour, business interests, or industrial relations scholars. Neither the enhancement of traditional collective bargaining nor a massive deregulation of labour markets is likely to be a politically viable or an economically desirable alternative. Were labour legislation reformed primarily to strengthen the ability of unions to organize, the monopoly costs of unionism would be increased in relatively noncompetitive sectors. At the same time, union power would remain in check in the most competitive sectors of the economy, leaving most of the private sector workforce uncovered by collective bargaining agreements.

Although critics of current labour law and the legal protection afforded to unions may find the promise of a deregulated labour law environment attractive, this approach is deficient in two important ways. First, a deregulated labour market will tend not to provide mechanisms for effective collective voice for workers. Second, a decentralized system of collective bargaining (or alternative mechanisms for collective voice for workers) are likely to be replaced not by a largely deregulated labour market but by one characterized by centralized and uniform regulations.

The general case that there will be a lack of participation by workers in firm-level decisions in the absence of legislative mandate has been supplied by Levine and Tyson (1990) and Freeman and Lazear (1995) among others. The logic is based on the thought experiment known as the Prisoner's Dilemma coupled with adverse selection. In these models, works councils or the exercise of a collective voice independent of management increase the joint (shareholder plus worker) surplus for some firms over some range of worker-council power. According to Levine and Tyson, market failure arises because participative firms require, among other things, compressed wage structures to encourage group cohesiveness, and dismissals protection to lengthen the time of employment and attachment of workers as compared to "traditional" nonparticipatory firms. Even though participation by workers will generate a higher joint product, a nonparticipatory equilibrium is likely to result owing to adverse selection. That is, the participatory firm will attract the less motivated workers while losing highly productive workers to traditional firms with a less compressed wage structure. In this way, so the argument runs, the market will be systematically biased against participatory workplaces and the economy will be locked in a suboptimal equilibrium. Although they downplay rent-seeking insider behaviour, Levine and Tyson argue that participation works better in unionized regimes because union workers have greater job security.

Freeman and Lazear (1995), on the other hand, are alert to the rent-seeking problem. Because unions or works councils not only encourage collective voice or participation by workers but also reduce profitability, they are either not established or are given insufficient authority by management. Again, an inefficient and insufficient provision of participation will exist in the absence of employment or labour law that facilitates its development. The sources of improved joint surplus identified by Freeman and Lazear are those emphasized by the collective-voice model, this time underwritten by exchange of high-quality information and the enhanced job security made possible by mandated participation. In recommending that participation be mandated, Freeman and Lazear seek to decouple pay from the non-pay aspects of participation. This explains why they light upon institutions in the German style as a template for participatory mandates.

It is not at all clear, however, that efficient levels of participation can be mandated. Even were it established that a systematic market bias against participation exists, there is scant knowledge of the type of public policies that might encourage effective participation by workers in what is largely a nonunion private sector. Nor is it obvious how to disentangle policies that might enhance participation by workers from the rather contentious debate over the appropriate role for unions and labour law. The National Labour Relations Act has undoubtedly strengthened the bargaining power of organized labour in the private sector, with net effects that may well have hastened union decline. This conclusion is of course quite consistent with the argument that the decline of unions raise legitimate grounds for concern regarding the availability of effective and protective participation and collective voice for workers.[10]

There is also a concern that, given a declining union sector, the political demand for regulations governing the entire labour market is enhanced. While unionism allows workers and firms to negotiate (implicitly or explicitly) the terms of labour contracts, union decline has been accompanied by legislation regulating such things as hours and overtime pay; discrimination on the basis of race, gender, national origin, age, and disabilities; workplace safety and notification of workplace dangers; notification of plant closings; pensions; drug use (for selected occupations); and family leave. Strong arguments can be made in support of many of these laws and there is likely to be substantial political support for uniform government regulation of the workplace as long as decentralized participation and collective voice for workers is limited. It is not at all clear that voluntary and decentralized negotiated workplace policies achieved through unions or mandated works councils are inferior to an increasing reliance on regulation, uniform standards, and litigation.[11] Indeed, causation works in both directions. Not only does an absence of effective unionism increase political demand for governmental regulation, the existence of such policies, strongly supported by organized labour, have almost certainly reduced support for unionization by workers since many of the benefits from collective bargaining are now provided to all workers.[12]

Labour unions are at a crucial juncture in their history. Increased foreign competition, deregulation of highly unionized domestic industries, and changes in technology have denied unionized companies access to rents and quasi-rents that have traditionally been shared by workers and shareholders. The organizing of new unions at the current rate is not sufficient to offset the attrition of existing union jobs, which leads to a continuing decrease in the extent of union coverage in the economy. Faced with new and more severe economic constraints, union leaders and the rank and file have been slow to adjust their expectations, strategies, and wage demands. Stated more bluntly, unions would have had to make large concessions to maintain union coverage at pre-1980 levels. It is not surprising that such substantial changes in union behaviour have been slow in coming, though substantial changes in union behaviour and in the industrial relations may yet emerge. But, given the rather weak relationship between unionization and productivity, combined with strong resistance by management to union organizing, the possibilities for sizable, union-induced improvements in workplace productivity appear meager. It is likely, therefore, that we will see a continued decline in union coverage in the United States and elsewhere until the economy in each finds a new steady state at a lower but sustainable level of union density.

The outline of an ideal system of labour law and regulation lies well beyond the scope of this paper. Such a system, however, would be one that simultaneously offers workers many of the types of organizing rights and legal protections offered by current labour law, while at the same time allowing considerably greater flexibility and enhancing worker participation and cooperation at both union and nonunion workplaces. That being said, it is difficult to be sanguine that such a system can evolve from current labour law or emerge in the current political and economic environment. The present system serves, on the one hand, as a less than ideal framework for a shrinking and rigid union labour relations system while, on the other hand, either restricting or doing little to facilitate a collective voice for workers in the mostly nonunion private sector. Employment law and regulations should facilitate the development of worker participation and collective voice. At the same time, it is important that labour law not be replaced with a plethora of federal mandates dictating specific terms of employment. Workplace outcomes would better be determined by market forces and decentralized communications and bargaining in union and nonunion workplaces.

Notes

1 The statistical issues discussed above are more formally known as omitted variable bias, selection and simultaneity bias, and external validity.
2 For purposes here, productivity simply means output for given levels of inputs. A firm that is more productive than another can produce more output using the same combination of inputs or, equivalently, produce the same output using fewer inputs. When we refer to a increase in productivity attributable to unions, we mean a real shift in the marginal product schedule, and not just a movement up the labour demand curve (implying a higher capital-labour ratio) in response to a higher wage. On this issue, see Reynolds 1986; Addison and Hirsch 1989; Addison and Chilton 1993.
3 Hirsch and Prasad (1995) show that if a union tax on the return to capital provides the source for wage gains, unions have an indeterminate effect on the capital-labour ratio.
4 Morgan (1994) uses aggregate cross-sectional manufacturing data across time. Although she finds estimates highly similar to Brown-Medoff for the years around 1972, the union coefficient declines steadily over time and is negative during the 1980s. It is unlikely that such large changes entirely reflect a true trend in the effect of unions upon productivity. Rather, these results illustrate the difficulty in estimating the productivity effect from aggregate industry data, since unionism is correlated with other industry-level determinants of productivity, some of which show trends over time.
5 An identical conclusion is reached in surveys by Addison and Hirsch (1989) and Booth (1995). Belman (1992) provides a more positive assessment of union effects on productivity.
6 See Addison and Hirsch 1989 and Booth 1995 for specific references. For an exception, see the analysis of hospitals in Register 1988.

7 Becker and Olson 1987, Addison and Hirsch 1989, and Hirsch 1991a provide surveys and analyses of the profit and market-value studies.
8 Using firm level data from Compustat and union density data collected by Hirsch (1991a), Cavanaugh (1996) shows that deleterious union effects on market value and investment are directly related to the ease with which quasi-rents can be appropriated.
9 This conclusion is based on results from the Worker Representation and Participation Survey, directed by Richard Freeman and Joel Rogers, and conducted by Princeton Survey Research Associates during Fall 1994. This report is summarized in United States Departments of Commerce and Labor 1994: app. A, 63-65.
10 For examples of reforms in labour law that attempt to promote collective voice or "value-added" unionism while limiting monopoly power, see Estreicher 1994, 1996.
11 Levine (1997), among others, proposes a system that would lessen direct regulation while maintaining a minimum set of labour standards for firms that voluntarily adopt alternative regulatory systems with employee oversight and approval. He would maintain the current system of standards for firms not adopting alternative systems. Levine argues that movement in this direction, while weakening workers' rights de jure, would strengthen their rights de facto and produce net welfare gains.
12 For a suggestive analysis, see Neumann and Rissman 1984. An explanation for union support of these policies is that such policies are costly, so union firms that provide such "services" in the absence of government mandates would be at a competitive disadvantage relative to nonunion firms.

References

Abowd, John M. (1989). The Effect of Wage Bargains on the Stock Market Value of the Firm. *American Economic Review* 79 (September): 774–800.

Addison, John T., and John B. Chilton (1993). Can We Identify Union Productivity Effects? *Industrial Relations* 32 (Winter): 124–32.

——— (1996). Self-Enforcing Union Contracts: Efficient Investment and Employment. Unpublished paper. Department of Economics, University of South Carolina.

Addison, John T., and Barry T. Hirsch (1989). Union Effects on Productivity, Profits, and Growth: Has the Long Run Arrived? *Journal of Labor Economics* 7 (January): 72–105.

Addison, John T., Claus Schnabel, and Joachim Wagner (1995). German Industrial Relations: An Elusive Exemplar. *Industrielle Beziehungen* 2, 1: 25–45.

Allen, Steven G. (1986a). The Effect of Unionism on Productivity in Privately and Publicly Owned Hospitals and Nursing Homes. *Journal of Labor Research* 7 (Winter): 59–68.

Allen, Steven G. (1986b). Unionization and Productivity in Office Building and School Construction. *Industrial and Labor Relations Review* 39 (January): 187–201.

Baldwin, Carliss Y. (1983). Productivity and Labor Unions: An Application of the Theory of Self-Enforcing Contracts. *Journal of Business* 56 (April): 155–85.

Becker, Brian E., and Craig A. Olson (1987). Labor Relations and Firm Performance. In M. Kleiner, R. Block, M. Roomkin, and S. Salsburg (eds), *Human Resources and the Performance of the Firm* (Madison, WI: Industrial Relations Research Association): 43–85.

—— 1992. Unionization and Firm Profits. *Industrial Relations* 31 (Fall): 395–415.

Belman, Dale (1992). Unions, the Quality of Labor Relations, and Firm Performance. In Lawrence Mishel and Paula P. Voos (eds), *Unions and Economic Competitiveness* (Armonk, NY: M.E. Sharpe): 41–107.

Betts, Julian R., and Cameron W. Odgers (1997). The Effects of Unions on Research and Development: An Empirical Analysis Using Multi-Year Data. Dep't of Economics, University of California, San Diego.

Blanchflower, David G., and Simon M. Burgess (1996). Job Creation and Job Destruction in Great Britain in the 1980s. *Industrial and Labor Relations Review* 50 (October): 17–38.

Blanchflower, David G., Neil Millward, and Andrew J. Oswald (1991). Unionization and Employment Behavior. *Economic Journal* 101 (July): 815–34.

Booth, Alison L. (1995). *The Economics of the Trade Union*. Cambridge: Cambridge University Press.

Bronars, Stephen G., and Donald R. Deere (1990). Union Representation Elections and Firm Profitability. *Industrial Relations* 29 (Winter): 15–37

—— (1993). Unionization, Incomplete Contracting, and Capital Investment. *Journal of Business* 66 (January): 117–32.

Bronars, Stephen G., Donald R. Deere, and Joseph S. Tracy (1994). The Effects of Unions on Firm Behavior: An Empirical Analysis Using Firm-Level Data. *Industrial Relations* 33 (October): 426–51.

Brown, Charles, and James Medoff (1978). Trade Unions in the Production Process. *Journal of Political Economy* 86 (June): 355–78.

Brunello, Giorgio (1992). The Effect of Unions on Firm Performance in Japanese Manufacturing. *Industrial and Labor Relations Review* 45 (April): 471–87.

Byrne, Dennis, Hashem Dezhbakhsh, and Randall King (1996). Unions and Police Productivity: An Econometric Investigation. *Industrial Relations* 35 (October): 566–84.

Cavanaugh, Joseph K. (1996). Asset Specific Investment and Unionized Labor. Unpublished paper. Department of Economics, Wright State University.

Clark, Kim B. (1980a). The Impact of Unionization on Productivity: A Case Study. *Industrial and Labor Relations Review* 33 (July): 451–69.

——— (1980b). Unionization and Productivity: MicroEconometric Evidence. *Quarterly Journal of Economics* 95 (December): 613–39.

——— (1984). Unionization and Firm Performance: The Impact on Profits, Growth, and Productivity. *American Economic Review* 74 (December): 893–919.

Connolly, Robert A., Barry T. Hirsch, and Mark Hirschey (1986). Union Rent Seeking, Intangible Capital, and Market Value of the Firm. *Review of Economics and Statistics* 68 (November): 567–77.

Denny, Kevin, and Stephen J. Nickell (1992). Unions and Investment in British Industry. *Economic Journal* 102 (July): 874–87.

Dunne, Timothy, and David A. Macpherson (1994). Unionism and Gross Employment Flows. *Southern Economic Journal* 60 (January): 727–38.

Estreicher, Samuel (1994). Employee Involvement and the "Company Union" Prohibition: The Case for Partial Repeal of Section 8(a)(2) of the NLRA. *New York University Law Review* 69 (April): 125–61.

——— (1996). Freedom of Contract and Labor Law Reform: Opening Up the Possibilities for Value-Added Unionism. *New York University Law Review* 71 (June): 827–49.

Fallick, Bruce C., and Kevin A. Hassett (1996). Investment and Union Certification. *Finance and Economics Discussion Series No. 1996-43* (November). Washinton, DC: Federal Reserve Board.

Farber, Henry S. (1986). The Analysis of Union Behavior. In Orley Ashenfelter and Richard Layard (eds), *Handbook of Labor Economics*, Vol. 2 (Amsterdam, NL: North-Holland): 1039–89.

Flanagan, Robert J. (1987). *Labor Relations and the Litigation Explosion.* Washington, DC: The Brookings Institute.

Freeman, Richard B. (1988). Contraction and Expansion: The Divergence of Private Sector and Public Sector Unionism in the United States. *Journal of Economic Perspectives* 2 (Spring): 63–88.

Freeman, Richard B. and Morris M. Kleiner (1990). Employer Behavior in the Face of Union Organizing Drives. *Industrial and Labor Relations Review* 43 (April): 351–65.

——— (1994). Do Unions Make Enterprises Insolvent? *Working Paper 4797* (July). Cambridge, MA: National Bureau of Economic Research.

Freeman, Richard B., and Edward P. Lazear (1995). An Economic Analysis of Works Councils. In Joel Rogers and Wolfgang Streeck (eds),

Works Councils: Consultation, Representation, and Cooperation in Industrial Relations (Chicago: University of Chicago Press).

Freeman, Richard B., and James L. Medoff (1979). The Two Faces of Unionism. *The Public Interest No.* 57 (Fall): 69–93.

——— (1984). *What Do Unions Do?* New York: Basic Books.

Gregg, Paul S., Stephen J. Machin, and David Metcalf (1993). Signals and Cycles? Productivity Growth and Changes in Union Status in British Companies, 1984-1989. *Economic Journal* 103 (July): 894–907.

Grout, Paul A. (1984). Investment and Wages in the Absence of Binding Contracts: A Nash Bargining Approach. *Econometrica* 52 (March): 449–60.

Hirsch, Barry T. (1990). Market Structure, Union Rent Seeking, and Firm Profitability. *Economics Letters* 32 (January): 75–79.

——— (1991a). *Labor Unions and the Economic Performance of Firms.* Kalamazoo, MI: W.E. Upjohn Institute for Employment Research.

——— (1991b). Union Coverage and Profitability Among U.S. Firms. *Review of Economics and Statistics* 73 (February): 69–77.

——— (1992). Firm Investment Behavior and Collective Bargaining Strategy. *Industrial Relations* 31 (Winter): 95–121.

——— (1993). Trucking Deregulation, Unionization, and Earnings: Is the Union Premium a Compensating Differential? *Journal of Labor Economics* 11 (April): 279–301.

Hirsch, Barry T., and Robert A. Connolly (1987). Do Unions Capture Monopoly Profits? *Industrial and Labor Relations Review* 41 (October): 118–36.

Hirsch, Barry T., and Albert N. Link (1984). Unions, Productivity, and Productivity Growth. *Journal of Labor Research* 5 (Winter): 29–37.

Hirsch, Barry T., and David A. Macpherson (1995). Earnings, Rents, and Competition in the Airline Labor Market. Unpublished paper. Department of Economics, Florida State University.

——— (1997). *Union Membership and Earnings Data Book: Compilations from the Current Population Survey* (1997 ed.). Washington, DC: Bureau of National Affairs.

——— (forthcoming). Earnings and Employment in Trucking: Deregulating a Naturally Competitive Industry. In James Peoples (ed), *Regulatory Reform and Labor Markets* (Dordrecht, NL: Kluwer).

Hirsch, Barry T., and Barbara A. Morgan (1994). Shareholder Risk and Returns in Union and Nonunion Firms. *Industrial and Labor Relations Review* 47 (January): 302–18.

Hirsch, Barry T., and Kislaya Prasad (1995). Wage-Employment Determination and a Union Tax on Capital: Can Theory and Evidence Be Reconciled? *Economics Letters* 48 (April): 61–71.

Hirsch, Barry T., Michael L. Wachter, and James W. Gillula (1997). Postal Service Compensation and the Comparability Standard. Unpublished paper. Department of Economics, Florida State University.

Karier, Thomas (1985). Unions and Monopoly Profits. *Review of Economics and Statistics* 67 (February): 34–42.

LaLonde, Robert J., Gérard Marschke, and Kenneth Troske (1996). Using Longitudinal Data on Establishments to Analyze the Effects of Union Organizing Campaigns in the United States. *Annales d' Économie et de Statistique* no. 41/42: 155–85

Leonard, Jonathan S. (1992). Unions and Employment Growth. *Industrial Relations* 31 (Winter): 80–94.

Levine, David I. (1997). They Should Solve Their Own Problems: Reinventing Workplace Regulation. In Bruce Kaufman (ed.), *Government Regulation of the Employment Relationship* (Madison, WI: Industrial Relations Research Association). Forthcoming.

Levine, David I., and Laura D'Andrea Tyson (1990). Participation, Productivity, and the Firm's Environment. In Alan S. Blinder (ed.), *Paying for Productivity: A Look at the Evidence* (Washington, DC: The Brookings Institute): 183–237.

Linneman, Peter D., Michael L. Wachter, and William H. Carter (1990). Evaluating the Evidence on Union Employment and Wages. *Industrial and Labor Relations Review* 44 (October): 34–53.

Long, Richard J. (1993). The Effect of Unionization on Employment Growth of Canadian Companies. *Industrial and Labor Relations Review* 46 (July): 691–703.

Machin, Stephen J., and Mark B. Stewart (1990). Unions and the Financial Performance of British Private Sector Establishments. *Journal of Applied Econometrics* 5 (October-December): 327–50.

Machin, Stephen J., and Mark B. Stewart (1996). Trade Unions and Financial Performance. *Oxford Economic Papers* 48 (April): 213–41.

Machin, Stephen J., and Sushil Wadhwani (1991). The Effects of Unions on Organisational Change and Employment. *Economic Journal* 101 (March): 835–54.

Maki, Dennis R. (1983). The Effects of Unions and Strikes on the Rate of Growth of Total Factor Productivity in Canada. *Applied Economics* 15 (February): 29–41.

Menezes-Filho, N.A., and John van Reenen (1996). R&D and Union Bargaining: Evidence from British Companies and Establishments. Unpublished paper. Institute for Fiscal Studies, London.

Mitchell, Merwin W., and Joe A. Stone (1992). Union Effects on Productivity: Evidence from Western Sawmills. *Industrial and Labor Relations Review* 46 (October): 135–45.

Morgan, Barbara A. (1994). Union Effects on Productivity, Growth and Profitability in U.S. Manufacturing. Doctoral dissertation. Department of Economics, Florida State University.

Neumann, George R., and Ellen R. Rissman (1984). Where Have All the Union Members Gone? *Journal of Labor Economics* 2 (April): 175–92.

Nickell, Stephen J., Sushil Wadhwani, and Martin Wall (1992). Productivity Growth in U.K. Companies, 1975–1986. *European Economic Review* 36 (June): 1055–85.

Odgers, Cameron W., and Julian R. Betts (forthcoming). Do Unions Reduce Investment? Evidence from Canada. *Industrial and Labor Relations Review.*

Olson, Craig A., and Brian E. Becker (1990). The Effects of the NLRA on Stockholder Wealth in the 1930s. *Industrial and Labor Relations Review* 44 (October): 116–29.

Ravenscraft, David J. (1983). Structure-Profit Relationships at the Line of Business and Industry Level. *Review of Economics and Statistics* 65 (February): 22–31.

Register, Charles A. (1988). Wages, Productivity, and Costs in Union and Nonunion Hospitals. *Journal of Labor Research* 9 (Fall): 325–45.

Reynolds, Morgan O. (1986). Trade Unions in the Production Process Reconsidered. *Journal of Political Economy* 94 (April): 443–47.

Ruback, Richard S., and Zimmerman, Martin B. (1984). Unionization and Profitability: Evidence from the Capital Market. *Journal of Political Economy* 92 (December): 1134–57.

Salinger, Michael A. (1984). Tobin's q, Unionization, and the Concentration-Profits Relationship. *Rand Journal of Economics* 15 (Summer): 159–70.

United States Departments of Commerce and Labor (1994). Commission on the Future of Labor-Management Relations: Report and Recommendations. Washington, DC: United States Departments of Commerce and Labor.

Voos, Paula B., and Lawrence R. Mishel (1986). The Union Impact on Profits: Evidence from Industry Price-Cost Margin Data. *Journal of Labor Economics* 4 (January): 105–33.

Weiler, Paul C. (1990). *Governing the Workplace: The Future of Labor and Employment Law.* Cambridge, MA: Harvard University Press.

Wessels, Walter J. (1985). The Effects of Unions on Employment and Productivity: An Unresolved Contradiction. *Journal of Labor Economics* 3 (January): 101–08.

Right-to-Work Laws
Evidence from the United States

JAMES T. BENNETT

Many economic studies have shown that the gross wages of union workers are higher than those of their counterparts who choose not to join a union (see, e.g., Lewis 1986). This finding raises a critical issue: are wages of unionized workers higher because of unionization, or do unions concentrate on organizing in industries where wages are high already? After an extensive survey of the economic studies of relative wage effects due to unions, C.J. Parsley answered this question in the following way: "It appears that wages affect unionization to a greater degree than unionism influences wages, but paradoxically, workers presumably become union members because they believe that the latter causal direction predominates" (1980: 29). Thus, it appears that high wages attract unions, not the other way round as much union publicity claims.

A second question concerns the difference in real incomes between states guaranteeing employees' right to work without joining a union, and those not doing so. In the 21 states that have Right-to-Work laws,[1] employees are not required to support

---

Notes will be found on pages 88–9.

financially the union that has monopoly bargaining privileges at the workplace in order to keep their jobs. In states that do not have Right-to-Work laws, employees must often financially support the union in order to keep their jobs. In short, in states without Right-to-Work laws, employees are coerced to pay union dues whether or not they desire union representation.

Supporters of monopolistic unions have often based upon the difference between the gross wages of unionized and non-unionized employees the claim that Right-to-Work laws are "right-to-work-for-less" laws, and that employees are worse off in states which have such laws. This claim deserves careful examination.

Asking the right question: the purchasing power of money income

Money income varies widely across states, regions, and cities, but so does the tax burden that reduces the family income and the prices of goods and services that are purchased with after-tax income. The appropriate comparison across cities, states, or regions in measuring economic well-being is the purchasing power of after-tax income. The relevant question is this: is money income, when adjusted for taxes and the cost of living, higher in non-Right-to-Work states than in Right-to-Work states?

Two earlier studies comparing adjusted incomes in Right-to-Work states with those in non-Right-to-Work states showed that while money income was higher in non-Right-to-Work states, adjusted income was higher in Right-to-Work states so that a higher money income does not imply that an employee is necessarily better off (see *World Report* 1977; Bennett 1985). These studies were conducted for the years 1977 and 1981 using family median income, tax, and cost-of-living data for each state. An interesting and important question is whether this finding remains valid.

Unfortunately, an updated replication of these earlier works is not possible because the United States Bureau of Labor Statistics no longer publishes the data series used in the earlier analyses. However, alternative data highly suitable for this purpose are available for 1993. In their book, *Places Rated Almanac*, Richard Boyer and David Savageau estimate family income, state and local taxes, and the cost of living for each of the 318 Standard Metropolitan Statistical Areas (SMSAs; i.e., central cities and surrounding suburbs) in the United States in which three-quarters or more of the American population live.[2] The remainder of the population resides in small towns and villages and in rural areas where labor unions are less prevalent.

Information for individual cities is preferable to information for states since cities and their surrounding suburbs are more homogeneous economically than are states, and a cost-of-living index is much more difficult to determine accurately for an entire state than for individual cities. The cost of living in New York City, for example, is quite different from that in Elmira, which is located upstate. Boyer and Savageau's cost-of-living index takes into account the costs of food, housing, health care, transportation, property taxes, and college tuition (Boyer and Savageau 1993: 23).

Seven of the 318 Standard Metropolitan Statistical Areas were omitted from the analysis because part of each lies in a Right-to-Work state and part in a non-Right-to-Work state; thus, there are 311 SMSAs in our sample.[3] In these 311 SMSAs, the entire SMSA lies entirely within either a Right-to-Work state or a non-Right-to-Work state. Right-to-work states tend to cluster in the South, the Plains States, and Rocky Mountain region. All have common borders with one or several of the other Right-to-Work states.

Appendix 1 lists alphabetically the 129 SMSAs located in the 21 Right-to-Work states and appendix 2 lists the 182 SMSAs located in non-Right-to-Work states. For each SMSA, typical family income (unadjusted income), state and local taxes, income after taxes, the cost-of-living index, and income adjusted for taxes and cost of living (adjusted income) are reported. Joplin, Missouri, is the least expensive SMSA in which to live, and the cost-of-living index was set equal to 100.0 for this SMSA so that the cost-of-living index for all other SMSAs is measured relative to the cost in Joplin. Averages for each variable are reported at the end of each appendix.

Before adjusting for taxes and cost of living, typical family income for the 129 SMSAs in states with Right-to-Work laws is US$46,883, US$6,747 less than the average (US$53,630) for the 182 SMSAs located in states without Right-to-Work laws. On average, however, families who reside in SMSAs with Right-to-Work laws pay US$1,779 less in state and local taxes than do families in non-Right-to-Work states, who pay an avereage of US$3,005 in taxes. Thus, there is less difference in after-tax average family income between Right-to-Work and non-Right-to-Work states; average annual after-tax family income in states with

Right-to-Work laws is US$45,104, only US$5,521 less than the average annual after-tax income of US$50,625 of families in states without Right-to-Work laws.

It is important to emphasize that these data include only state and local taxes; federal taxes also reduce the income that families have available for purchasing goods and services. Federal taxes are based on money income and are progressive, i.e., the tax rate rises with income. Thus, since average income is greater in non-Right-to-Work states than in Right-to-Work states, the amount taken by federal tax is greater in non-Right-to-Work states and this further narrows the difference in after-tax income between Right-to-Work and non-Right-to-Work states. If it were possible to adjust for federal taxes, the difference in after-tax family income between Right-to-Work and non-Right-to-Work states would be smaller than US$5,521.

It is adjusting for the cost of living, however, that corrects the impression caused by higher gross incomes that workers in non-right-to work states are better off economically. After-tax income buys much more in states with Right-to-Work laws because the cost of living is considerably higher in SMSAs in non-Right-to-Work states than for those located in Right-to-Work states. The average cost-of-living index for the 129 SMSAs in Right-to-Work states is 123.8 in comparison with 154.1 for the 182 SMSAs in non-Right-to-Work states. Stated in money terms, the same package of goods and services that can, on average, be purchased for US$123.80 in Right-to-Work states would cost US$154.10 in non-Right-to-Work states. Thus, on average, residents in SMSAs in states without Right-to-Work laws pay 24.5 percent more for food, housing, health care, transportation, utilities, property taxes, and college tuition than in Right-to-Work states.

What, then, is the result after adjustments are made for the cost of living and for state and local taxes? Average after-tax income in Right-to-Work states is US$36,540 but only US$33,688 in non-Right-to-Work states. Thus, a typical urban family in a Right-to-Work state has US$2,852 more in after-tax purchasing power than the same family would have in a non-Right-to-Work state—a statistically significant difference.[4] In SMSAs where incomes are high, taxes and the cost of living are generally high as well. In states without Right-to-Work laws, high taxes and the high cost of living erode the purchasing power of income so much that families in states with Right-to-Work laws are, on average, actually better off. As the evidence presented in this chapter shows, low taxes and low or moderate living costs can easily compensate for lower hourly rates of pay.

Three additional points are noteworthy. First, unions may collect dues, fees, fines, assessments, and per capita taxes from all employees whom they represent in states without Right-to-Work laws, where financial support of the union is a condition of employment.[5] Payments to the union can further reduce the income of families in non-Right-to-Work states relative to their counterparts in Right-to-Work states who choose not to join the union.

Second, the gap in living standards between Right-to-Work and non-Right-to-Work states appears to be growing over time. A study using the same data source and methodology employed here for 1993 was compiled using statistics for 1987 (see Bennett 1990). In 1987, Right-to-Work states had only US$1,377 more in after-tax purchasing power compared to US$2,852 for 1993. Thus, the size of the difference in after-tax purchasing power between Right-to-Work and non-Right-to-Work states more than doubled in the six years from 1987 to 1993.

Third, the evidence presented here is strengthened by a recent study by Thomas J. Holmes at the Federal Reserve Bank of Minneapolis. Holmes investigated the effects of "pro-business policies" on manufacturing activity in states of the United States (Holmes 1995). He classified a state as "pro-business" if the state had a Right-to-Work law, and noted that "states with such laws tend to adopt a variety of other pro-business policies" such as low taxes and a less restrictive regulatory environment (Holmes 1995: 2). He found that "over the period 1947 [when federal legislation was passed permitting states to adopt Right-to-Work laws] to 1992, manufacturing employment increased by 148 percent in states that currently have Right-to-Work laws. Over the same period, growth in manufacturing employment was virtually zero (less than 2 percent) in states without such laws" (Holmes 1995: 1–2). Although Holmes limited his analysis to manufacturing activity, the location of other types of industry are likely to be similarly affected by the "pro-business" policies adopted by Right-to-Work states.

Conclusion

In the pro-business climate created in states that have adopted Right-to-Work laws, then, employees are economically better off and also have greater employment opportunities than those living in the states that have not adopted such laws.

Appendix 1

Income, state and local taxes, after-tax income, and adjusted income for the 129 standard metropolitan statistical areas (SMSAs) in Right-to-Work states

Standard Metropolitan Statistical Area	Income (US$)	Taxes (US$)	Income Taxes (US$)	COL Index	Adjusted Income (US$)
Abilene (TX)	47,223	986	46,237	109.4	42,264
Albany (GA)	45,500	2,655	42,845	116.7	36,714
Alexandria (LA	44,614	2,097	42,517	108.7	39,114
Amarillo (TX)	47,137	985	46,152	114.3	40,378
Anniston (AL)	39,776	2,151	37,625	104.3	36,074
Asheville (NC)	43,827	2,674	41,153	125.6	32,765
Athens (GA)	40,586	2,368	38,218	125.6	30,428
Atlanta (GA)	56,098	3,273	52,825	140.5	37,598
Augusta/Aiken ((GA/SC)	48,794	2,847	45,947	121.1	37,941
Austin/San Marcos (TX)	46,426	970	45,456	138.7	32,773
Baton Rouge (LA)	50,983	2,397	48,586	122.0	39,825
Beaumont/Port Arthur (TX)	51,184	1,069	50,115	112.2	44,666
Biloxi/Gulfport/Pascagoula (MS)	41,835	1,699	40,136	112.4	35,708
Birmingham (AL)	49,945	2,702	47,243	121.2	38,979
Bismarck (ND)	47,229	1,429	45,800	121.9	37,572
Boise City (ID)	50,107	3,145	46,962	123.2	38,119
Brazoria (TX)	55,176	1,153	54,023	126.3	42,774
Brownsville/Harlingen/San Benito (TX)	37,607	786	36,821	108.2	34,030
Bryan/College Station (TX)	36,152	755	35,397	129.0	27,440
Casper (WY	48,084	674	47,410	112.0	42,330
Cedar Rapids (IA)	51,896	2,660	49,236	120.6	40,826
Charleston/N. Charleston (SC)	46,195	2,676	43,519	127.8	34,052
Charlotte/Gastoni/Rock Hill (NC/SC)	49,530	3,022	46,508	132.8	35,021

Appendix 1 continued

Standard Metropolitan Statistical Area (SMSA)	Income (US$)	Taxes (US$)	Income Taxes (US$)	COL Index	Adjusted Income (US$)
Charlottesville (VA)	54,773	2,560	52,213	151.1	34,555
Chattanooga (TN/GA)	47,276	1,190	46,086	112.7	40,893
Cheyenne (WY)	47,143	660	46,483	121.9	38,132
Columbia (SC)	49,906	2,891	47,015	125.2	37,552
Columbus (GA/AL)	43,811	2,556	41,255	116.6	35,382
Corpus Christi (TX)	48,790	1,019	47,771	110.0	43,428
Dallas (TX)	57,704	1,206	56,498	147.9	38,200
Danville (VA)	43,525	2,034	41,491	108.7	38,170
Daytona Beach (FL)	41,421	743	40,678	131.9	30,840
Decatur (AL)	44,036	2,382	41,654	111.0	37,526
Des Moines (IA)	54,261	2,781	51,480	126.1	40,825
Dothan (AL)	42,643	2,307	40,336	109.8	36,736
Dubuque (IA)	48,865	2,504	46,361	118.2	39,223
El Paso (TX)	42,225	882	41,343	122.1	33,860
Fayetteville/Springdale/Rogers (AR)	42,126	2,090	40,036	111.7	35,842
Fayetteville (NC)	41,447	2,529	38,918	119.3	32,622
Florence (AL)	38,578	2,087	36,491	106.7	34,200
Florence (SC)	44,048	2,552	41,496	110.1	37,689
Fort Lauderdale (FL)	58,000	1,041	56,959	155.8	36,559
Fort Meyers/Cape Coral (FL)	49,557	890	48,667	145.5	33,448
Fort Pierce/Port St. Lucie (FL)	46,986	843	46,143	147.4	31,305
Fort Walton Beach (FL)	44,821	805	44,016	129.8	33,911
Fort Worth/Arlington (TX)	52,486	1,096	51,390	137.0	37,511
Gadsden (AL)	37,504	2,028	35,476	101.8	34,849
Gainesville (FL)	42,200	757	41,443	123.3	33,612
Galveston/Texas City (TX)	50,694	1,059	49,635	127.3	38,991
Goldsboro (NC)	37,980	2,317	35,663	115.8	30,797

Appendix 1 continued

Standard Metropolitan Statistical Area (SMSA)	Income (US$)	Taxes (US$)	Income Taxes (US$)	COL Index	Adjusted Income (US$)
Greensboro/Winston-Salem/High Point (NC)	48,929	2,985	45,944	125.5	36,609
Greenville/Spartanburg/Anderson (SC)	44,679	2,588	42,091	116.7	36,068
Greenville (NC)	40,965	2,499	38,466	119.6	32,162
Hickory-Morgantown (NC)	43,568	2,658	40,910	115.5	35,420
Houma (LA)	43,749	2,057	41,692	108.6	38,390
Houston (TX)	56,795	1,187	55,608	139.7	39,805
Huntsville (AL)	49,118	2,657	46,461	126.4	36,757
Iowa City (IA)	48,250	2,473	45,777	141.7	32,306
Jackonsville (NC)	35,527	2,167	33,360	117.2	28,464
Jacksonville (FL)	50,836	913	49,923	131.0	38,109
Jackson (MS	47,577	1,932	45,645	119.5	38,197
Johnson City/Kingsport/Bristol (TN/VA)	41,120	1,035	40,085	107.8	37,185
Killeen/Temple (TX)	42,028	878	41,150	113.2	36,352
Knoxville (TN)	44,052	1,109	42,943	118.1	36,362
Lafayette (LA)	44,296	2,082	42,214	109.4	38,587
Lake Charles (LA0	46,575	2,189	44,386	111.9	39,666
Lakeland/Winter Haven (FL)	42,871	769	42,102	121.3	34,709
Laredo (TX)	36,720	767	35,953	115.2	31,209
Las Vegas (NV/AZ)	49,228	931	48,297	142.8	33,821
Lawrence (KS)	40,687	1,690	38,997	120.4	32,390
Lincoln (NE)	49,601	2,416	47,185	126.0	37,448
Little Rock/N. Little Rock (AR)	47,622	2,363	45,259	119.2	37,969
Longview-Marshall (TX)	44,873	937	43,936	111.4	39,440
Lubbock (TX)	44,785	936	43,849	117.4	37,350
Lynchburg (VA)	47,132	2,202	44,930	117.6	38,206
Macon (GA)	48,931	2,855	46,076	118.3	38,948
McAllen-Edinburg-Mission (TX)	34,690	725	33,965	104.2	32,596

Appendix 1 continued

Standard Metropolitan Statistical Area (SMSA)	Income (US$)	Taxes (US$)	Income Taxes (US$)	COL Index	Adjusted Income (US$)
Melbourne/Titusville/Palm Bay (FL)	47,408	851	46,557	138.5	33,615
Memphis (TN/AR/MS)	52,543	1,323	51,220	126.6	40,458
Miami (FL)	55,316	993	54,323	154.2	35,229
Mobile (AL)	43,873	2,373	41,500	117.8	35,229
Monroe (LA)	43,151	2,028	41,123	112.3	36,619
Montgomery (AL)	48,718	2,635	46,083	117.6	39,186
Myrtle Beach (SC)	37,401	2,167	35,234	129.8	27,145
Naples (FL)	65,617	1,178	64,439	188.2	34,240
Nashville (TN	52,365	1,318	51,047	129.9	39,297
New Orleans (LA)	50,488	2,373	48,115	127.1	37,856
Norfolk/Virginia Beach/ Newport News (VA/NC)	51,376	2,401	48,975	145.2	33,729
Ocala (FL)	36,716	659	36,057	121.8	29,603
Odessa-Midland (TX)	48,564	1,015	47,549	119.8	39,690
Omaha (NE/IA)	55,906	2,723	53,183	124.9	42,580
Orlando (FL)	48,537	871	47,666	141.0	33,806
Panama City (FL)	41,364	742	40,622	121.9	33,324
Pensacola (FL)	43,633	783	42,850	120.4	35,590
Phoenix-Mesa (AZ)	50,740	2,085	48,655	144.9	33,578
Pine Bluff (AR)	40,293	1,999	38,294	105.9	36,161
Provo/Orem (UT)	44,741	3,031	41,710	125.8	33,156
Punta Gorda (FL)	40,273	723	39,550	136.7	28,932
Raleigh/Durham/Chapel Hill (NC)	49,546	3,023	46,523	136.8	34,008
Rapid City (SD)	46,231	839	45,392	120.7	37,607
Reno (NV)	58,499	1,106	57,393	163.9	35,017
Richmond-Petersburg (VA)	60,197	2,813	57,384	143.0	40,129
Roanoke (VA)	53,678	2,508	51,170	125.3	40,838
Rocky Mount (NC)	43,229	2,637	40,592	115.5	35,145

Appendix 1 continued

Standard Metropolitan Statistical Area	Income (US$)	Taxes (US$)	Income Taxes (US$)	COL Index	Adjusted Income (US$)
Salt Lake City/Ogden (UT)	50,486	3,420	47,066	129.9	36,232
San Angelo (TX)	46,632	974	45,658	113.6	40,192
San Antonio (TX)	48,257	1,008	47,249	126.8	37,263
Sarasota-Bradenton (FL)	54,532	979	53,553	145.5	36,806
Savannah (GA)	50,632	2,954	47,678	126.1	37,810
Sherman-Denison (TX)	46,476	971	45,505	111.1	40,959
Shreveport-Bossier City (LA)	46,531	2,187	44,344	111.2	39,878
Sioux City (IA/NE)	49,810	2,553	47,257	112.0	42,194
Sioux Falls (SD)	51,118	928	50,190	118.9	42,212
Sumter (SC)	36,768	2,130	34,638	109.6	31,604
Tallahassee (FL)	43,879	788	43,091	127.5	33,797
Tampa/St. Petersburg/Clearwater (FL)	47,695	856	46,839	131.8	35,538
Texarkana (TX/AR)	42,022	2,085	39,937	104.7	38,144
Topeka (KS)	54,568	2,267	52,301	118.0	44,323
Tucson (AZ)	42,988	1,766	41,222	136.7	30,155
Tuscaloosa (AL)	42,069	2,275	39,794	115.8	34,364
Tyler (TX)	49,210	1,028	48,182	116.9	41,216
Victoria (TX)	49,542	1,035	48,507	116.9	41,494
Waco (TX)	44,208	923	43,285	114.4	37,837
Waterloo/Cedar Falls (IA)	47,430	2,431	44,999	114.7	39,232
West Palm Beach/Boca Raton (FL)	61,937	1,112	60,825	165.4	36,774
Wichita Falls (TX)	49,261	1,029	48,232	112.5	42,873
Wichita (KS)	54,939	2,283	52,656	122.3	43,055
Wilmington (NC)	45,418	3,826	41,592	133.0	31,272
Yuma (AZ)	37,173	1,527	35,646	127.1	28,046
AVERAGES	46,883	1,779	45,104	123.8	36,540

Source: Boyer and Savageau 1993.

Appendix 2

Income, state and local taxes, after-tax income, and adjusted income for the 182 standard metropolitan statistical areas (SMSAs) in states without Right-to-Work laws

Standard Metropolitan Statistical Area	Income (US$)	Taxes (US$)	Income Taxes (US$)	COL Index	Adjusted Income (US$)
Akron (OH)	52,151	3,231	48,920	129.7	37,718
Albany/Schenectady/Troy (NY)	54,154	4,919	49,235	165.3	29,785
Albuquerque (NM)	48,564	2,318	46,246	137.7	33,585
Allentown/Bethlehem/Easton (PA-NJ)	56,800	5,022	51,778	162.8	31,805
Altoona (PA)	42,567	3,763	38,804	117.6	32,997
Anchorage (AK)	72,833	0	72,833	180.4	40,373
Ann Arbor (MI)	62,165	4,099	58,066	164.2	35,363
Appleton/Oshkosh/Neenah (WI)	49,598	3,077	46,521	125.3	37,128
Atlantic City-Cape May (NJ)	68,878	2,534	66,344	173.9	38,151
Bakersfield (CA)	49,696	2,169	47,527	142.3	33,399
Baltimore (MD)	61,695	4,122	57,573	156.1	36,882
Bangor (ME)	46,599	2,500	44,099	131.0	33,663
Barnstable/Yarmouth (MA)	60,629	4,121	56,508	219.6	25,732
Bellingham (WA)	43,447	924	42,523	146.3	29,066
Benton Harbor (MI)	46,045	3,036	43,009	129.4	33,237
Billings (MT)	47,091	1,581	45,510	123.8	36,761
Binghamton (NY)	48,598	4,414	44,184	143.7	30,747
Bloomington-Normal (IL)	54,754	2,526	52,228	133.3	39,181
Bloomington (IN)	37,934	1,892	36,042	127.0	28,380
Boston (MA)	68,411	4,650	63,761	229.1	27,831
Boulder-Longmont (CO)	59,528	3,215	56,313	162.4	34,675
Bremerton (WA)	49,777	1,059	48,718	150.7	32,328

Appendix 2 continued

Standard Metropolitan Statistical Area (SMSA)	Income (US$)	Taxes (US$)	Income Taxes (US$)	COL Index	Adjusted Income (US$)
Bridgeport (CT)	66,100	3,263	62,837	175.2	35,866
Buffalo-Niagara Falls (NY)	50,659	4,601	46,058	146.8	31,375
Burlington (VT)	52,103	2,143	49,960	175.3	28,500
Canton-Massillon (OH)	48,059	2,977	45,082	120.7	37,350
Central New Jersey (NJ)	81,411	2,995	78,416	222.8	35,196
Champaign-Urbana (IL)	48,711	2,247	46,464	138.7	33,500
Charleston (WV)	45,101	2,375	42,726	115.7	36,928
Chicago (IL)	66,300	3,059	63,241	176.6	35,810
Chico-Paradise (CA)	42,406	1,851	40,555	146.4	27,702
Cincinnati (OH/KY/IN)	54,870	3,399	51,471	138.2	37,244
Cleveland/Lorain/Elyria (OH)	56,848	3,522	53,326	147.8	36,080
Colorado Springs (CO)	51,065	2,758	48,307	137.4	35,158
Columbia (MO)	48,567	2,939	45,628	126.4	36,098
Columbus (OH)	51,630	3,199	48,431	136.0	35,611
Cumberland (MD/WV)	40,444	2,702	37,742	108.0	34,946
Danbury (CT)	68,780	3,363	65,417	187.8	34,833
Dayton-Springfield (OH)	51,551	3,194	48,357	129.3	37,399
Decatur (IL)	51,558	2,378	49,180	118.9	41,362
Denver (CO)	58,114	3,189	54,925	147.7	37,187
Detroit (MI)	58,890	3,883	55,007	147.2	37,369
Dover (DE)	44,567	2,154	42,413	136.1	31,163
Duluth-Superior (MN/WI)	43,857	2,691	41,166	115.0	35,797
Dutchess County (NY)	63,374	5,756	57,618	203.3	28,341
Eau Claire (WI)	43,409	2,693	40,716	119.5	34,072
Elkhart/Goshen (IN)	47,738	2,382	45,356	116.1	39,066
Elmira (NY)	45,423	4,126	41,297	129.7	31,840
Enid (OK)	44,392	2,511	41,881	101.4	41,303

Appendix 2 continued

Standard Metropolitan Statistical Area (SMSA)	Income (US$)	Taxes (US$)	Income Taxes (US$)	COL Index	Adjusted Income (US$)
Erie (PA)	48,381	4,277	44,104	128.0	34,456
Eugene/Springfield (OR)	43,095	1,572	41,523	131.4	31,600
Evansville/Henderson (IN/KY)	47,631	2,376	45,255	114.5	39,524
Flint (MI)	48,837	3,220	45,617	128.9	35,389
Fort Collins-Loveland (CO)	49,546	2,676	46,870	141.4	33,147
Fort Wayne (IN)	50,509	2,520	47,989	115.5	41,549
Fresno (CA)	52,046	2,272	49,774	141.9	35,077
Gary (IN)	49,409	2,465	46,944	129.5	36,250
Glen Falls (NY)	44,944	4,082	40,862	154.9	26,380
Grand Rapids/Muskegon/Holland (MI)	52,007	3,429	48,578	137.1	35,433
Great Falls (MT)	46,750	1,569	45,181	121.9	37,064
Greeley (CO)	50,437	2,724	47,713	126.8	37,629
Green Bay (WI)	50,598	3,139	47,459	126.3	37,576
Hagerstown (MD)	47,681	3,186	44,495	131.7	33,785
Hamilton/Middletown (OH)	49,185	3,047	46,138	134.7	34,252
Harrisburg/Lebanon/Carlisle (PA)	50,405	4,456	45,949	146.7	31,322
Hartford (CT)	69,989	2,311	67,678	208.8	32,413
Honolulu (HI)	74,744	4,979	69,765	262.0	26,628
Huntington/Ashland (WV/KY/OH)	40,764	2,147	38,617	108.9	35,461
Indianapolis (IN)	52,633	2,626	50,007	124.7	40,102
Jackson (MI)	45,276	2,985	42,291	125.8	33,618
Jamestown (NY)	43,608	3,961	39,647	125.4	31,616
Janesville/Beloit (WI)	46,187	2,865	43,322	118.4	36,590
Johnstown (PA)	42,529	3,760	38,769	119.7	32,388
Joplin (MO)	40,606	2,457	38,149	100.0	38,149

Appendix 2 continued

Standard Metropolitan Statistical Area (SMSA)	Income (US$)	Taxes (US$)	Income Taxes (US$)	COL Index	Adjusted Income (US$)
Kalamazoo/Battle Creek (MI)	47,979	3,163	44,816	129.1	34,714
Kankakee (IL)	51,749	2,387	49,362	130.3	37,883
Kenosha (WI)	52,491	3,256	49,235	135.3	36,390
Kokomo (IN)	47,755	2,382	45,373	116.2	39,047
La Crosse (WI/MN)	45,768	2,839	42,929	124.9	34,371
Lafayette (IN)	44,068	2,199	41,869	121.0	34,602
Lake County (IL)	84,060	3,878	80,182	211.6	37,893
Lancaster (PA)	55,290	4,888	50,402	155.1	32,496
Lansing/East Lansing (MI)	50,571	3,334	47,237	140.9	33,525
Las Cruces (NM)	35,339	1,687	33,652	126.6	26,581
Lawton (OK)	40,577	2,295	38,282	111.2	34,426
Lewiston-Auburn (ME)	46,905	2,516	44,389	140.3	31,639
Lexington (KY)	47,509	3,741	43,768	125.1	34,986
Lima (OH)	48,226	2,988	45,238	119.0	38,015
Long Island (NY)	88,415	9,506	78,909	251.1	31,425
Los Angeles/Long Beach (CA)	71,029	4,251	66,778	250.5	26,658
Louisville (KY/IN)	50,905	4,009	46,896	121.8	38,502
Madison (WI)	53,757	3,335	50,422	148.2	34,023
Manchester/Nashua (NH)	67,289	0	67,289	193.6	34,757
Mansfield (OH)	43,675	2,706	40,969	114.4	35,812
Medford/Ashland (OR)	42,447	1,548	40,899	141.6	28,883
Merced (CA)	48,839	2,132	46,707	144.3	32,368
Milwaukee/Waukesha (WI)	55,757	3,459	52,298	147.5	35,456
Minneapolis/St. Paul (MN/WI)	61,029	3,744	57,285	151.5	37,812
Modesto (CA)	46,010	2,008	44,002	161.6	27,229
Monmouth-Ocean (NJ)	72,548	2,669	69,879	208.2	33,563

Appendix 2 continued

Standard Metropolitan Statistical Area (SMSA)	Income (US$)	Taxes (US$)	Income Taxes (US$)	COL Index	Adjusted Income (US$)
Muncie (IN)	42,549	2,123	40,426	111.9	36,127
New Bedford/Fall River/Attleboro (MA)	53,155	3,613	49,542	185.1	26,765
New Haven/Meriden (CT)	65,474	3,742	61,732	195.7	31,544
New London/Norwich (CT/RI)	57,783	2,667	55,116	194.5	28,337
New York (NY)	67,201	6,104	61,097	280.0	21,820
Newark/Jersey City (NJ)	73,817	2,716	71,101	238.6	29,799
Northern New Jersey (NJ)	84,416	3,106	81,310	250.3	32,485
Oakland (CA)	66,538	2,905	63,633	238.7	26,658
Oklahoma City (OK)	46,056	2,605	43,451	112.6	38,589
Olympia (WA)	47,906	1,019	46,887	138.5	33,853
Orange County (CA)	73,145	4,378	68,767	259.1	26,541
Orange County (NY)	61,322	5,570	55,752	198.8	28,044
Owensboro (KY)	44,186	3,480	40,706	108.5	37,517
Parkersburg/Marietta (WV/OH)	43,368	2,284	41,084	107.5	38,218
Peoria/Pekin (IL)	52,136	2,405	49,731	124.1	40,073
Philadelphia (PA/NJ)	63,701	5,632	58,069	198.0	29,328
Pittsburgh (PA)	52,108	4,607	47,501	158.8	29,912
Pittsfield (MA)	55,800	3,793	52,007	172.7	30,114
Portland (ME)	57,821	3,102	54,719	169.2	32,340
Portland (OR)	53,763	1,961	51,802	152.1	34,058
Portsmouth/Dover/Rochester (NH)	61,354	0	61,354	198.8	30,862
Providence/Warwick/Cranston (RI)	52,340	2,088	50,252	185.2	27,134
Pueblo (CO)	44,230	2,389	41,841	110.6	37,831
Racine (WI)	54,196	3,362	50,834	136.7	37,187
Reading (PA)	56,680	5,011	51,669	151.6	34,082

86 Unions and Right-to-Work Laws

Appendix 2 continued

Standard Metropolitan Statistical Area	Income (US$)	Taxes (US$)	Income Taxes (US$)	COL Index	Adjusted Income (US$)
Redding (CA)	46,232	2,018	44,214	144.2	30,662
Richland/Kennewick/Pasco (WA)	50,710	1,079	49,631	125.4	39,578
Riverside/San Bernardino (CA)	52,760	2,303	50,457	178.3	28,299
Rochester (MN)	61,954	4,230	57,724	141.0	40,939
Rochester (NY)	58,139	5,281	52,858	161.5	32,729
Rockford (IL)	51,911	2,395	49,516	133.7	37,035
Sacramento (CA)	54,026	2,358	51,668	180.4	28,641
Saginaw/Bay City/Midland (MI)	51,531	3,397	48,134	125.4	38,384
Salem (OR)	47,543	1,734	45,809	128.7	35,594
Salinas (CA)	62,064	3,714	58,350	226.5	25,762
San Diego (CA)	56,542	2,468	54,074	223.1	24,238
San Francisco (CA)	80,087	4,793	75,294	299.4	25,148
San Jose (CA)	75,157	4,498	70,659	279.8	25,253
San Luis Obispo/Atascadero/Paso Robles (CA)	49,835	2,175	47,660	228.0	20,904
Santa Barbara/Santa Maria/Lompoc (CA)	64,354	3,851	60,503	254.9	23,736
Santa Cruz/Watsonville (CA)	62,645	3,749	58,896	257.3	22,890
Santa Fe (NM)	51,047	2,437	48,610	168.9	28,780
Santa Rosa (CA)	61,392	3,674	57,718	221.7	26,034
Scranton/Wilkes/Barre/Hazleton (PA)	46,355	4,098	42,257	131.7	32,086
Seattle/Bellevue/Everett (WA)	57,884	1,231	56,653	184.4	30,723
Sharon (PA)	43,811	3,873	39,938	115.3	34,638
Sheboygan (WI)	52,669	3,267	49,402	126.9	38,930
South Bend (IN)	48,817	2,436	46,381	111.2	41,710
Spokane (WA)	46,466	988	45,478	117.1	38,837

Appendix 2 continued

Standard Metropolitan Statistical Area (SMSA)	Income (US$)	Taxes (US$)	Income Taxes (US$)	COL Index	Adjusted Income (US$)
Springfield (IL)	55,258	2,549	52,709	125.0	42,167
Springfield (MA)	54,997	3,738	51,259	175.6	29,191
Springfield (MO)	45,172	2,733	42,439	117.2	36,211
Stamford/Norwalk (CT)	96,760	1,632	95,128	233.0	40,827
State College (PA)	45,533	4,026	41,507	145.1	28,606
Steubenville/Weirton (OH/WV)	42,206	2,615	39,591	111.2	35,603
Stockton/Lodi (CA)	51,269	2,238	49,031	163.1	30,062
St. Cloud (MN)	44,960	2,758	42,202	129.8	32,513
St. Joseph (MO)	47,499	2,874	44,625	104.2	42,826
St. Louis (MO/IL)	58,697	3,552	55,145	137.5	40,105
Syracuse (NY)	51,716	4,697	47,019	147.3	31,921
Tacoma (WA)	46,556	990	45,566	146.9	31,018
Terre Haute (IN)	41,815	2,086	39,729	106.9	37,165
Toledo (OH)	51,398	3,184	48,214	131.0	36,805
Trenton (NJ)	78,772	2,898	75,874	198.7	38,185
Tulsa (OK)	49,050	2,775	46,275	113.5	40,771
Utica/Rome (NY)	45,754	4,156	41,598	141.9	29,315
Vallejo/Fairfield/Napa (CA)	56,022	2,445	53,577	191.7	27,948
Vancouver (WA)	46,082	980	45,102	135.9	33,188
Ventura (CA)	67,036	4,012	63,024	252.3	24,980
Vineland/Millville/Bridgeton (NJ)	55,018	2,024	52,994	140.8	37,638
Visalia/Tulare/Porterville (CA)	49,003	2,139	46,864	134.9	34,740
Waterbury (CT)	61,256	1,033	60,223	172.9	34,831
Wausau (WI)	48,432	3,004	45,428	120.4	37,731
Wheeling (WV/OH)	42,857	2,257	40,600	107.1	37,908
Williamsport (PA)	45,135	3,990	41,145	124.3	33,101

Appendix 2 continued

Standard Metropolitan Statistical Area	Income (US$)	Taxes (US$)	Income Taxes (US$)	COL Index	Adjusted Income (US$)
Wilmington/Newark (DE/MD)	62,712	2,195	60,517	164.0	36,901
Worcester/Fitchburg/ Leominster (MA)	56,517	3,842	52,675	183.5	28,706
Yakima (WA)	49,201	1,047	48,154	113.5	42,426
Yolo (CA)	56,202	2,453	53,749	181.9	29,549
York (PA)	55,683	4,923	50,760	150.9	33,638
Youngstown/Warren (OH)	45,470	2,817	42,653	117.1	36,424
Yuba City (CA)	46,004	2,008	43,996	141.7	31,049
AVERAGES	53,630	3,005	50,625	154.1	33,688

Source: Boyer and Savageau 1993.

Notes

1 The 21 states that have adopted Right-to-Work laws are Alabama, Arizona, Arkansas, Florida, Georgia, Idaho, Iowa, Kansas, Louisiana, Mississippi, Nebraska, Nevada, North Carolina, North Dakota, South Carolina, South Dakota, Tennessee, Texas, Utah, Virginia, and Wyoming.
2 Boyer and Savageau 1993. Boyer and Savageau also include information on 25 SMSAs in Canada but, since Canada has no counterpart to the Right-to-Work law in the United States, these cities were omitted from the analysis.
3 The seven SMSAs are Clarksville/Hopkinsville (TN/KY); Davenport/Rock Island/Moline (IA/IL); Fargo/Moorehead (ND/MN); Fort Smith (AR/OK); Kansas City (MO/KS); Washington (DC/MD/VA); and Grand Forks (ND-MN).
4 The mean (standard deviation) of adjusted income in the 129 SMSAs in Right-to-Work states is US$36,540 (3,696.9); for non-Right-to-Work states, the mean adjusted income in 182 SMSAs in non-Right-to-Work states is US$33,688 (4,559.3). The computed value of the t-statistic used to determine whether the difference in the means is

statistically significant is 6.08, which is statistically significant at better than the 99.9 percent level for a one-tailed test.
5 The costs of unionization to employees vary widely, and precise estimates are difficult to find. However, such costs can be significant. One estimate of the annual per-capita cost of unionization in the private sector exceeded US$500 in 1987. See Bennett 1991: 4, table 2.

References

Bennett, James T. (1985). *Does a Higher Wage Really Mean You Are Better Off?* Springfield, VA: National Institute for Labor Relations Research.

——— (1990). *A Higher Standard of Living in Right To Work States.* Springfield, VA: National Institute for Labor Relations Research.

——— (1991). Private Sector Unions: The Myth of Decline. *Journal of Labor Research,* 12 (Winter): 1–12.

Boyer, Richard, and David Savageau (1993). *Places Rated Almanac.* New York: Simon and Schuster.

Holmes, Thomas J. (1995). *The Effects of State Policies on the Location of Industry.* Staff Report 205. Minneapolis, MN: Federal Reserve Bank of Minneapolis.

Lewis, H. Gregg (1986). *Union Relative Wage Effects: A Survey.* Chicago, IL: University of Chicago Press.

Parsley, C.J. (1980). Labor Unions and Wages: A Survey. *Journal of Economic Literature,* 18 (March): 1–31.

World Report: Is Mississippi Richer than New York? (1977). Chicago: First Chicago Bank.

Economic Development and the Right to Work
Evidence from Idaho and other Right-to-Work States

David Kendrick

Passing Right-to-Work legislation: the start of the economic boom

Idaho became the nation's twenty-first Right-to-Work state in 1985, when the state Senate and the state House of Representatives overrode then-Governor John V. Evans's veto of House Bill 2. Idaho's status as a Right-to-Work state was immediately challenged by the state's labour unions, which obtained enough signatures to place the law on the 1986 general election ballot.

Having run the gauntlet of numerous committee hearings, votes in both houses of the legislature, second votes in the legislature on overriding the Governor's veto, the idea of Right-to-Work was clearly popular. However, union officials in Idaho had US$1.3 million in forced union dues handed to them by the American Federation of Labor-Congress of Industrial Organizations (AFL-CIO) in Washington, DC, to spend on their drive to

---

Notes will be found on page 102.

repeal the law. All in all, opponents of Right-to-Work had nearly twice as much money to spend as the supporters of the Right-to-Work law.

By election day, last minute polls seemed to indicate a photo finish, but the Right-to-Work law was upheld by Idaho voters on November 4, 1986 by a surprisingly strong 54 to 46 percent margin. Since then, Idaho has enjoyed sustained economic growth—so much so that a recent publication by the Idaho Department of Commerce describes "six consecutive years of growth and stability that is the envy of many," beginning in 1987, the year Right-to-Work legislation finally took effect (Idaho Dep't of Commerce 1993). It is no exaggeration to say that the enactment of Right-to-Work laws has done more for the Idaho economy than has any other legislative measure in the last decade.

Economic decline in the pre-Right-to-Work era

In the period before the passage of the Right-to-Work legislation, Idaho was beset with serious economic problems. And, perhaps nothing illuminates better the need, in the midst of these problems, to enlarge employees' rights against the interests of the unions than the tragedy of Bunker Hill. This Bunker Hill does not refer to American minutemen being forced to give up Boston to the British in 1776, but rather to the loss of 1,500 Idaho mining jobs due to the intransigence of the national executive of the Steelworkers union in 1982.

In January of 1982, the union leaders in Pittsburgh overruled the employees of Bunker Hill Mining Company -in Cour d'Alene, Idaho. The employees had voted to accept pay cuts and other concessions to save the firm from going out of business. But, to their surprise, they were informed by the local president that, as far as union leaders in Pittsburgh were concerned, their vote in favour of the proposed contract was merely "advisory." In desperation, the local union members voted out of office the local president, who was following the instructions of the leadership in Pittsburgh. Prospective buyers of the company, however, did not believe that they could proceed with their buyout unless the cost savings from the proposed contract were approved by union officials in Pittsburgh. The deal fell through and all 1,500 jobs were lost. "Remember Bunker Hill" took on a new meaning in Idaho in 1986.

In the five years previous to the enactment of Right-to-Work legislation in 1985, manufacturing employment in Idaho had declined by 8 percent. At the same time, neighbouring states such as Nevada, Utah, Wyoming and Arizona, which had enacted Right-to-Work laws, saw their manufacturing employment increase by no less than 16 percent, and as much as 36 percent, over the same five year period.

Right-to-Work laws bring new businesses and new jobs

Many businesses looking to relocate were waiting on the results of the vote. In June 1986, Phillip D. Phillips, a vice-president of the Fantus Company—one of the nation's largest industrial relocation firms—wrote in a letter to Michael Dolton of the Chamber of Commerce in Greater Twin Falls, Idaho: "Approximately 50 percent of our clients ... do not want to consider locations unless they are in Right-to-Work states. As a result, states that are not Right-to-Work states, and the communities in them, are eliminated from consideration in the initial phase of the site selection process, no matter how strong their other advantages for a facility might be." That "deal sweeteners" like tax incentives or other bonuses for companies considering relocation were still inadequate was also clear from a study conducted by the Center for Business and Economic Research of the University of Tennessee in 1985. According to this survey, even incentives such as low taxes, tax concessions, government support for site acquisition, and quality of life were ranked less important than Right-to-Work laws as factors in deciding where to relocate (Hake, Ploch, and Fox 1985).

Since Idaho's Right-to-Work law took effect in 1987, the state has enjoyed growth in virtually all major areas of business. According to the United States Bureau of Labour Statistics, 142,500 new jobs were added to Idaho's payroll between 1986 and 1995, bringing the total non-agricultural employment to 476,900. High-technology industries continue to expand in Idaho, with the 1993 employment level at 27,000 compared to 17,100 in 1987. Over 1,000 net new businesses opened their doors in Idaho in 1992; since 1987, net new business starts have totalled 5,000 (Idaho Dep't of Commerce 1993).

Manufacturing employment in Idaho has grown at a rate far exceeding the growth of the pre-Right-to-Work era. Idaho's 36.2

percent growth in manufacturing employment from 1987 through 1995 was the fifth-highest rate of growth in the United States for that eight-year period. By way of contrast, manufacturing employment in Idaho declined 2.1 percent in the six years before the Right-to-Work law went into effect.[1] Neighbouring Montana, which lacks a Right-to-Work law, had only a 9 percent increase in manufacturing jobs between 1986 and 1993—less than one-third of Idaho's 36.2 percent growth.[2]

Construction employment doubled in Idaho between 1986 and 1994. Its 105 percent increase was the second-highest rate of growth in the nation in a period during which the number of construction jobs in non-Right-to-Work states rose by only 5.5 percent.[3] Mining employment, according to the United States Commerce Department, rose by 106 percent between 1986 and 1994.

Across the board, Right-to-Work states created 118,400 more non-agricultural jobs than did non-Right-to-Work states from 1987 through 1993.[4] Clearly, since 1986, Idaho has managed to achieve economic stability and promote growth in nearly all sectors of its economy.

Right-to-Work laws are a key factor for companies deciding to relocate in Idaho

The survey conducted by the Fantus Company demonstrated that half of all businesses looking to relocate will not even consider moving to a state without a Right-to-Work law. In other words, states allowing forced-unionism automatically cut in half their opportunities for job creation because they lack a right-to-work law. A survey undertaken by Area Development magazine of those responsible for selecting industrial sites revealed similar results: 39.1 percent of respondents considered a Right-to-Work law "very important" in determining where to relocate. Another 32.3 percent considered it "important," and 19.9 percent said Right-to-Work was at least a "minor consideration." All told, 91.3 percent of the business leaders surveyed reported that Right-to-Work laws are a positive factor for businesses looking to relocate (Glenn 1991, citing *Area Development*, December 1990). The conclusion is clear: a state Right-to-Work law is an essential part of the sort of business climate that attracts new businesses and encourages development and expansion by existing businesses.

Right-to-Work laws produce lower unemployment

When labour unions must compete in a free market—where employees have a choice about whether or not to join or support a union—union leadership must be attentive to the real needs and desires of the rank-and-file members. Right-to-Work states thus offer a business environment free from much of the onerous mandatory union-imposed regulation, feather-bedding, and work rules that raise labour costs and reduce jobs in non-Right to Work states. As a result, businesses in Right-to-Work states have lower costs, allowing them to produce goods and services less expensively, and to employ more people without cutting wages.

Unemployment rates tend to be lower in Right-to-Work states than they are in non-Right-to-Work states. For example, in 1995, forced-unionism states had an average unemployment rate of 5.6 percent. In Right-to-Work states, however, that average was only 4.8 percent, and Idaho mirrored this national trend (USBLS 1987, 1989, 1991, 1992, 1993, 1994, 1995).

In 1986—before the enactment of the Right-to-Work law—despite a strong national economy the unemployment rate in Idaho was 8.7 percent. In 1990—after passage of Right-to-Work legislation—with a nationwide recession underway the unemployment rate was 5.8 percent. In 1996, the unemployment rate was down to 5.4 percent (Idaho Dep't of Employment 1993).

Right-to-Work laws bring higher wages and more personal income

Perhaps, the best indicator of how Right-to-Work laws benefit a state economy is the level of personal disposable income. The more income individuals have, the more goods and services they can buy, which in turn stimulates the economy and contributes directly to economic growth. Since 1977, Professor James T. Bennett has pioneered research showing that, on average, real income adjusted for taxes and inflation is, in fact, higher in Right-to-Work states than non-Right-to-Work states (Bennett 1994). In 1994, per capita personal income in Idaho grew by 8.8 percent, well above the national average of 5.1 percent. The only two states with greater rates of growth in this period—Arizona and Nevada—were also Right-to-Work states. Over the longer range, 1987 to 1995, Idaho's personal income growth rate was 71.7 percent, the highest in the United States, and well above the average growth of 57.1 percent in the non-Right-to-Work states.[5]

Right-to-Work laws enhance the performance of the unions

The unions have also benefitted from the passage of Right-to-Work laws. Once Idaho voters approved the law in November 1986, the unions had a new task at hand. Jim Kerns, the Idaho AFL-CIO chief, explained their dilemma very well: "Business agents have to learn something about contacting workers and asking him to join," Kerns said, "which they haven't had a great amount of experience in" (quoted in Glenn 1987). According to the National Labor Relations Board, in 1986, private-sector unions in Idaho won fewer than half the elections where they sought to represent employees in a particular workplace. In 1994, they won 63 percent of those elections. Since the passage of Right-to-Work legislation, the experience gained in actually "asking" someone to join a union voluntarily has benefitted unions.

Further, Right-to-Work laws encourage unions to perform better at the bargaining table. Sam Ervin, a Senator from North Carolina and leading Democrat in the fight to preserve the states' freedom to enact Right-to-Work laws when President Lyndon Johnson sought to repeal that right in 1965, put it well in his autobiography: "Right-to-Work laws remove the motive of the union to subordinate the interests of the employees to its wish, and thus leaves it free to conduct negotiations for the sole purpose of obtaining an employment contract advantageous to the employees" (Ervin 1984: 190).

Right-to-Work laws produce fiscal flexibility

Idaho has long had a budget surplus, a "rainy day" fund providing it with a degree of fiscal flexibility. But in the years prior to the passing of Right-to-Work legislation, the "rainy day" surplus was marginal: in fiscal year 1980, Idaho had total expenditures of US$360,527,000 and a surplus of US$6,571,000; by 1986, the surplus was down to only US$1 million. After the enactment of Right-to-Work laws, however, the budget surplus grew nearly 400-fold from the amount available in 1986. In 1994, Idaho's "rainy day fund" of US$38 million was nearly 400 times larger than the paltry US$1 million surplus Idaho had in 1986 (US Dept. of Commerce 1988: 267; 1995: 311). This was due in large part to the expanding job market.

The boom in job creation resulting from passage of Right-to-Work legislation has led to a similar expansion in the state tax base and an increase in state revenue, despite the fact that Idaho's tax rates are lower than those of any other western state (Idaho Dep't of Commerce, Div. of Economic Development 1992: 4-1, citing US Bureau of Census 1990).

Idaho's prosperity and the "regional boom"

Is Idaho's prosperity since the introduction of Right-to-Work legislation merely the result of the economic growth of the entire region? It is certainly true, as the AFL-CIO argued before the Alberta Joint Review Committee on Right-to-Work, that Idaho's economic resurgence was "part of the regional boom in the Pacific Northwest states" (Alberta Economic Development Authority 1995: 20, citing AFL-CIO 1994). Since 1986, while Idaho has seen 36.2 percent growth in manufacturing jobs, Nevada's manufacturing employment has risen by 65.3 percent, Utah's by 34.5 percent, and Wyoming's by 22.5 percent. All of these states are Right-to-Work jurisdictions. (See figure 1 for a map showing states with Right-to-Work laws.)

On the other hand, the rates of growth in manufacturing employment for the non-Right-to-Work states in the region are not nearly so high: Colorado, 3.2 percent; Montana, 9.9 percent; Or-

Figure 1 States with Right-to-Work legislation.

egon, 15.7 percent; Washington, 9.1 percent. Thus, this "regional boom" seems to be occurring only in the Right-to-Work states. In fact, the average rate of growth in manufacturing jobs since 1987 has been 39.6 percent for the four Right-to-Work states but only 9.5 percent for the non-Right-to-Work states in the region.

The positive effects of Right-to-Work laws are also evident when one looks at growth in manufacturing productivity between 1987 and 1992. In Idaho, manufacturing output per hour grew by nearly 5 percent during that five year period, while the neighbouring, non-Right-to-Work, state of Montana saw a decline of 4.4 percent during the same period. Overall, manufacturing output per hour in the four Right-to-Work states of Idaho, Utah, Nevada and Wyoming grew by 2.7 percent, while in the non-Right-to-Work states of Montana, Washington, Oregon and Colorado, it fell by 2.45 percent.

Since the passage of the Right-to-Work legislation, Idaho has had sustained economic growth, and Boise, Idaho, is considered by many to be the fastest growing metropolitan area in the country (The Conference Board 1993: 14). Idaho's economic success has attracted international attention. According to the *Economist* magazine of February 11, 1995, Idaho's "economy would be unrecognizable to the early pioneers. Job growth is roaring at 5.8 percent a year, the third fastest in the nation ... A decade ago, Idaho had a recession in which it lost jobs for three consecutive years." Today, *The Economist* continues, "[e]mployers in the Boise area find it so hard to hire enough workers that fast-food restaurants have abandoned the minimum wage and replaced billboards for hamburgers with signs pleading for applicants." Going on, *The Economist* reports that Idaho's job growth has been

> an impressively broad-based boom. Construction, tourism, food-processing, retail, and forest products are all prospering. But Idaho also has a fine display of high-tech industries. Micron Technologies, based in Boise [and] launched in 1987 ... now employs 5,600 people in state-of-the-art plants fabricating memory chips and personal computers. At the other end of town, Hewlett-Packard builds laser printers in a plant that employs 5,000 workers. A crowd of smaller high-tech operations are springing up around Boise as former Micron or HP engineers launch their own companies. (*The Economist* 1995: 30)

The same pattern seen in the Pacific Northwest of prosperity in states with Right-to-Work laws and slow growth in states without such laws has also been observed in other parts of the United States. Between 1960 and 1993, according to the United States Bureau of Labor Statistics, the 21 Right-to-Work states[6] increased their manufacturing payrolls by 2.68 million while those states subject to federally imposed mandatory unions lost 1.36 million manufacturing jobs. Further, we now have evidence of a dramatic shift in manufacturing employment that one can see simply by stepping over the border from a forced-unionism state to a Right-to-Work state.

Dr. Thomas J. Holmes, in a study published by the Federal Reserve Bank of Minneapolis (1995), breaks new ground in our understanding of how state policies can encourage or discourage industrial development. Holmes first drew a border between Right-to-Work and non-Right-to-Work states in the eastern part of the continental United States (see figure 2). His border begins at the Right-to-Work state of North Dakota and the non-Right-to-Work state of Minnesota. The line runs south to Texas (Right-to-Work) and Oklahoma (non-Right-to-Work), then turns east, ending at the Atlantic coast between Virginia (Right-to-Work) and Maryland (non-Right-to-Work). Using data from the United States Census Bureau's County Business Patterns for 1992, Holmes then compared manufacturing employment on both sides of the border and found that, in 1992, manufacturing constituted 21 percent of total employment in those non-Right-to-Work counties within 25 miles of the border while, on the Right-to-Work side of the border, manufacturing accounted for 28.6 percent of total employment. Holmes writes: "[O]n average, manufacturing employment increases by one-third when one steps over the border" to a Right-to-Work state. (1995: 3).

To measure the long-term effect of Right-to-Work laws, Holmes contrasts the total growth of manufacturing employment during the period from 1947 to 1992 in those counties within 100 miles of the border between Right-to-Work and non-Right-to-Work states. Of the nine Right-to-Work states on Holmes's border (North Dakota, South Dakota, Nebraska, Iowa, Kansas, Texas, Askansas, Tennessee, Virginia), all but Kansas had enacted their laws by the end of 1947. Within 100 miles of the border, manufacturing employment in Right-to-Work states

Figure 2 Holmes's border between states with, and states without Right-to-Work legislation

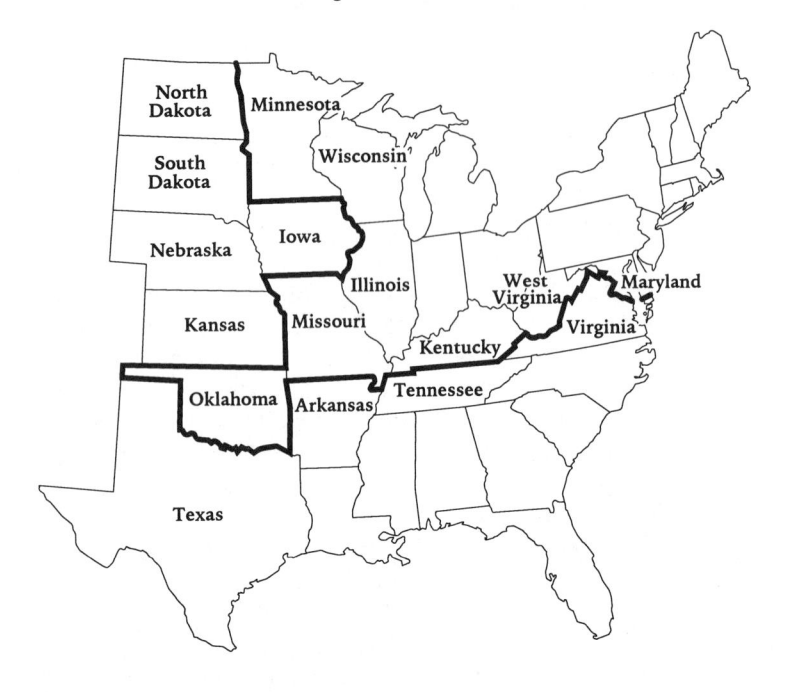

Source: adapted from figure 2, County boundaries, in Holmes 1995.

grew more than twice as fast as that in the non-Right-to-Work states. And, within 25 miles of the border, Right-to-Work states increased their manufacturing employment by 170 percent—more than triple the 54 percent growth on the non-Right-to-Work side (Holmes 1995: 12).

This gap in manufacturing employment between Right-to-Work states and non-Right-to-Work states has expanded without interruption since 1947. Holmes discovered this by comparing manufacturing employment as a percentage of total population in those counties within 25 miles of the border. A difference of 10 percentage points in 1947 had become a spread of 30 percentage points by 1963, and had widened to 45 percentage points by 1992 (Holmes 1995:13).

Some have pointed to accidental factors such as the South's warmer weather and the advent of air conditioning as the principal cause of this shift in manufacturing activity. But by comparing manufacturing employment on the border between Right-to-Work and non-Right-to-Work states, Holmes eliminates weather, which does "not change discontinuously at state borders," and highlights state policies, which do change at the border (1995: 3). In short, Holmes has uncovered the most conclusive evidence to date that state policies encouraging cooperative and voluntary relations between labour and management have played a crucial role in the exodus of manufacturers to the 21 Right-to-Work states.

While the evidence Holmes has gathered is new, the economic wisdom behind it certainly is not. Many employers know firsthand the costly burdens of union work rules and violent strikes. But back in 1960, Nobel-Prize winning economist Friedrich Hayek discerned that in the final analysis, "whatever true coercive power unions may be able to wield over employers is a consequence of this primary power of coercing other workers" (Hayek 1960: 269).

Using their control over the employer's labour to drive up his production costs, union officials inhibit job creation, as Holmes shows. They also liquidate existing jobs, leading to an average unemployment rate seven percent higher in non-Right-to-Work states than in Right-to-Work states since 1981.[7]

With a new factual certainty, Dr. Holmes has shown that Right-to-Work laws are a major spur to the creation of manufacturing growth and new jobs. That is a winning proposition for employees and employers alike.

Conclusion

Having permitted a budget surplus, low unemployment, positive new job creation, and low taxes, Idaho's Right-to-Work law provides business recruitment leverage, a solid economic foundation, and a secure climate for sustained growth well into the next century. What Idahoans now enjoy as a way of life began at the 1986 watershed, the enactment of the state's Right-to-Work law. And the first seven years of Idaho's Right-to-Work law bode well for that state's future prosperity, so long as markets remain free and individuals maintain their right to chose whether or not to join or support a labour union.

Notes

1. Based on figures from United States Bureau of Labor Statistics [USBLS] 1995.
2. Based on figures from USBLS 1995.
3. Based on figures from USBLS 1995.
4. Based on figures from USBLS 1994.
5. Idaho Department of Commerce n.d., using statistics from the US Bureau of Labor Statistics and the US Bureau of Economic Analysis.
6. The 21 states that have adopted Right-to-Work laws are Alabama, Arizona, Arkansas, Florida, Georgia, Idaho, Iowa, Kansas, Louisiana, Mississippi, Nebraska, Nevada, North Carolina, North Dakota, South Carolina, South Dakota, Tennessee, Texas, Utah, Virginia, and Wyoming.
7. Compiled from unemployment figures published by the United States Bureau of Labor Statistics, 1981 to 1994.

References

AFL-CIO (1994). *A Tale of Two Nations: What's Wrong with Right-to-Work*. Washington, DC: American Federation of Labor-Congress of Industrial Organizations.

Alberta Economic Development Authority (1995). *Final Report*. Joint Review Committee: Right-to-Work Study (November 30).

Bennett, James T. (1990). *A Higher Standard of Living in Right to Work States*. Springfield, VA: National Institute for Labor Relations Research.

The Conference Board (1993). *Regional Economies and Markets: A Quarterly Report* (Second Quarter). New York: The Conference Board.

Ervin, Sam J.J. (1984). *Preserving the Constitution*. Charlottesvill, VA: Michie.

The Economist (1995). February 11.

Glenn, Gary (1987). Idahoans Were Right When They Approved Right-to-Work. Times-News (September 4). Twin Falls, Idaho.

——— (1991). Right to Work Led to Idaho Resurgence. Times-News (September 2). Twin Falls, Idaho.

Hake, David A., Donald R. Ploch, and William F. Fox (1985). *Business Location Determinants in Tennessee*. Knoxville, TN: Center for Business and Economic Research, College of Business Administration, University of Tennessee.

Hayek, Friedrich A. (1960). *The Constitution of Liberty*. Chicago, IL: University of Chicago Press.
Holmes, Thomas J. (1995). *The Effects of State Policies on the Location of Industry: Evidence from State Border*. Research Department Staff Report 205. Minneapolis, MN: Federal Reserve Bank of Minneapolis.
Idaho Department of Commerce, Division of Economic Development (1992). *Idaho Facts*. Boise, ID: Idaho Dep't of Commerce.
Idaho Department of Commerce (1993). *1993 Annual Report*. Boise, ID: Idaho Dep't of Commerce.
Idaho Department of Commerce (n.d.). *Economic Highlights: Idaho and Leading States*. Boise, ID: Idaho Dep't of Commerce.
Idaho Department of Employment, Bureau of Analysis and Research (1993). *State of Idaho Labor Force Data—Place of Work—Annual Averages*. Boise, ID: Idaho Dep't of Employment.
Jones, Sybil (1992) *Jobs Up in Right to Work States, 1986–1991*. Springfield, VA: National Institute for Labor Relations Research.
United States Bureau of the Census (1990). *Government Finances, 1989-1990*. Washinton, DC: US Dep't of Commerce.
United States Bureau of the Census (1992). *County Business Patterns 1990, Idaho*. Washington, DC: US Government Printing Office.
United States Bureau of Labor Statistics (1987). *Employment and Earnings* (May). Washington, DC: US Bureau of Labor Statistics.
——— (1989). *Employment and Earnings* (May). Washington, DC: US Bureau of Labor Statistics.
——— (1991). *Employment and Earnings* (May). Washington, DC: US Bureau of Labor Statistics.
——— (1992). *Employment and Earnings* (May). Washington, DC: US Bureau of Labor Statistics.
——— (1993). *Employment and Earnings* (May). Washington, DC: US Bureau of Labor Statistics.
——— (1994). *Employment and Earnings* (May). Washington, DC: US Bureau of Labor Statistics.
——— (1995). *Employment and Earnings* (May). Washington, DC: US Bureau of Labor Statistics.
United States Department of Commerce (1988). *Statistical Abstract of the United States, 1988*. Washington, DC: US Dep't of Commerce.
United States Department of Commerce (1995). *Statistical Abstract of the United States, 1995*. Washington, DC: US Dep't of Commerce.

The Process of Labour Market Reform in the United Kingdom

*JOHN T. ADDISON AND
W. STANLEY SIEBERT*

Over the course of the past 30 years in Britain, industrial relations law and practice has been subject to sharp changes. In the 1970s collective bargaining and closed shops were actively encouraged. Indeed, as we shall see, individuals were virtually forced to become union members and statutory wage fixing together with collective bargaining came to involve at least 80 percent of the work force. In the 1980s and 1990s the opposite policy was pursued, with six major pieces of union reform legislation being enacted by successive Conservative administrations. Nevertheless, the coverage of collective bargaining remains high—around 45 percent—and, although formal closed shops have been made unlawful, questions remain as to the present extent of informal union restrictions on recruitment and whether these will multiply now that the Labour Party has regained power. The effect of the laws attacking union immunities

---

Notes will be found on pages 130–31.

on British economic performance has also been questioned, and some have wondered if they are worth preserving.

In this chapter, we first consider the historical development of union organization and, in particular, of the closed shop. We then describe the legal changes affecting union power over the period, contrasting Labour and Conservative legislation. Finally, we assemble empirical evidence concerning the effects of the law on union membership and the links between the decline in union power and Britain's improved economic performance.

Trends in union security

Table 1 shows trends in union density (i.e., percentage unionization) and in collective-bargaining coverage since 1960. Union density increases to a peak in 1980 and then declines continuously, falling to 32 percent in 1995. Collective-agreement coverage, including coverage under statutory wage-fixing machinery (the Wages Councils), shows a similar pattern. Collective-agreement coverage has always exceeded density, and has declined faster. Factors underlying the decline in coverage include the ending of the extension of collective agreements in 1980, the rescission of the "fair wages resolution" in 1982 (under which government contractors paid union rates), and also the abolition of Wages Councils in 1993.

Table 1 Union density and collective-agreement coverage (percentage of employees in employment)

Year	Union Density (%)*	Collective-agreement coverage (%) (including Wages Councils)
1960	41	70–74†
1970	48	76–80†
1975	49	84–86†
1980	53	83‡
1990	38	65‡
1995	32	47**

Sources: *Metcalf (1994: 127); Cully and Woodland (1996: 216). †Milner (1995: 82). Wages Councils covered roughly 10 percent of employees when abolished in 1993. ‡Interpolated from Milner (1995: 76), whose estimates are most likely on the high side. **Cully and Woodland (1996: 222). Figure refers to proportion of employees in workplaces where unions are recognized for purposes of negotiating pay and conditions.

On some estimates, at their peak in the middle-to-late 1970s collective agreements plus statutory wage fixing covered almost all the workforce. Indeed, it was probably only in the late 1980s that collective-agreement coverage dropped below the 1960 level of 70 to 74 percent. Thus, Britain has a tradition of strong national wage-fixing arrangements and it is to be expected that it will be hard to break this mould.

Table 2 provides measures of the extent of the closed shop. The closed shop is important because it is the most coercive aspect of trade unionism. Closed-shop legislation also epitomizes the political differences between the main parties, with Labour encouraging their formation in the 1970s.

Closed shops are difficult to measure because of definitional problems. Conventionally, a distinction is made between "preentry" closed shops ("closed shops" proper in American parlance) and "post-entry" closed shops (or "union shops"). Under pre-entry closed shops, the worker has to be a union member before being considered for the job and owes the job to the union. With post-entry closed shops, the member has to join the union once hired in the job. In both cases, the worker will lose the job if expelled from the union—say, for not supporting a strike—but the pre-entry variety clearly confers more power on the union. Famous closed shops include craft qualification closed shops in printing (still important in general printing though not in newspapers; see Dunn and Wright 1993: 19) and labour-pool closed shops for seamen and for actors. Shipbuilding workers and dock labour have also had pre-entry closed shops.[1]

The estimates given in table 2 indicate that the total of those employed in closed shops appears to have peaked around 1980, and to have then declined in step with the path of union density. However, the extent of the decline since 1980 is controversial. A specially commissioned government survey of workers in 1989 gives much higher estimates (2.6 million) than does the 1990 Workplace Industrial Relations Survey (WIRS) survey of firms (0.3 to 0.5 million).[2] It seems as though workers, when asked whether union membership was a condition of their employment, are more aware of union pressures than are managers. The latter might only be aware of closed shops if there is a formal agreement to that effect between management and a trade union (Stevens et al. 1989: 618; Wright 1996: 590).

Table 2 Extent of the closed shop

Year	Extent of Closed Shop (million workers) total	pre-entry	Notes and Sources
1964	3.76	0.75	Hanson et al. 1982: 66, 70, using data from McCarthy's (1964) survey.
1979	4.3	0.84 69% of union firms employing craftsmen	Gennard et al. 1980, survey of firms. Wright 1996: 502, survey of union firms.
1980	4.7–4.9* 32% of union firms	0.9†	*Millward and Stevens 1984: 107, survey of establishments; †Daniel and Millward 1980: 71, 281, survey of establishments. Millward and Stevens 1984: 102, percentage of establishments recognizing manual unions with any workers in closed shop.
1984	3.5–3.7* 26% of union firms	0.5†	*Millward and Stevens 1984: 107, survey of establishments; †Dunn and Wright 1993: 8. Millward and Stevens 1984: 102, percentage of establishments recognizing manual unions with any workers in closed shop.
1989	2.6	0.8–1.3	Stevens et al. 1989: 617, survey of workers; true figure could be only 40% of given figure as only 40% of closed-shop members said they would be dismissed if they lost union membership (Stevens et al. 1989: 620).
1990	0.3–0.5* 23% of union firms†	0.1–0.15*	*Millward et al. 1992: 99, 101; survey of establishments. Note that in a further 15% of establishments management "strongly recommends" union membership. †Geroski et al. 1995: 43, survey of unionized quoted companies.
1991		55% of union firms employing craftsmen	Wright 1996: 502, survey of union firms.
1993	20% of union firms		Geroski et al. 1995: 43, survey of unionized quoted companies.

But it must be admitted that only 40 percent of the workers who believed they were in closed shops in the 1989 survey also stated that they would definitely lose their jobs if they lost their union membership (although other sanctions against non-membership were mentioned). Applying this fraction to the 1989 survey values would reduce the (1989) estimate for the total number of workers in closed shops to around 1 million and those in pre-entry closed shops to some 0.5 million. Still, these figures are well above the corresponding magnitudes derived from the 1990 WIRS, which puts the total number in closed shops at under 0.5 million, and the number in pre-entry closed shops at only 100,000—even if management in a further 15 percent of establishments "strongly recommends" that workers be in a union (and this figure is little changed from the 1984 WIRS; see Millward et al. 1992: table 3.17).

Other surveys of movements in the numbers covered by closed shops also suggest a less precipitous decline in the 1980s and 1990s. Thus, a survey of unionized companies traded on the stock exchange by Geroski et al. (1995) found that 23 percent had a closed shop in 1990, a figure that had fallen only slightly to 20 percent by 1993. These figures may be roughly compared with earlier WIRS values: according to the 1984 WIRS, 26 percent of union firms had at least some manual workers in a closed shop; the corresponding figure from the 1980 WIRS is 32 percent. On these data, therefore, there has not been a great decline in the prevalence of the closed shop, and there is room to doubt that David Metcalf (1994: 129) is correct in his verdict that the closed shop has "virtually withered away."

It is also interesting to note that the 1990 WIRS indicates that nearly half the workplaces with 100 percent (manual) union membership had, according to management, neither a comprehensive manual closed shop nor a management that strongly recommended union membership. (About 14 percent of establishments reported 100 percent unionization for manual employees, 12 percent reported this for employees other than manual labourers; see Millward et al. 1992: 61.) The question arises, therefore, as to what was causing 100 percent union density (that is, effectively a closed shop) in the absence of a management-union agreement. A plausible answer, according to Wright (1996: 509), is that "some form of mandatory unionism may been maintained without overt senior management approval, either with supervisory management complicity, and/or unilateral work group regulations." The policy problem is, of course, that it is difficult to legislate against closed shops, and to prevent firms from discriminating against nonunion workers in hiring and promotion, if they are under union pressure to do so. The next section will examine government efforts to tackle this problem.

In conclusion, the current position regarding the closed shop can perhaps best be gauged from Wright's (1996: 502) research findings on highly unionized firms in 1991. He reports that only 16 percent of highly unionized firms had a pre- or post-entry closed shop for non-manual workers (compared with 44 percent of the same sample of firms in 1979). But 68 percent operated a closed shop of some variety for manual workers (compared with 96 percent in 1979), and virtually all firms continued to operate a closed shop for craftsmen. Although there has been a decline in the closed shop, then, it remains strong among manual workers, particularly craftsmen, despite legislation attacking the device.

Laws affecting union security

A summary of the development of the laws affecting the density of union representation and the closed shop is given in Appendix 1. The list starts with the 1971 Industrial Relations Act because this particular piece of legislation signals the onset of legal activism in British industrial relations. Until 1971 industrial relations law was based on the 1906 Trade Disputes Act, which protected the right to strike by conferring "immunity" on union funds from liability for damages in actions in tort for inducing workers to breach their contracts of employment when pursuing a "trade dispute." Collective agreements were not legally enforceable. Union officials, it is worth remembering, have never had immunity, but this has not been particularly relevant since officials do not provide a rich target for damage claims. It has always been possible, however, to subject union officials to injunctions. (On the immunities system, see Deakin and Morris 1995: 758ff.) It must also be noted that individual striking workers have never enjoyed immunity.

Workers can be dismissed for breach of contract while striking, so long as their dismissal cannot be shown to be discrimination on the grounds of their union activities.[3] The 1971 Act attempted to impose an American-style industrial relations framework that included (1) a labour court; (2) a mechanism for recognizing unions, which could then form "agency shops" similar to those permitted by the Taft-Hartley Act of 1947; (3) a set of "unfair labour practices" (including unfair dismissal for the first time in British law); and (4) legally enforceable collective agreements. The Trades Union Congress (TUC) discouraged unions from registering under the Act, however, so that in practice few agency shops were formed. The 1971 Act also made provision for approved closed shops, that is, full pre-entry closed shops. Exceptionally, the National Union of Seamen and the actors' union, Equity, decided to register and establish these arrangements in 1973 (Hanson et al. 1982: 314).

In February 1974, the Conservative government was replaced by a Labour administration that brought in the Trade Union and Labour Relations Act (TULRA), amended in 1976. Although TULRA replaced the Industrial Relations Act and essentially restored the immunities of the 1906 Trade Disputes Act, the concept of unfair dismissal was retained and it has been built on ever since. Currently, there are about 40,000 unfair dismissals cases a year (Department for Education and Employment 1996a).[4]

The TULRA and the Employment Protection Act of 1975 used the concept of unfair dismissal to strengthen the closed shop. This was achieved by removing protection from workers who were dismissed for not belonging to a union in workplaces where union membership was a condition of employment. In other words, dismissal for non-membership of a union was "fair" when a firm had a closed shop. This law led to the expansion of closed shops because uncertainties about the law on unfair dismissal raised difficulties for firms because they might or might not lose an unfair dismissal case when a non-union worker was dismissed, depending upon whether the courts concluded that union membership was in fact a condition of employment for the person in question. Such problems gave rise to the view that "the personnel manager with closed shop problems deserves everyone's sympathy" (*Industrial Relations Legal Information Bulletin* [IRLIB] 1976: 6). The response of many managements was to write tightly specified "union membership agreements" (UMAs) and to ensure that workers complied with these, thereby spreading the closed shop. It became usual practice for a notice to be posted stating that within a certain period—say, a month—employees had to become union members unless they had a valid objection (Hanson et al. 1982: 59).

While under many union membership agreements existing non-union status was a valid reason for remaining outside the union (in two-thirds of the sample analyzed by Gennard et al. 1979: 1091), many others were more rigid and recognized only religious objection. A famous example of the latter is the UMA negotiated between British Rail and its three railway unions—the National Union of Railwaymen, the Associated Society of Locomotive Engineers and Firemen, and the Transport Salaried Staff Association. Some 43 employees were unwilling to join a union but, having no religious objections, were duly dismissed. A number of these workers then petitioned the European Commission of Human Rights for relief. The case went on to be heard by the European Court of the Council of Europe, which found for the dismissed railwaymen in 1981, stating that their dismissal was incompatible with the "pluralism, tolerance and broad-mindedness" of a democratic society (see Hanson et al. 1982: 102).

The rise of the formal UMA underlies the extension of the closed shop to almost 5 million workers in 1980, as shown in table 2. The new closed shops would have been mainly of the post-entry variety. As can be seen from the table, the number of pre-entry closed shops increased only slightly. The pre-entry closed shop needs to exclude, so as to drive up wages; expansion would defeat this object. The post-entry closed shop, on the other hand, needs to include so as to reduce the threat of nonunion workers being substituted for union labour; expansion is the objective.

The Employment Protection Act of 1975 put in place further measures to "encourage the extension of collective bargaining" (under Section 1(2) of the legislation). These measures caused controversy at the time but their effects in increasing union presence are admittedly hard to assess. In the first place, the Central Arbitration Committee (CAC), when called upon by a union, was empowered to secure the observance of "recognized" terms and conditions in an industry. If the CAC identified an employer as engaged in an industry covered by an industry-wide agreement, it could make an award bringing that employer's terms and conditions up to the recognized level.[5] Nearly 400 claims a year were being made by unions under the legislation in the late 1970s when the practice was at its height (Advisory Conciliation and Arbitration Service [ACAS] 1981: table 10).

In the second place, the Employment Protection Act provided that the Arbitration Conciliation and Advisory Service (ACAS) could be called upon by a union to make a recommendation that it be recognized by an employer for the purposes of collective bargaining. The process involved ACAS in organizing a union election within the plant in question. This led to the famous case involving Grunwick Film Processing Laboratories Ltd., where the owner defied ACAS by preventing attempts to elicit the workers' opinions on union recognition (ACAS 1981: 77). Overall, ACAS heard about 1,600 union claims for recognition during the period from 1976 to 1980, when the procedure was operative (it ended with the 1980 Employment Act), and has estimated that its efforts resulted in the extension of recognition to about 65,000 workers (ACAS 1981: 99). This might seem a small number in the national context and none of the firms considered in the Workplace Industrial Relations Survey (WIRS) for 1980 had been involved in any such statutory union-recognition process (Millward and Stevens 1986: 303). That said, these measures helped union organizing activities by establishing that public policy was favourable to union organization, and encouraging employers to recognize unions voluntarily to avoid the public scrutiny attendant upon a reference to ACAS (see Davies and Freedland 1993: 421).

When the Conservative government came to power under Margaret Thatcher, one of its election pledges was to change the law on the closed shop. Successive Conservative administrations have passed six principal pieces of industrial relations legislation, all of which have a bearing on the closed shop and the associated issue of union power. Yet even now there is doubt as to whether the closed shop is broken. Part of the reason for the persistence of the closed shop is that trade unions are a powerful force in a class-conscious society. Their objections to the 1971 Industrial Relations Act had been instrumental in bringing down the Conservative government of Edward Heath. A clear idea of the mood at the time can be gained from the fact that the new administration, despite its commitment to reform the law on the closed shop, refused to assist the railwaymen who were then petitioning the European Commission on Human Rights against British Rail's closed shops. (The railwaymen had recourse only to the support of Mr. Norris McWhirter and the Freedom Association; see Hanson et al. 1982: 101). Yet two years later a special fund was set up by the 1982 Employment Act to compensate retrospectively all such workers dismissed between 1974 and 1980 (see IRLIB 1982a: 2).

In 1980—and indeed subsequently—Conservative governments felt the need to move cautiously so as to avoid the dislocation from major strikes, such as occurred in the cases of miners and printers in 1984 and 1987, respectively. In the 1980 Employment Act, although new UMAs were submitted to the tough electoral hurdle of an 80 percent majority, the government decided to leave existing UMAs alone. But union strike-threat power was somewhat reduced by removing unions' immunity from liability for damages for actions in tort when organizing "secondary" strikes. The Act also introduced the idea of secret ballots (rather than a show of hands) but, at this stage, ballots were only voluntary and a fund was established from which trade unions could be reimbursed for expenditures in connection with such postal ballots. The response of the TUC was to boycott the scheme and it looked as if the scene was set for a replay of the events of 1971. However, on this occasion the boycott was to be successfully overridden by the 1984 Trade Union Act (see below).

The 1982 Employment Act was much bolder. All UMAs were now required to clear the voting hurdle every 5 years. Dismissal for non-membership of a union where there was an existing UMA remained lawful but only so long as the UMA had secured the necessary majority within the previous 5 years. Punitive compensation of up to £20,000 was available for individuals wrongfully dismissed (the limit is now £26,800; see Deakin and Morris 1994: 445). Measures were also adopted to stop discrimination against nonunion workers: contracts could not be enforced if they specified union-only labour, nor could tenders be awarded on this basis. The secretary of state for Employment, Norman Tebbit, believed that such union-only labour requirements in contracts were being "widely used to extend the closed shop," and that some Labour-controlled local authorities in particular had been "blatant" in awarding contracts only to 100 percent unionized firms (IRLIB 1982a: 3–4). The practice of "fair lists" was thus meant to be ended.

The 1982 Act also removed trade unions' blanket immunity from liability for damages for actions in tort. Prior to the legislation, the only real remedy for employers was against the individual organizers of labour disputes, who lacked the means to pay substantial damages and who would likely assume the mantle of martyrs were they to be sued (see Deakin and Morris 1995: 808). As Tebbit said: "What incentive is there for the union to restrain unlawful action by its officials if the union's funds are never to be at risk?" (IRLIB 1982b: 2). From now on, the union could be sued for unlawful industrial action. Given the large damages to which unions could be exposed, the Act also placed upper limits on damages that could be awarded against unions.

In the wake of the 1982 Act, there was to be a steady increase in legal action by employers against unions (see McKay 1996) and also against striking workers. In 1986, for example, News International dismissed 5,500 striking print workers (Heery 1987: 303). Most action against unions has taken the form of injunctions, that is, court orders to prevent an action starting or continuing, issued at the discretion of the High Court pending a full trial. The alternative to the injunction is the action for damages, which was hardly considered before the 1982 Act, because such an action could only be brought against union officials and not the union itself (see Deakin and Morris 1995: 806). Between 1980 and 1995, there were 201 legal actions against unions, including 166 injunctions (McKay 1996: 11, 14). Prior to 1980 injunctions were also uncommon, partly because the definition of a lawful trade dispute was wider and partly because the Labour government made the granting of injunctions more difficult by the use of rules such as that which restricted the granting of injunctions in circumstances where only one party was present (see Deakin and Morris 1995: 760).

The next major piece of legislation is the 1984 Trade Union Act, following Thatcher's victory in the 1983 "Falklands" election. The legislation developed the balloting idea presaged in the 1982 Act. Secret voting was now required in three areas: prior to industrial action, when electing union officials, and over political funds. Secret ballots for industrial action have apparently done most to reduce union power, because they are "extremely complex, technical and, in parts, ambiguous, thus leaving unions vulnerable to potential challenge in the courts on several counts" (Deakin and Morris 1995: 794). The Act and its associated Code of Practice put forward principles governing such matters as the balloting constituency, content of the voting paper, conduct of the ballot, and the time limit (4 weeks) within which action had to be taken after a ballot. Approximately one-third of the injunctions taken out since 1980 have been based on these balloting provisions (McKay 1996: 16). Large financial penalties have been imposed, including a £650,000 fine imposed on the National Graphical Association in

1984, and also sequestration of £707,000 of the National Mineworkers Union's assets (Marsden 1985: 157).

In 1988 and again in 1990, two more Employment Acts were passed. The 1988 Act followed another heavy election defeat for Labour in which union power was again a major issue. This Act sought to remove the ability of trade unions to enforce the closed shop via industrial action. It became unlawful to take any form of industrial action to establish or maintain a closed shop irrespective of whether or not the closed shop had been approved in a ballot. (Note that industrial action to force another firm to establish or maintain a closed shop had already lost immunity under the 1980 Employment Act.) It was now also unfair to dismiss an employee for non-membership of a union, even if that arrangement had been sanctioned by ballot.

The 1988 Act also made it "unjustifiable" for unions to discipline members for refusing to take part in industrial action. The courts are able to award up to £22,000 for such infringements, the same maximum amount as applies in the case of unjustifiable expulsion from a union. An example of the use of the Act is the case brought against the Local Government Officers' Union by 9 ex-members who were disciplined for refusing to join a properly balloted strike. They were each awarded £2,520 in compensation (see McMullen 1991: 4).

The 1990 Employment Act attempted a different approach against the closed shop. Hitherto, the legislative attack had attempted to eliminate the threat of dismissal based on non-membership; now attention turned to the point of hire. The Act made it unlawful to discriminate against non-union workers when hiring. By the same token, it is also unlawful to discriminate against union workers when hiring (that is, the "black-listing" of union activists is also unlawful), though a closed shop agreement, oddly enough, is not in and of itself unlawful (see Hendy 1993: 65).

The aggrieved job applicant has to make a complaint to an Industrial Tribunal, and the difficulty with this approach is that it will always be difficult to prove an allegation of refusal to hire because of an individual's union membership, or lack thereof (see lrd 1994: 24). As in the case of gender or race discrimination in hiring, without monitoring union density in the firm and comparing this with union density measured across all firms, it seems that nothing much concrete can be done to prove discrimination in hiring.

The final substantive piece of industrial relations legislation considered here is the 1993 Trade Union Reform and Employment Rights Act. This legislation also followed a Conservative victory, in the 1992 election. The Act's most far-reaching change for unions is its requirement that union members give written authorization for the check-off every 3 years. The Act also requires that an individual be permitted to join any union at the workplace. This requirement aims to override trade union procedures (the so-called Bridlington rules) preventing unions from "poaching" members from each other. In turn, the requirement could weaken union control over particular jobs and so lead to increased flexibility at the workplace.

Looking back over changes in industrial relations legislation in Britain since 1971, the difference in legal approach between the Labour and Conservative periods is dramatic. In the 1970s we see laws radically supportive of closed shops and collective bargaining. In the 1980s and the 1990s we see equally radical changes in the opposite direction. The 1982 Employment Act, which removed the blanket union immunity in tort and so exposed their funds to actions for damages was a particularly hard blow against closed shops and collective bargaining. This immunity, long established, had provided the only real basis for strike action because individual strikers enjoy very little protection under British law. Given such marked legal changes, coinciding with equally marked changes in union density and closed shop power, it is hard not to conclude that one caused the other.

Determinants of union density

Three main factors can be advanced to explain changes in union density. Firstly, there are "compositional" factors, namely, those associated with changes in the structure of the workforce. One such a change would be the increased importance of female workers who traditionally are less unionized. In the British context, however, the magnitude of the compositional factor is arguably quite small. Thus, for example, changes in the composition of the labor force unfavorable to unionization, such as increases in the proportion of female workers and white-collar workers, were also a feature of the 1970s when union density increased apace (see Disney 1990: 171). Although Green (1992: 454) reports that 30 percent of the fall in union density between 1983 and 1989 may be attributed to compositional factors (including gender, full-time/part-time status, firm size, age, industry, and occupation), Freeman and Pelletier's (1990: 144) well-known study finds nowhere near as strong a compositional effect between 1980 and 1986; specifically, at most 0.4 percentage point of the observed 8.6 percentage point drop in density is attributed to compositional factors.

Secondly, there are economic factors such as unemployment, inflation, and real wage growth. The most thorough British study in this vein is by Carruth and Disney (1988: 10), who find real wage growth to be most important: real wage growth of 1 percent per annum is associated with a steady-states union density of 59 percent, while a corresponding growth rate of 3 percent is associated with a steady-state density of only 27 percent. Union density is also found to react negatively to unemployment. The model is estimated over the period from 1896 to 1970, with 1971 to 1987 as the forecast period. Although the authors' use of actual lagged values of union density to forecast union density (see Disney 1990: 169) seems questionable, the model forecasts with little error. In particular, it closely tracks the decline in union density in the 1980s.

While economic factors seem to have reasonable time-series associations with trends in union density, the problem of why there should be these associations remains. The theory is weak: that workers are said to "credit" unions with the high nominal wage increases that occur in times of inflation (see, for example, Mason and Bain 1993: 334) aptly conveys the flavour of applied theorizing in this area. The unemployment variable is just as difficult to assess. High unemployment may increase employers' opposition to unions or reduce unions' organizing resources but it may also make workers more keen to join unions. Carruth and Disney (1988: 7) admit to a "lack of clear a priori theorization" in the literature, and move on.

Cross-sectional economic modeling of union density seems more convincing and can also illuminate trends through time. Using data from the Workplace Industrial Relations Surveys for 1980, 1984, and 1990 on the founding of new establishments, Disney et al. (1995: 413–14) report that union recognition is positively related to profits per worker at the date the plant was established. This is reasonable since profitable companies are likely to be more heavily targeted by union organizers, who may not be so actively opposed by management. Union recognition is also found to be positively related to the degree of industry organization at the time the plant was set up. This result implies that recognition is a once-for-all decision taken early in the plant's existence, and depends upon conditions prevailing at that time.

Most important, Disney et al. estimate that private-sector (but not public-sector) establishments founded in the 1980s are almost one-third less likely to recognize unions than establishments set up before this date, *ceteris paribus*. This finding serves to underscore the point that the decline in unionization is an intrasectoral phenomenon, such that compositional factors are not likely to prove very important. But the result does not of itself, of course, explain why union recognition was so much harder to achieve in the 1980s. We are left with changes in the law as the explanation.

The law is the third category of influences on union density. Our preceding detailed discussion of the law would, on the face of it, suggest that legal changes have played an important role. Indeed, Freeman and Pelletier's analysis (1990: 155) accords to the law pride of place: changes in their legal index account for virtually all the decline in union density during the period from 1980 to 1986. The main problem here—apart from the obviously subjective nature of the authors' measure of the coerciveness of the law—is one of causality. Disney (1990: 171), for example, argues that the Conservative government's "step-by-step" approach was primarily reactive during the 1980s, responding to rather than causing weaker unions.

It might be argued that Labour and Conservative governments alike have simply attempted to follow public opinion—this is, after all, one aspect of the role of government in a democracy. As union members become less numerous, there are fewer union voters, and this, in turn, affects legislation. Marsh's (1990) interesting analysis of public opinion finds that while Gallup polls have consistently shown that a majority of members of the public feel that "trade unions are a good thing" (1990: table 1), until the mid-1980s at least they also thought that unions were "too powerful" (1990: table 2). The laws of the 1980s have, on this view, merely "given the public what it has always wanted" (1990: 63). This argument is echoed in Farber (1984: 319), whose research for the United States indicates that "right-to-work laws simply mirror pre-existing preferences against union representation." However on this analysis, if the

Conservatives gave the public what they wanted, they were slow about doing it; while Labour's earlier actions buttressing union power were at variance with public opinion.

The economic effects of changes in the law

We have seen that there are good reasons to suppose that changes in the law over the past 15 years or so have had a material impact on union membership and density. What signs are there these changes in labour legislation have in turn influenced economic performance? To answer this question we shall first examine the effects of unionization on the performance of firms along the principal dimensions of productivity, profitability, and investment. Some other aspects of declining unionization are also touched upon, including the strike record, pay and employment determination, and wage inequality.

Productivity

Although there is some dispute as to the effects of British unions on productivity, the balance of the evidence for manufacturing industry clearly points to a negative effect, despite a pay differential of roughly 10 percent between union and non-union workers (the evidence is reviewed in Metcalf 1989). There is, one must admit, ambiguity as to whether there is a "hierarchy of effects;" that is, with worse outcomes being observed where union presence is stronger (see Machin 1991; Fernie and Metcalf 1995). There is also ambiguity about the mediating role of employee involvement. But the unfavorable impact of collective bargaining is a dominant theme of the empirical literature, although this observation is, of course, subject to the standard statistical problems raised by the cross-sectional nature of the British studies.

This point-in-time evidence is qualified by the empirical evidence that productivity growth was higher in unionized than in non-unionized plants during the 1980s (in contrast to the 1970s when the reverse was the case), even if productivity levels still remain higher in the latter.[6] The acceleration of productivity growth in unionized plants has been called a reduction in the "disadvantages of unionization" by Oulton (1990: 5). Other studies have confirmed that the most densely organized firms improved their productivity most in the 1980s (e.g., Bean and Symons 1989; Layard and Nickell 1989). This turnaround has been fairly uniformly interpreted as indicating that antiunion legislation had the intended effect, even if the relative contributions of the law and other factors such as greater market competition for products, greater risk of job loss, and decentralized bargaining cannot be precisely calculated. Gregg, Machin, and Metcalf (1993), however, report that productivity growth in the latter half of the 1980s, although greater in union than in nonunion companies, was actually highest in those companies that rid themselves of the closed shop and either partially or totally withdrew their recognition from unions.

Profitability

There is near unanimity among British studies that profits are lower in unionized workplaces. (The principal exception is Geroski et al. 1993; the various studies are reviewed in Metcalf 1993, 1994). The traditional indicators have been union recognition and the closed shop: both are negatively related to subjective measures of firm profitability. A handful of studies have used accounting measures and reach the same conclusion (e.g. Cable and Machin 1991).

Corporate profitability in Britain improved markedly from 1981 onward. This improvement not only is consistent with such factors as the abolition of exchange controls (in 1979) but has also been directly linked to the decrease in unionization. Thus, for example, Haskel's (1993) industry-level study reports that union decline contributed materially to rising corporate earnings, an interpretation that ties in with the studies of productivity growth mentioned earlier. More directly, both panel data and WIRS data suggest that the tendency of unions to reduce profit margins weakened throughout the 1980s (see, respectively, Menezes-Filho 1994; Millward et al. 1992).

Using WIRS data, Machin and Stewart (1996) have examined hierarchy of effect by distinguishing between union recognition and the closed shop (including in the latter classification circumstances where management "recommends" union membership). Of the two, only the closed shop is found to be statistically significant in a profit regression that includes the full array of control variables, suggesting that, at least for 1990, trade unions only reduced profitability in a subset of unionized establishments, namely, where they were strongest. This is in sharp contrast with earlier studies where, as we have seen, both variables were found to have a statistically significant depressing effect on profitability. (The authors also argue that the closed-shop variable does not simply proxy union density; that is, its effect is robust to the inclusion of a density variable.) Widening their analysis to encompass earlier WIRS data, Machin and Stewart conclude that the negative effects of unions on the financial performance of firms decreased by half between 1984 and 1990, and that it had collapsed entirely for the union-recognition variable.

It is of course conventional to argue that the profit effect may merely be redistributive and not distorting, that it simply shares out the quasi-rents due to market power. Unlike the situation in the United States, there is partial evidence to suggest that the size of the gap in Britain between union and non-union wages is associated with the degree of monopoly power in the product market. This result is reflected in Machin and Stewart's study (1996), where it is reported that, in addition to the closed shop, it is also necessary for there to be market power (as proxied by the relative size of establishments) to observe the negative effect upon profits. Interestingly, this study also finds that the effect upon profits is greater where there are limits on the exercise of managerial prerogative via demarcation rules and other protective and restrictive practices.

We may reasonably conclude that the effect of the unions upon profitability declined markedly during the 1980s, a result that seems consistent with the decline in the unions' bargaining power attributable to labour-reform legislation. But the obdurate effects of the closed shop are notable, despite the shrinkage of that sector. Also, it remains to be established that the profit effect can, after all, be glossed over as a simple redistributive exercise.

Investment

The effects of the unions upon investment—a key to evaluating the hypothesis that the effects upon profits can be explained as a simple redistributive exercise that is neutral from an efficiency perspective—have been less studied for Britain than for the United States (see Addison and Chilton 1997: 429–37). Moreover, as noted by Metcalf (1993: 16), time-series studies and cross-sectional studies produce contradictory findings. On the one hand, time-series studies have indicated that unions discourage investment. Denny and Nickell (1992), for example, find that the rate of investment is approximately 28 percent lower in firms that recognize unions relative to those firms that do not have to deal with unions. The tendency for unionization to discourage investment is also found to be more pronounced in competitive sectors. On the other hand, cross-sectional analyses indicate that recognition of unions has encouraged the introduction of "advanced technological change" or "the use of microelectronic technology" (e.g., Machin and Wadwhani 1991; Latreille 1992).

It might be argued that the time-series evidence, since it focuses upon investment rates, is more directly relevant to the notion that unions may exploit the quasi-rents accruing from long-lived specialized plant and equipment. But pending further analysis we simply note that there is again some evidence that the negative effects of unions on investment rates became less pronounced in the 1980s than in previous decades (Metcalf 1994: 151).

Pay and employment

Blanchflower's (1996) calculations suggest that, despite the diminution in the unions' bargaining power, the gap between the wages of unionized and non-unionized workers has remained more or less constant at around 10 percent since 1970. That differential does, however, apply to a considerably smaller portion of the British workforce given the decline in union density and collective-bargaining coverage. Blanchflower's results are based on individual-earnings data. Estimates based on establishment-earnings data point to a decline in the union premium through time. They also suggest that union security is material. Thusm for examply, summarizing data for semiskilled workers from the 1984 WIRS, Metcalf (1994: 141–42) reports that union density exceeding 95 percent was necessary to achieve the premium (of 8 percent) observed, on average, for union recognition. A post-entry closed shop yielded no additional wage advantage over that generated by high union density although its pre-entry counterpart produced a differential of no less than 17 to 19 percent.

Studies by Ingram (1990) and Gregg and Machin (1992) point to lower wage growth in unionized than in nonunionized plants in the 1980s. At issue is the extent to which these observed differences in the growth of wages act to modify the broad stability of the differential observed in studies using individual data. The narrowing of the differential may in practice have been rather too modest to yield any increase, ceteris paribus, in union employment.

Blanchflower, Millward, and Oswald (1991) have argued that, even independent of their wage effects, unionized workplaces grow less or shrink more than their nonunionized counterparts. However, using more recent WIRS data, Millward et al. (1992) suggest that this negative effect upon employment may have moderated in the latter half of the 1980s, which may again be consistent with labour law having reduced the disadvantages of unionization. Furthermore, research (using a fairly extensive set of controls) by Machin (1995) on plant closings fails to indicate that union recognition affected the probability of closure over the interval between 1984 and 1990.

Strikes

Strikes have decreased by a factor of 10 since 1979. Specifically, the number of stoppages declined from 2,125 in 1979 to just 235 in 1995, and the numbers of workers involved fell from 4.61 million to 174,000 (Department for Education and Employment 1996b: table 3). The legislation detailed in Appendix 1 has clearly increased the costs of strikes to unions. Yet these legal impediments to strike action do not speak for themselves. That is, one needs to know how the law has been used by employers. Moreover, on theoretical grounds (and, in particular, from the perspective of a Pareto-optimal accident model) it could be argued that the main effect of the law should have been to reduce settlements by eroding union bargaining power rather than to reduce the frequency of strikes (Siebert and Addison 1981; Hirsch and Addison 1986: ch. 4). On this view, strikes relect incomplete or asymmetric information in bargaining, leading either or both of the parties to miscalculate the position of the other's concession curve. The legislation is not easily diagnosed in these terms, although the undoubted ambiguities as to what constituted lawful industrial action under the evolving law may have caused unions to be overly cautious in exercising their bargaining power. From a different theoretical perspective having a basis in socio-political considerations, the changes in the law narrowing the range of (legal) industrial action may be expected to have curbed strikes arising from a desire to show solidarity with other workers or advance political goals.

It is perhaps unsurprising that empirical analysis has been unable to disentangle the effects of changes in the law from other factors likely to reduce strikes—heightened unemployment, falling union membership, and compositional factors attendant on the decline of sectors with traditionally high levels of strike activity (see, for example, Dunn and Metcalf 1994). Even though there is no firm indication that the legislation reduced strikes at a given unemployment rate (Blanchflower and Freeman 1994: 57), the evidence seems to suggest that the influence of the law has increased. But that influence is subtle. It is not simply reflected in an increased number of legal challenges in the courts but also in a greater willingness on the part of management to use an implied threat of legal action.

There are also some other empirical regularities concerning the decline in the closed shop and in multiunionism (i.e., the presence of a number of bargaining groups at the workplace). Whatever the theoretical pedigree of the argument, the closed shop has been linked empirically to higher propensity to strike (Machin, Stewart, and Van Reenan 1993). Here the decline in the closed shop offers one possible explanation for the observed reduction in industrial action. Perhaps more important in view of the greater robustness of the association has been the decline in multiunionism (see, for example, Millward et al. 1992: 282), with the offsetting (mechanical) effect of decentralized bargaining countered by a corresponding growth in single-table bargaining.

Some other performance outcomes

The institutional reforms designed to reduce union power are but one component of an internally self-consistent reform package adopted by successive Conservative administrations to improve Britain's poor economic performance. Other labour market measures have included a reduced role for government in the labour market (through, inter alia, privatization and the abolition of statutory wage-fixing machinery) and alterations to the welfare state to increase the incentive to work. Although there is some disagreement on individual components of the latter measures such as the reduction in the unemployment insurance replacement rate (see Blanchflower and Freeman 1994; Jackman, Layard, and Nickell 1996), the general conclusion is that the incentive to work has indeed increased. An additional element of the government's strategy was, of course, the removal of exchange controls in 1979.

Comparing the decade of the 1980s with that of the 1970s, data provided by Blanchflower and Freeman (1994) suggest, on the one hand, that these reforms may have succeeded in decreasing inflation and unit labour-costs and increasing economic growth in the United Kingdom relative to other nations of the Organization of Economic Cooperation and Development (OECD). They also observe some domestic improvement in the speed of adjustment of the labour market and in the responsiveness of wages to local conditions. On the other hand, Blanchflower and Freeman note that the reforms were not associated with any improvement in the responsiveness of real wages to unemployment and even appeared to be accompanied by a relative increase in unemployment (for males, if not for females). By way of explanation, they speculate that the reform package failed to recognize the rent-seeking power of unionized insiders, while the policies themselves produced greater segmentation in the labour market at a time of high unemployment. They also argue (Blanchflower and Freeman 1994: 75) that the type of reform measures adopted since 1980 may require tight labour markets to achieve their traction. We would argue that, to the contrary, comparative unemployment data suggest that the unemployment of less skilled workers relative to that of their more skilled counterparts has actually decreased in the United Kingdom at a time when it increased in countries such as France and Germany.[7] In short, the decline in the power of unionized insiders may have helped maintain job opportunities for the unskilled.

To be sure, there remain a number of other problems. There is, for example, a sharply rising inequality of earnings that has been linked, in the United Kingdom (Leslie and Pu 1996) as in the United States, to the decline of the unions. Yet, unlike their American counterparts, the bottom decile of British wage earners have enjoyed rising real incomes (Katz, Loveman, and Blanchflower 1994), which blurs the picture even if it is consistent with the facts of union decline and an improving economy. Schmitt (1995) has calculated that roughly one-fourth of the rise in wage inequality in the United Kingdom can be attributed to wider wage differentials due to fewer workers being covered by union contracts. Schmitt does not consider the consequences of preventing wage structures from widening, namely, increased unemployment inequality and the corrosive effects on workers of exposure to protracted unemployment. The real question is whether the United Kingdom would have managed to achieve its relatively successful employment record in the face of the challenges of increased trade and technological change (see Addison forthcoming), if the position of unionized insiders had been left unchallenged.

Conclusion

We have seen that there has been a profound change in the industrial-relations infrastructure in Britain. In a radical departure, successive Conservative administrations have sought fundamental reform of unions and collective bargaining. The legal changes in question have sought to limit the permissible range of industrial action, to strengthen union democracy, to attack the closed shop, and to remove the support of statutory procedures for union recognition. The consequence has been to undermine a system of wage setting via collective and statutory mechanisms that, at one point, covered over 80 percent of the workforce and that was widely perceived to produce distortions in the labour market. At issue, of course, is the effect of the reforms.

It seems that the attack on old-style collective bargaining and industrial relations has reduced union membership and collective bargaining coverage, eroded the closed shop, and diminished the disadvantages of unionization to society. There is also some suggestion in the data of an improvement in the responsiveness of wages and employment at the micro level and in a number of relative performance indicators such as inflation and growth. It is impossible, however, to quantify with any precision the particular contribution of union reform given the interlocking nature of the government's agenda that encompassed a reduced governmental role in the labour market, sharpened work incentives, and other measures generally supportive of economic competition.

It is perhaps too early to expect more of the reforms than a reduction of the disadvantages of unionization and a modest improvement in aggregate outcomes. But already there are signs that one major criticism leveled at the measures—that they have been accompanied by an increase in unemployment—has now to confront the reality of a rapidly improving labour market marked by robust job creation in the private section and by lower joblessness. Improvement over the medium term depends upon whether the new incentives will be maintained and, in particular, whether the power of the unions and the closed shop will be resurrected by the present Labour government.

Appendix 1
Summary of laws affecting union density and the closed shop (see discussion in text for sources)

1971: *Industrial Relations Act (Conservative government)*
- gave a statutory right not to be a union member, but permitted registered unions to negotiate "agency" shops if approved in workplace election
- also permitted "approved" closed shops to be negotiated in certain circumstances (where ratified by National Industrial Relations Court)

1974, 1976: *Trade Union and Labour Relations Acts (Labour government)*
- repealed the right not to be a union member (except in cases of genuine religious belief)
- established that dismissal of workers for non-membership of union is fair where a firm and a union negotiate a "union membership agreement" (closed shop)
- denied workers the right of appeal to Industrial Tribunal when dismissed for non-membership of union

1975: *Employment Protection Act (Labour government)*
- established a Trade Union Certification Officer to certify union independence from management
- established an Arbitration Conciliation and Advisory Service to supervise elections for statutory union recognition
- established a Central Arbitration Committee to hear claims from unions in support of extension to third parties of the terms and conditions of collective agreements

1980: *Employment Act (Conservative government)*
- required that new union membership agreements be approved in secret ballot by at least 80 percent of those entitled to vote
- withdrew immunity in tort from unions in cases of "secondary" industrial action, including action to compel union membership

- established a fund to reimburse unions for postal secret ballots on industrial action and union elections

1982: *Employment Act (Conservative government)*
- required that all union membership agreements be approved in secret ballot every 5 years, again by not less than 80 percent of those entitled to vote, or 85 percent of those voting
- set punitive compensation of up to £20,000 for workers unfairly dismissed on grounds of non-membership of unions
- declared unlawful both contracts requiring union entry labour and tenders awarded on a basis of union-only labour
- removed trade union funds from automatic shelter from liability for damages in tort and provided for damages in any proceedings of up to £250,000 for unions with more than 100,000 members

1984: *Trade Union Act (Conservative government)*
- required that there be secret ballots (postal or work-place) prior to industrial action (postal ballot expenses to be reimbursed by the Certification Officer)
- required that there be elections with secret ballots for union executives every 5 years, and for political funds every 10 years

1988: *Employment Act (Conservative government)*
- established a Commissioner for the Rights of Trade Union Members to assist union members with advice and in applications to the High Court
- gave union members the right not to be disciplined by their union for failure to support industrial action and provided for remedies for union members from their union of up to £13,420 plus a compensatory award of £8,500
- established that it is automatically unfair to dismiss a worker for non-membership of a union, irrespective of whether the closed shop has been supported by a ballot
- removed immunity from tort liability from industrial action to impose a closed shop

1990: *Employment Act (Conservative government)*
- established that it is unlawful to discriminate against non-union members (or union members) at the time of recruitment
- prohibited job advertisements specifying union membership and established that any practice under which employment is afforded only to union members is to be presumed discriminatory
- required that unions repudiate unofficial industrial action, permitted summary dismissal of unofficial strikers, and removed immunity for industrial action in support of dismissed strikers

1993: *Trade Union and Employment Rights Act (Conservative government)*
- prohibited unions from refusing to accept anyone into membership (or expel anyone) except on grounds of the individual's conduct
- required that the union-dues check-off must be authorized in writing by every member every 3 years
- established a Commissioner for Protection against Unlawful Industrial Action to advise and finance individuals claiming to have been affected by unlawful industrial action, who can apply to the High Court for an order against the union to discontinue that action

Notes

1 In dock work, the closed shop hinged on restriction of entry to "Registered Dock Workers" under the National Dock Labour Scheme which ended in 1989 (see Davis 1988).
2 The Workplace Industrial Relations Survey is a survey of a nationally representative sample of 2,000 establishments employing 25 workers or more (see Millward et al. 1992). The 1990 survey is the third and most recent, the other surveys having been undertaken in 1984 and 1980 (see Millward and Stevens 1986; Daniel and Millward 1983).

3 In practice, so long as all strikers are dismissed, and none are selectively re-hired for a period of three months, the employer cannot be sued for unfair dismissal.
4 Unfair dismissals are heard before tripartite Industrial Tribunals, chaired by a barrister or solicitor and assisted by 2 lay members drawn from separate panels of employer and employee representatives. Industrial Tribunals are intended to be more informal and less costly than the regular courts, and date from the Industrial Training Act of 1964, when they were set up to hear appeals by firms against the training levies imposed by that Act.
5 Where no recognized terms existed, unions could bring a claim before the CAC to raise wages and conditions to the "general level" for comparable employees—although this was obviously difficult to define (IRLIB 1975: 10).
6 Differential productivity growth in favour of unionized establishments is not universally observed. Thus, Heywood, Siebert, and Wei (1997), using WIRS data, report a negative (albeit statistically insignificant) coefficient estimate for union recognition in an equation explaining productivity growth from 1987 to 1990.
7 We derive this inference from data supplied in Nickell and Bell 1996: table1, while noting that this is emphatically not the interpretation advanced by these authors.

References

Advisory Conciliation and Arbitration Service (1981). *Annual Report 1980.* London: ACAS.

Addison, John T., and John B. Chilton (1997). Models of Union Behavior. In David Lewin, Daniel J.B. Mitchell, and Mahmood A. Zaidi (eds.), *Handbook of Human Resource Management* (Greenwich, CT: Connecticut Press): 407–44.

Addison, John T. (forthcoming). Sectoral Change and the State of the Labor Market in the United States. In Horst Siebert(ed.), *Sectoral Structural Change and Labour Market Flexibility: Experience in Selected OECD Countries* (Tübingen: J.C.B. Mohr).

Bean, Charles, and James Symons (1989). Ten Years of Mrs. T. Working Paper No. 1119. London: Centre for Labour Economics, London School of Economics.

Beaumont, Phillip B., and Richard I.D. Harris (1995). Union Derecognition and Declining Union Density in Britain. *Industrial and Labor Relations Review* 48 (April): 389–402.

Blanchflower, David (1996). The Role and Influence of Trade Unions in the OECD. Discussion Paper No. 310. London: Centre for Economic Performance, London School of Economics.

Blanchflower, David, and Richard Freeman (1994). Did Mrs. Thatcher's Reforms Change British Labour Market Performance? In Ray Barrell (ed.), *The U.K. Labour Market: Comparative Aspects and Institutional Developments* (Cambridge: Cambridge University Press): 51–92.

Blanchflower, David, Neil Millward, and Andrew J. Oswald (1991). Unionism and Employment Behaviour. *Economic Journal* 101 (July): 815–34.

Cable, John, and Stephen Machin (1991). The Relationship between Union Wage and Profitability Effects. *Economics Letters* 37 (November): 315–21.

Carruth, Alan, and Richard Disney (1988). Where Have Two Million Trade Union Members Gone? *Economica* 55 (February): 1–19.

Cully, Mark, and Stephen Woodland (1996). Trade Union Membership and Recognition: An Analysis of Data from the 1995 Labour Force Survey. *Labour Market Trends* 104 (May): 216–25.

Daniel, W.W., and Neil Millward (1983). *Workplace Industrial Relations in Britain*. London: Heinemann Educational Books.

Davies, Paul, and Mark Freedland (1993). *Labour Legislation and Public Policy*. Oxford: Clarendon Press.

Davis, David (1988). *Clear the Decks: Abolish the National Dock Labour Scheme*. Policy Study No. 101. London: Centre for Policy Studies.

Deakin Simon, and Gillian S. Morris (1995). *Labour Law*. London: Butterworths.

Department for Education and Employment (1996a). Industrial and Employment Appeal Statistics, 1993–94 and 1994–95. *Labour Market Trends* 104 (July): 305–10.

——— (1996b). Labour Market Disputes in 1995. *Labour Market Trends* 104 (June): 271–85.

Denny, Kevin, and Stephen J. Nickell (1992). Unions and Investment in British Industry. *Economic Journal* 102 (July): 874–87.

Disney, Richard (1990). Explanations of the Decline in Trade Union Density in Britain: An Appraisal. *British Journal of Industrial Relations* 28 (July): 165–77.

Disney, Richard, Amanda Gosling, and Stephen Machin (1995). British Unions in Decline: Determinants of the 1980's Fall in Union Recognition. *Industrial and Labor Relations Review* 48 (April): 403–19.

Dunn, Stephen, and David Metcalf (1993). Labour Legislation 1980–1993: Intent, Ideology and Impact. Working Paper No. 12. London: Centre for Economic Performance, London School of Economics.

Dunn, Stephen, and Martyn Wright (1993). Managing without the Closed Shop. Discussion Paper No. 118. London: Centre for Economic Performance, London School of Economics.

Fernie, Sue, and David Metcalf (1995). Participation, Contingent Pay, Representation and Workplace Performance: Evidence from Great Britain. *British Journal of Industrial Relations* 33 (September): 379–415.

Freeman, Richard, and Jeffrey Pelletier (1990). The Impact of Industrial Relations Legislation on British Union Density. *British Journal of Industrial Relations* 29 (July): 141–64.

Gennard, John, Stephen Dunn, and Michael Wright (1980). The Extent of Closed Shop Arrangements in British Industry. *Employment Gazette* 88 (January): 16–22.

Gennard, John, Stephen Dunn, and Michael Wright (1979). The Content of British Closed Shop Agreements. *Employment Gazette* 87 (November): 1088–92.

Geroski, Paul, Paul Gregg, and Thibault Desjonqueres (1995). Did the Retreat of UK Trade Unionism Accelerate During the 1990–1993 Recession? *British Journal of Industrial Relations* 33 (March): 36–54.

Geroski, Paul, Stephen Machin, and John Van Reenan (1993). The Profitability of Innovating Firms. *Rand Journal of Economics* 24 (Summer): 198–211.

Green, Francis (1992). Recent Trends in British Trade Union Density: How Much of a Compositional Effect? *British Journal of Industrial Relations* 30 (September): 445–58.

Gregg, Paul, and Stephen Machin (1992). Unions, the Demise of the Closed Shop and Wage Growth in the 1980s. *Oxford Bulletin of Economics and Statistics* 54 (February): 53–72.

Gregg, Paul, Stephen Machin, and David Metcalf (1993). Signals and Cycles: Productivity Growth and Changes in Union Status in British Companies. *Economic Journal* 103 (July): 894–907.

Hanson, Charles, Sheila Jackson, and Douglas Miller 1982). *The Closed Shop*. Aldershot: Gower.

Haskel, Jonathan (1993). Why Did U.K. Manufacturing Profitability Rise over the 1980s? *Empirica* 20: 51–67.

Heery, Edmund (1987). Chronicle: Industrial Relations in the United Kingdom December 1986–March 1987. *British Journal of Industrial Relations* 25 (July): 295–305.

Hendy, John (1993). *A Law unto Themselves: Conservative Employment Laws*. London: Institute of Employment Rights.

Heywood, John, W. Stanley Siebert, and Xiangdong Wei (1997). Payment by Results Systems: British Evidence. *British Journal of Industrial Relations* 35 (March): 1–22.

Hirsch, Barry T., and John T. Addison (1986). *The Economic Analysis of Unions: New Approaches and Evidence*. London/Boston: Allen & Unwin.

Ingram, Peter (1991). Ten Years of Manufacturing Wage Settlements. *Oxford Review of Economic Policy* 7 (March): 93–106.

Industrial Relations Legal Information Bulletin (1975). The IRLIB Guide to the Employment Protection Act: Part 1. New Rights for Trade Unions. *Industrial Relations Legal Information Bulletin* 55 (December 17): 2–14.

—— (1976). The IRLIB Guide to the Employment Protection Act: Part 3. New Rights on Termination of Employment. *Industrial Relations Legal Information Bulletin* 57 (January 21): 2–15.

—— (1982a). The IRLIB Guide to the Employment Bill: Part 1. Closed Shops Dismissals. *Industrial Relations Legal Information Bulletin* 204 (March 9): 2–10.

—— (1982b). The IRLIB Guide to the Employment Bill: Part 3. Trade Union Immunities. *Industrial Relations Legal Information Bulletin* 208 (May 11): 2–7.

Jackman, Richard, Richard Layard, and Stephen Nickell (1996). Combatting Unemployment: Is Flexibility Enough? Discussion Paper No. 293. London: Centre for Economic Performance, London School of Economics.

Katz, Lawrence F., Gary W. Loveman, and David G. Blanchflower (1995). A Comparison of Changes in the Structure of Wages in Four OECD Countries. In Richard B. Freeman and Lawrence F. Katz (eds.), *Differences and Changes in Wage Structures* (Chicago: University of Chicago Press): 25–66.

Latreille, Paul (1992). Unions and the Inter-Establishment Adoption of New Microelectronic Technologies in the British Private Manufacturing Sector. *Oxford Bulletin of Economics and Statistics* 54 (February): 31–51.

Layard, Richard, and Stephen Nickell (1989). The Thatcher Miracle? *American Economic Review: Papers and Proceedings* 79 (May): 215–19.

Leslie, Derek, and Yonghao Pu (1996). What Caused Rising Pay Inequality in Britain: Evidence from Time Series, 1970–1993. *British Journal of Industrial Relations* 34 (March): 111–30.

Labour Research Department (1994). *The Law at Work 1994*. London: Labour Research Department.

Machin, Stephen (1991). The Productivity Effects of Unionization and Firm Size in British Engineering Firms. *Economica* 58 (November): 479–90.

—— (1995). Plant Closures and Unionization in British Establish 1995): 55–68.

Machin, Stephen, and Mark Stewart (1996). Trade Unions and Financial Performance. *Oxford Economic Papers* 48 (April): 213–41.

Machin, Stephen, Mark Stewart, and John Van Reenan (1993). Multiple Unionism, Fragmented Bargaining, and Economic Outcomes in

Unionized U.K. Establishments. In David Metcalf and Simon Milner (eds.), *New Perspectives on Industrial Disputes* (London: Routledge).

Machin, Stephen, and Sushil Wadhwani (1991). The Effects of Unions on Investment and Innovation: Evidence from WIRS. *Economic Journal* 101 (March): 324–30.

Marsden, David (1985). Chronicle: Industrial Relations in the UK, August-November 1984. *British Journal of Industrial Relations* 23 (March): 139–58.

Marsh, David (1990). Public Opinion, Trade Unions and Mrs. Thatcher. *British Journal of Industrial Relations* 28 (March): 57–65.

Mason, Bob, and Peter Bain (1993). The Determinants of Trade Union Membership in Britain: A Survey of the Literature. *Industrial and Labor Relations Review* 46 (January): 332–51.

McCarthy, W.E.J. (1964). *The Closed Shop in Britain.* Oxford: Blackwell.

McKay, Sonia (1996). *The Law on Industrial Action under the Conservatives.* London: Institute of Employment Rights.

McMullen, Jeremy (1991). *Labour Law Review 1991.* London: Institute for Employment Rights.

Menezes-Filho, N. (1994). Unions and Profitability over the 80s: Some Evidence on Union-Firm Bargaining in the U.K. Discussion Paper No. 94–17. London: Dep't of Economics, University College London.

Metcalf, David (1989). Trade Unions and Economic Performance: The British Evidence. *LSE Quarterly* 3: 21–42.

——— (1993). Industrial Relations and Economic Performance. *British Journal of Industrial Relations* 31 (June): 255–83.

——— (1994). Transformation of British Industrial Relations? Institutions, Conduct and Outcomes. In Ray Barrell (ed.), *The U.K. Labour Market: Comparative Aspects and Institutional Developments* (Cambridge: Cambridge University Press): 126–57.

Millward, Neil, and Mark Stevens (1986). *British Industrial Relations 1980–1984.* Aldershot: Gower.

Millward, Neil, Mark Stevens, David Smart, and W. Hawes (1992). *Workplace Industrial Relations in Transition.* Aldershot: Dartmouth.

Milner, Simon (1995). The Coverage of Collective Pay-setting Institutions in Britain, 1895–1990. *British Journal of Industrial Relations* 33 (March): 69–91.

Moher, Jim (1995). *Trade Unions and the Law: The Politics of Change.* London: Institute of Employment Rights.

Nickell, Stephen, and Brian Bell (1996). Changes in the Distribution of Wages and Unemployment in OECD Countries. *American Economic Review, Papers and Proceedings* 86 (May): 302–308.

Oulton, Nicholas (1990). Labour Productivity in U.K. Manufacturing in the 1970s and the 1980s. *National Institute Economic Review* 132 (May): 71–91.

Schmitt, John (1995). The Changing Structure of Male Earnings in Britain, 1974–1988. In Richard B. Freeman and Lawrence F. Katz (eds.), *Differences and Changes in Wage Structures* (Chicago: University of Chicago Press): 177–204.

Siebert, W. Stanley, and John T. Addison (1981). Are Strikes Accidental? *Economic Journal* 91 (June): 389–404.

Stevens, Mark, Neil Millward, and David Smart (1989). Trade Union Membership and the Closed Shop in 1989. *Employment Gazette* 97 (November): 615–23.

Wright, Martyn (1996). The Collapse of Compulsory Unionism? Collective Organization in Highly Unionized British Companies 1979–1991. *British Journal of Industrial Relations* 34 (December): 497–513.

The Economic Impact of Labour Reform:
Evidence from the United Kingdom

CHARLES HANSON

The British disease: a way out

Britain has not yet reached an ideal labour situation because unemployment at 7.2 percent is still too high, but it is difficult to exaggerate the contrast with the position in the 1970s. Let me remind you briefly of the way things were at that time, and then review the significant improvement in the British labour market since 1979 and the reasons for that improvement. The British disease—of which the main symptoms were a high level of strikes, a low level of labour productivity and poor quality products—was rampant. The automobile industry, which had been a world leader up to the 1960s, was especially badly affected. Sir Michael Edwardes was asked to rescue British Leyland in October 1977. Edwardes wrote that over a 6 month period in 1977 both British Leyland and Ford had experienced 350 disputes—that is more than two disputes in each working day and went on: "A motor business cannot be run on that basis" (see Edwardes 1983: 280).

Note will be found on page 147.

This disastrous state of affairs had political as well as economic implications. Early in 1974, when the coal miners went on strike, industry had to go on a three-day week because of reduced supplies of electricity (most power stations were coal-fired). Edward Heath, the prime minister, called a general election and was defeated, and many people felt that the trade unions were virtually running the country. That feeling was confirmed a few years later when several public-sector trade unions went on strike in the winter of 1978/79 (the "winter of discontent") and caused chaos in numerous essential public services, including the health service and garbage collection. This turmoil also precipitated a general election but, on this occasion, it brought to power Margaret (now Baroness) Thatcher, who was determined not to repeat her predecessors' mistakes. When she left office 11 years later perhaps her single most important achievement had been the radical reform of trade union law and practice

The Thatcher appoach: incremental change

Intelligent politicians and commentators had understood since the 1960s that Britain's trade union laws required reform. But as the Labour Party was financed and dominated by the unions and the Conservatives had vainly attempted to do too much, too quickly in their Industrial Relations Act of 1971, it seemed that the problem was insoluble. Prime Minister Thatcher disagreed: her plan was to adopt a step-by-step approach so that the excessive legal privileges that had previously been granted to the unions were progressively cut back or eliminated. Since 1979, there have been eight Employment and/or Trade Union Acts (1980, 1982, 1984, 1988, 1989, 1990, 1992 and 1993; for details, see Addison and Siebert, this volume). Contrary to pessimistic predictions, this massive program of legislative reform has been extremely effective. I will concentrate on three essential elements of Thatcher's program: (1) the closed shop (Right to Work); (2) trade union democracy; (3) trade union immunities.

The closed shop

Frederick Hayek taught us in *The Constitution of Liberty* that the coercion by trade unions of fellow workers (that is to say, the existence of the closed shop and the absence of a right to work) is "contrary to all principles of freedom under the law" (1960: 269). Those words were written 36 years ago, so it would now be reasonable to expect that the lesson has been learned in free, democratic societies. But that was certainly not the case in Britain in the 1970s. On the contrary, legislation passed by a Labour government in 1974 and 1975 actually encouraged the expansion of the closed shop and by 1978 a thorough survey indicated that "at least 5.2 million" out of 13 million trade unionists were members of closed shops (Gennard, Dunn, and Wright 1980).

Clauses in the Employment Acts of 1980, 1982, 1988 and 1990 radically reformed the previous state of affairs. In the introduction to *The Downing Street Years* (1993: 3–15), Thatcher referred to F.A. Hayek's *Road to Serfdom* (1944) as one of two texts that influenced Tory rethinking after World War II, and her personal commitment to individual freedom strongly influenced the reform of the closed shop. In the United Kingdom this was linked to the right not to be unfairly dismissed, which had been introduced in 1971. The introduction of such a right raised the question: is it lawful to dismiss an employee for not being a member of a trade union? In 1979, the answer to that question was "Yes." Between 1980 and 1989, the answer was "Sometimes." But, by 1990, it was an emphatic "No." The 1993 Act went even further by making it illegal to refuse employment on the grounds of non-membership of a trade union. So law in the United Kingdom has gone about as far as it can to eliminate closed shops, and they have almost disappeared. Actors and musicians are now among the few groups of workers for whom it is very difficult to find employment without a union card.

A similar situation exists in the other 14 member states of the European Union, all of whom have accepted the "Community Charter of the Fundamental Social Rights of Workers," which was signed by the heads of state or government in 1989. The first clause of the Section "Freedom of Association and Collective Bargaining" reads as follows:

> Employers and workers of the European Community shall have the right of association in order to constitute professional organisations or trade unions of their choice for the defence of their economic and social interests. Every employer and every worker shall have the freedom to join *or not to join* such organisations without any personal or occupational damage being thereby suffered by him. (Foster 1990: 97–102; emphasis added).

Thus it is clear that in Western Europe freedom to join or not to join a trade union is now generally regarded as an essential element in working life. And both the spirit and the letter of this part of the Social Charter are usually observed in practice.

Trade union democracy

In 1979, it was widely thought that instead of being answerable to the majority of their members, most British trade unions were manipulated by a minority of political militants. The object of the Trade Union Act 1984 was to reverse this situation by laying down strict conditions for the conduct of trade union affairs. In particular, secret ballots had to be held at least every five years for the election of every voting member of a union's Executive Council and every ten years if a union wished to establish and maintain a political fund. These provisions were important, but much more important was that part of the Act that obliged trade unions to ballot those of their members who would be involved in industrial action before a union could take such a step. While senior trade union officials were unanimously opposed to this provision, several surveys and opinion polls showed that a large majority of their members were in favour. For instance, 94 percent of the members of the Inland Revenue Staff Federation favoured pre-strike ballots, yet a delegate conference rejected a proposal to make such ballots obligatory!

Opponents of pre-strike ballots insisted that this reform spelled the end of trade union rights, but by 1987 such ballots had become commonplace and today no one would recommend a return to the pre-1984 situation. This is a classic example of the way in which even a desirable, common-sense reform can be opposed by an hysterical, extremist minority.

Trade union immunities

The third and final element in the reform of the unions was the drastic reduction of trade union legal immunities. In contrast to those countries that have provided their unions with positive legal rights, since the late nineteenth century, trade unions in the United Kingdom have received certain legal immunities. In other words, the law has protected unions and their officials from legal action in some circumstances. This process reached its peak in the Trade Disputes Act 1906, about which a constitutional lawyer wrote: "It makes a trade union a privileged body exempted from the ordinary law of the land. No such privileged body has ever before been deliberately created by an English Parliament"(Dicey 1914: xlvi). And in 1980 Hayek wrote: "There can be no salvation for Britain until the special privileges granted to the trade unions three-quarters of a century ago are revoked" (1984: 58). The need was obvious, but was there a politician bold and subtle enough to grasp this nettle? Clearly it is much easier to grant a privilege than to revoke it. Fortunately in the United Kingdom we had not one but two politicians with the necessary acumen and political courage: Margaret Thatcher as the prime minister who set the strategy and Norman (now Lord) Tebbit as the secretary of state for Employment who worked out the details formed an almost unique partnership during the period September 1981 to October 1983. Tebbit was the architect of the Employment Act 1982 and the Trade Union Act 1984, and it was these two measures that significantly cut back the trade union immunities (privileges) to which Hayek had referred. By a stroke of extreme political boldness the previously sacrosanct power of the unions was undermined, and it seems that the effect of this will be permanent.

Since 1906, a trade union in the United Kingdom had been virtually immune from legal action. The 1982 Employment Act changed that arrangement, and unless a union now operates strictly within the legal framework, which includes a pre-strike secret ballot, it may be subject to very large damages. The wings of the unions have been severely clipped and there is no popular support for a reversal of this reform.

Thus it can be seen that a radical and permanent reform of trade union law and practice in the United Kingdom took place between 1980 and 1993. Some of the particular, beneficial effects of this reform have been discussed elsewhere (Hanson 1991: ch. 8), but here I mention three.

(1) *Cure of the British disease* The British disease of frequent industrial disputes, low labour productivity and poor quality goods and services has been practically cured. Table 1 shows the dramatic decline in the number of days lost in industrial disputes and in the number of disputes since 1976:

Table 1: Industrial stoppages in the United Kingdom, 1976–95

	Annual Averages		
	1976–85	1986–95	1991–95
Working days lost in stoppages	11.1 million	1.8 million	526,000
Number of stoppages	1,693	539	249

Source: Employment Gazette/Labour Market Trends 1977–96.

A continuous statistical series of the number of working days lost in stoppages and of the number of stoppages in the United Kingdom has been published since 1893. Both series show record low figures in the past few years: 1992 showed a record low of 528,000 working days lost but this was surpassed in 1994, when the figure dropped to 278,000. In 1992, the low number of stoppages (240) set a record but, in 1993 and in 1994, it dropped even lower—to 203. Therefore it can be stated with confidence that since 1991 the incidence of industrial disputes in the United Kingdom has been negligible.

This general picture can be supported by examples of particular firms and industries. Nissan built a major car plant a few miles from Newcastle upon Tyne in the mid-1980s. They have yet to experience their first stoppage, and most people will be very surprised if one occurs. Naturally the absence of stoppages has helped to improve labour productivity and product quality, and for many companies these improvements have been almost as dramatic as the reduction in stoppages, although they are not so easily measured. In 1994 the famous German car manufacturer, BMW, bought the last major British motor firm, Rover Group. This would have been unthinkable in 1979. In a lecture in the United Kingdom last October, Bernd Pischetsrieder, Chairman of BMW, stated that Britain was "the most attractive country among all European locations for the production of cars" and added: "This results from the structural reforms initiated by Margaret Thatcher in the early 1980s, the most significant factor being the re-arrangement of industrial relations between companies and trade unions" (quoted in *The* [London] *Times*, October 12, 1995). If anyone had predicted in 1979 that Britain would become the most attractive European location for the production of cars, his friends would have quickly called some men in white coats to take him away and calm him down.

(2) *Inward investment* The second benefit of the reforms has been a large amount of inward investment like that by Nissan mentioned above. Instead of being seen as a pariah, Britain is now a magnet for companies from the Far East, North America and elsewhere wishing to establish a base for the European market. This inward investment creates employment and stimulates innovation in manufacturing processes and systems. It has played a major part in transforming the whole manufacturing sector of the British economy, which is much more productive than it was 17 years ago.

(3) *The development of an enterprise economy* The significance of enterprise in the mysterious process of economic growth has been underrated by too many economists. Again, it is difficult to quantify; but who can doubt its importance?[1] The reduction of trade union power and influence in the United Kingdom has encouraged many people, who in the 1970s would have joined a trade union to secure a pay increase by collective bargaining, to maintain and improve their incomes by self-employment and similar means. Over the past ten years there has been a resurgence of entrepreneurial activity, especially in the service sector, where a new business can be started with a modest amount of capital. The present government claims that Britain is now the enterprise centre of Europe and there is evidence to support that claim. Sadly, in most of the 15 member states of the European Union there is a marked lack of enterprise. Bureaucracy normally takes precedence, particularly in Brussels where an unelected Commission churns out far too many regulations and directives.

Indeed, labour relations in Britain have been transformed and the legislative program of the period from 1980 to 1993 played a crucial part in that transformation. I have focused on the European approach to the closed shop and suggested it might be seen as a model for other countries to follow. It would be quite wrong, however, to give you the impression that in most respects the European labour market is working well. On the contrary, the evidence—particularly the high and rising unemployment—indicates that there are serious problems right across the European Union. Figure 1 provides evidence to support this statement.; it also shows that the European Union's labour market has performed very badly in comparison with the United States since 1974. Figure 2 shows the main reason for that.

Figure 1 Unemployment in the community (percentage of the civilian labour force)

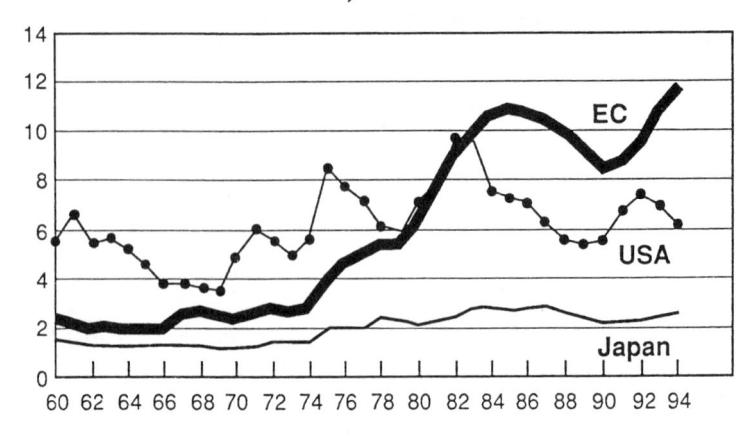

[Line graph showing unemployment from 1960 to 1994 for EC, USA, and Japan. EC rises from about 2% to nearly 12%; USA fluctuates between 4% and 10%; Japan remains low, around 1-3%.]

Figure 2 Job creation in the European Community, United States and Japan (index: 1960 to 1973 = 100)

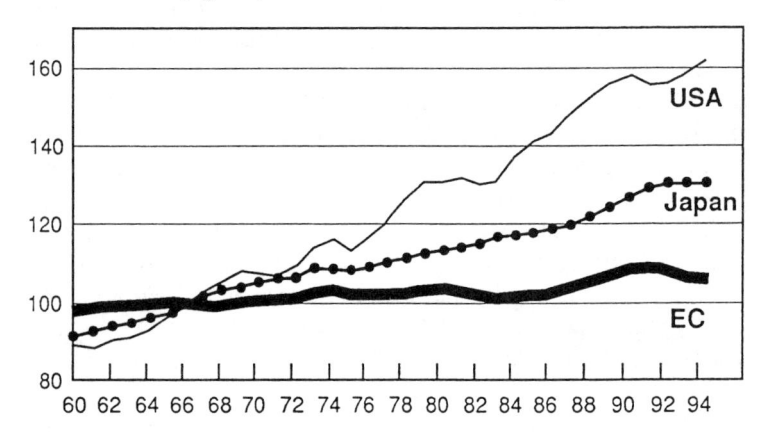

[Line graph showing job creation index from 1960 to 1994. USA rises to about 160; Japan rises to about 130; EC remains around 100-105.]

The United States created over 30 million additional jobs in the private sector between 1974 and 1994, while the member states of the European Union created none. We need to explore the reasons for this absence of job creation.

The attitude of private sector employers—and especially small employers—to employing people is really quite simple. The basic question which they ask themselves is: "Will it pay me to take on one or more additional employees?" In other words: "Is it worth my while to accept the cost and the effort involved in employing additional people?" Why has the answer to these questions normally been positive in the United States but negative in the European Union over the past 20 years?

The cost of employment can be separated into three elements. First—and most obvious—is the wage or salary paid to the employee. Second—and just as real for the employer—are the social costs, that is the taxes and social insurance charges levied by the state on the employer. Third is the cost of meeting the legal obligations of employment, which start at the time of recruitment. In some countries today, disappointed job applicants are quick to take legal action on the grounds of sex, race, or other kind of discrimination, and this action may be supported by public funds channelled (in Britain) through the Equal Opportunities Commission or the Commission for Racial Equality.

Recently all three elements have become a severe deterrent to private sector employers in the European Union. Wages and salaries in Germany are now the highest in the world for a major economy. Social costs are also very high, so that the total cost of employing people in that country is exorbitant and cannot now be offset by the efficiency of many manufacturing firms. When the numerous social rules and regulations are included, it is not at all surprising that German car firms are now building plants in the United States and that unemployment exceeds four million in Germany. German workers have literally priced and regulated themselves out of the world labour market

What is surprising is that the social and employment system is designed to encourage other member states to follow the German example. Wage competition—or "social dumping" as it is usually called—is severely frowned upon. Sections 7 and 8 of the Social Charter (which come under the heading of "Improvement of living and working conditions") spell out this approach. Section 7 states:

> The completion of the internal market must lead to an improvement in the living and working conditions of workers in the European Community. This process must result from an approximation of these conditions while the improvement is being maintained, as regards in particular the duration and organization of working time and forms of

employment other than open-ended contracts, such as fixed term contracts, part-time working, temporary work and seasonal work. (Foster 1990: 99)

And Section 8 states:

> Every worker of the European Community shall have a right to a weekly rest period and to annual paid leave, the duration of which must be progressively harmonised in accordance with national practices. (Foster 1990: 99)

The whole thrust of social and employment policy in the European Union is to harmonize upwards wages and conditions of work or, in other words, to make all of the other member states as uncompetitive as Germany. The level of unemployment when this objective is achieved is best left to your imagination, but you will readily understand why the British government is trying—without complete success—to opt out of this "social" legislation.

The European Union is now paying the price of some very serious mistakes in social and employment policy. These mistakes have been made by the governments of the member states and compounded by the European Commission in Brussels. The whole labour market in the European community is now grossly over-regulated in a way that suffocates enterprise and prevents the creation of new jobs in the private sector. Minor reforms would be a waste of time. As the joint chairmen of the Anglo-German Deregulation Group said in their recent report, commissioned by Chancellor Kohl and Prime Minister Major: "The specific proposals for deregulatory reform that we make are only part of the story. We believe that there needs to be a change of culture within all the European institutions including the Commission, the Council and the European Parliament."

Conclusion

In conclusion I offer brief answers to four questions.

(1) *What can we learn from the United Kingdom?* —that when it comes to employment reform, we must never give up hope. Most of our experts thought in 1979 that it would be impossible, but now it has been done.

(2) *What can we learn from the European Union?* —that unduly high wages and work benefits coupled with an excess of regulation can severely damage the labour market and create mass unemployment.

(3) *What can we learn from the United States?* —a lot. You might find a few tips in my paper, Employment Policy in the European Community: Lessons from the USA (1995).

(4) *What about the right to work?* —that it is a necessary but not a sufficient condition for a healthy labour market. In an increasingly competitive world, realistic wages, low social costs, light regulation, and a vigorous spirit of enterprise are also very important.

Note

1 For a discussion on the effect of entrepreneurship and technological change on economic growth, see Gilder 1981 and Lipsey 1996.

References

Dicey, A.V. (1914). *Lectures on the Relation between Law and Public Opinion in England during the Nineteenth Century.* 2nd ed. London: Macmillan.
Edwardes, M. (1983). *Back from the Brink.* London: Collins.
Foster, Nigel G., ed. (1990). *Blackstone's EEC Legislation.* Blackstone Press.
Gennard, J., S. Dunn and M. Wright (1980). The Extent of Closed Shop Arrangements in British Industry. *Employment Gazette* (January).
Gilder, George (1981). *Wealth and Poverty.* New York: Basic Books.
Hanson, Charles (1991). *Taming the Trade Unions.* London: Macmillan and Adam Smith Institute.
——— (1995). Employment Policy in the European Community: Lessons from the USA. London: Institute of Directors.
Hayek, F.A. (1944) *Road to Serfdom.* London: Routledge & Kegan Paul.
——— (1960). *The Constitution of Liberty.* London: Routledge & Kegan Paul.
——— (1984) 1980s Unemployment and the Unions. 2nd ed. London: Institute of Economic Affairs.
Lipsey, Richard G. (1996). *Economic Growth, Technological Change, and Canadian Economic Policy.* Toronto: C.D. Howe Institute.
Potter, Edward, and Judith Youngman. *Keeping America Competitive.* Glenbridge.
Thatcher, Margaret (1993). *The Downing Street Years.* New York: Harper Collins.
White Paper on Growth, Competitiveness and Employment (1993). Brussels: European Commission.

Free to Work
The Liberalization of Labour Markets in New Zealand

WOLFGANG KASPER

> We passed through this difficult economic period ... when there was a tremendous period of adjustment. When things are tough, people do new things and pull themselves up by their shoestrings to become successful again ... Not only did we remove all our subsidies but there were major changes to union power. In order to survive in the world we had to diversify, and this is finally bearing fruit.
>
> Sir Edmund Hillary
> *The Australian*, 10-11 June 1995

Economic failures drive comprehensive reform
God's Own Country

New Zealand shares with immigrant societies (Australia, South Africa, Argentina, Chile, Canada) a pattern of (a) relatively late and thin white settlement, (b) a history of almost instantaneous wealth thanks to easily exploited land or resources, (c) an historic aspiration to protect the newly rich societies from undue competitive

---

Notes will be found on pages 206–07.

pressures, and (d) heavy reliance on governmental protection and redistribution. In addition, a strong—almost utopian—aspiration to create a "better Britain down-under" pervades New Zealand's short history from the start of white settlement in the nineteenth century; this is coupled with a late-nineteenth-century belief in the perfectibility of man, a trust in government "can-do-ism" and a reformist zeal to create a materially safe, egalitarian society (Kasper 1990: ch. 1; also Hawke 1985: 4).

Late in the nineteenth century, New Zealand placed strong central controls on the labour market and industrial relations and, as early as the 1920s, foreign trade and domestic product markets were tightly controlled. After the Second World War, New Zealand was one of the most prosperous countries on earth, with living standards not far behind those of contemporary Switzerland. Prosperity was based on pastoral farming and the exploitation of natural resources, and benefited from high demand in the world market for natural resources and food products. New Zealand's prosperity also owed much to the innovative use of technologies and, in particular, innovations to overcome perpetual labour shortages.[1]

In response to the shock of the Depression in the 1930s, policy was committed (in 1938) to full employment and the establishment of a welfare state. Post-war prosperity made it possible to promise more comprehensive social security, providing universal family benefits, state assistance for young children, education, health and a comprehensive government pension scheme. The government directly produced and distributed these services. As well, many utilities, transport, energy, and financial services were socialized. These arrangements responded to strong, popularly held, preferences for predictability and security. They also relied on the self-motivation and self-discipline of a fairly homogenous population that was predominantly of the lower middle class and of British stock. In 1951, 92 percent of New Zealanders claimed British descent, and 7 percent Maori. The demand for security was also met by political and military alliances and close cultural ties with Britain. In the 1950s, New Zealand society was self-contented and inward-looking, considering theirs as "God's Own Country."

Collective action and government intervention in the post-war economy were pervasive. Imports were licensed; foreign exchange was rationed; many types of investment required prior government approval. Government intervened directly in many markets to guarantee prices, subsidised interest rates for many types of borrowers and gave farmers tax incentives. The workplace was heavily regulated and collectively organized; the five-day week was mandated; and closed-shop legislation was implemented that required most workers to belong to state-registered occupational unions. Wages were fixed centrally in tax-financed conciliation meetings between unions and employer representatives and subject to the quasi-legal rulings of the Arbitration Court. In a pattern of "egalitarian creep," wages tended to move up without much change in relative wages. Rewards for skills were small, if they existed at all. The political culture stressed equality and "social justice" (Hawke 1985). Only 10 percent of the workforce had formal qualifications. Where occupational bottlenecks arose, government-assisted immigration, mainly from England, was an easy "quick-fix" to fill the gap (Kasper 1990). Businesses operated on a cost-plus basis in protected markets. Economic growth was taken for granted, and living standards were perceived as internationally underwritten by the country's rich endowments of natural resources and its special access to British markets.

The fall from grace

In the 1960s and 1970s, New Zealanders gradually and, often reluctantly, discovered that they were not living in a paradise on earth any more; indeed that their relative productivity and living standards were slipping (table 1). The power of Britain—still called "home" by New Zealanders—and of Europe was waning, and eastern Asia was increasingly in the ascendancy. In 1973, when Britain joined the EEC, New Zealand began to lose its preferential access to traditional markets, especially for agricultural produce. New Zealand's primary exporters increasingly suffered from the European Community's dumping of subsidized surpluses in third markets as well as the politicization of access to American markets. Attempts to find new markets were normally left to governmental marketing boards—compulsory monopsonies for New Zealand primary producers. The attempts were not very successful. The oil shocks of 1973/74 and 1979/81 created further problems and uncertainties.

Table 1 Trend in productivity growth

	GDP per person employed, percent, per annum				
	1961–73	1974–79	1980–86	1987–92	1993–97*
New Zealand	1.2	0.2	1.1	1.1	1.8
OECD average†	4.0	1.9	1.6	1.6	1.4

* own estimate for 1996 and 1997.
† aggregated with 1990 GDP weights.
Sources: OECD, Economic Survey; Australia (Paris: OECD, 1994); OECD, World Economic Outlook (Dec.) 1996.

Another challenge to New Zealand's secure, established order came from the rapid growth of the Maori population and high immigration from the Pacific islands. By 1981, 14 percent of the population was non-white. Many Maoris more assertively challenged the concept of outright integration into the predominant British-derived culture. And, female participation in the workforce rose, reflecting another major social change.

Import protection was no longer capable of safeguarding New Zealand's high-cost domestic industries. Protected managers and a protected workforce had cared little about productivity and work practices adapted to a competitive world. Industries had ossified; international competitiveness declined steeply while the prices of New Zealand's traditional raw material exports fell. Between the mid-1960s and mid-1970s, New Zealand's terms of trade deteriorated by 30 percent. International competitiveness was further damaged by rapid wage increases mandated under the quasi-judicial, union-dominated, centralized award system. In 1971, the General Wage Order system broke down, and a 25 percent wage hike was the result. All through the 1970s, nominal wage rises exceeded both productivity improvement and the inflation rate. Investment remained fairly high but the pervasive system of industrial regulation, with its low utilisation rates and rigid work practices worked against efficient use of capital. One prominent economic historian concluded that "New Zealand has something of a genius for wasting capital" (Gould 1985: 65).

The current account of the balance of payments began to register big deficits in the 1970s, a move accelerated by the oil shocks. Initially, it was easy to borrow overseas but, as foreign debts piled up, interest payments rose and New Zealand's international credit rating slipped. Total public debt—borrowed to finance increased expectations—rose from NZ$4 billion in 1975 to NZ$28 billion ten years later, despite increases in income-tax rates. The existing social arrangements and economic institutions conspired to produce a poor and deteriorating record of economic growth (table 1). Between 1975 and 1982, the annual growth rate averaged a mere 0.4 percent.

In the early 1980s, average New Zealanders began to realise what well-informed insiders had concluded for well over a decade, namely that their productivity was the poorest among the countries of the Organization for Economic Cooperation and Development (OECD). Increasing numbers of observers began to conclude that this had much to do with New Zealand's being the most heavily regulated economy in the OECD (James 1992). Many critical observers began to accept that in particular the increasingly comprehensive and generous provision of public cradle-to-grave welfare and highly politicized labour-market arrangements were undermining economic growth. These institutions had shifted the emphasis of policy more and more from efficiency to security but they had broad electoral support. Poor economic prospects and the sterility of pervasively regulated economic and social life at home combined with better information about the outside world to induce many young New Zealanders to migrate elsewhere, and expecially to Australia (Kasper 1990).[2] This brought home the message to many families that all was not well in "God's Own Country."

New Zealanders had enjoyed full employment from the 1950s to the 1970s but that pillar of private welfare and material security began to crumble from the mid-1970s, when unemployment went up rapidly reflecting, in part, low incentives to search for work. Underlying conditions for social stability and cohesion began to deteriorate and the incidence of serious crime tripled between the 1950s and early 1980s; ex-nuptial births rose from 4 percent in the 1940s to 38 percent in the early 1980s; divorce rates increased enormously. While these developments have their parallels in other Western societies, they came as a serious disillusionment to New Zealanders, who had prided themselves of being able to create a more perfect, more secure life for the average citizen.

Macroeconomic conditions deteriorated from the mid-1970s to the early 1980s: as mentioned, the current account showed big deficits from 1974. Welfare costs climbed to over 25 percent of GDP, helping to push the government deficit to 7 percent of GDP by 1984. Inflation and legislative changes pushed up income taxes, so that the average wage earner paid 24 percent of gross income in tax and social security contributions in the early 1980s (up from 14 percent in 1950/51). Inflation was fuelled by quasi-automatic wage indexation and direct interventions in financial markets had no lasting effect.

The National Party government under Prime Minister Robert Muldoon frequently saw the way out of the growing social and economic crisis through more centralized intervention, which culminated in a freeze of wages and prices in 1983/84. The National Party's "Think Big" strategy aimed to develop a number of new, capital-intensive, industries either by direct public investment or by the government's assuming the risk for private investments. This expansion policy raised national income temporarily, especially in the election year, 1984, but it increased the budget deficit (9.5 percent of GDP in 1985-86), the current account deficit, and international debt (70 percent of GDP by the mid-1980s). New Zealand's credit rating dropped further. The OECD diagnosed at that time that New Zealand "risked entering a vicious circle of uncontrollable deficits and debt" (OECD 1989: 11), and the New Zealand government came perilously close to bankruptcy (Prebble, 1996).

It is true that the conservative Muldoon government took some half-hearted steps towards deregulating transport, import quotas, interest rates and international payments, but it did so hesitantly, timidly and late, caving in to pressure groups. As these changes were tried out piecemeal and without a clear strategy, they met with political resistance and were perceived as too marginal to affect general economic behaviour.

Two waves of economic reform

In 1984, a national election took place in the midst of a perception of a widening economic crisis. This feeling was accentuated by a 20 percent devaluation of the New Zealand dollar immediately after the election of a Labour Party government (appendix 2). The incoming government used the foreign exchange crisis to give a sense of urgency to its program of pervasive and fundamental economic reform.

The reforms were based on a strategy to implement new thinking that issued from a critical analysis in the New Zealand Treasury. This encouraged the adoption of a new economic paradigm (see below) and the reform program promoted by the energetic incoming Labour finance minister, Roger Douglas (Douglas 1982). The package of energetic, rapid reforms deregulated many aspects of private business, opened the economy to freer trade and investment, abolished producer subsidies, and reshaped or privatised parts of the public sector, while putting a tight monetary policy into place (Douglas 1990; Walker 1989; James 1992). The reforms were based on a critical new look at what collective action could achieve and relied heavily upon market forces and the resolute action by a few economic ministers and their advisers.

The reforms were supported by substantial sections of the business community, most notably after the formation of the New Zealand Business Roundtable. The reforms were tolerated by the Labour government team, many of whom held basic philosophies opposed to what became known as "Rogernomics." At the least, many Labour politicians were slightly perplexed, but the new administration was not beholden to entrenched lobbies and tolerated the reformist zeal of Roger Douglas and his associates.

The support of the Labour Party was won by quarantining much of the public welfare system from reform, by exempting the labour market from comprehensive exposure to competitive forces, and by a cautious reduction of public spending. The economic reformers in the Labour government also gathered support for their radical program by supporting the foreign policy of the prime minister, David Lange, who lacked interest in economic affairs. However, that alliance crumbled when the costs of reform became felt: Lange and his allies withdrew support from Roger Douglas in 1988 and he resigned as finance minister, finding his position untenable. By that time, however, many of the essential reforms were already in place (see appendix 2) and key supporters of "Rogernomics" held many of the top policy-making positions. David Caygill, his successor, supported reform of the public sector and implemented the Reserve Bank Act that made the central bank independent of government and committed it to the task of providing stable money. Richard Prebble, the privatization minister, was able to continue the program of rationalizing government-owned enterprises (Prebble, 1996).

Goaded by electoral defeats in 1984 and 1987, the National Party opposition underwent a thorough conversion from collectivist statism to free-market ideas. The intellectual and generational change was even more dramatic than in the governing Labour Party and in the national election of 1990 they campaigned confidently on a platform of more complete deregulation. They made it clear from the outset that they would extend reform to welfare benefits and liberate the labour market. The National Party's manifesto was explicit about taking government out of the labour market and withdrawing all privileges under the law from the trade unions.

The election was won by the National Party. They faced a dire fiscal outlook, since Labour had spent a great deal and weakened the economy. The new government implemented a second round of quick economic reforms, many of which were pushed through by the energetic new finance minister, Ruth Richardson (appendix 2). As a result of sweeping reforms in the public sector, budget accounting began to be done virtually according to the same standards as business accounting, including not only accounts of annual flows of revenues and outlays, but also balance sheets on assets and liabilities (Richardson 1995). These accrual accounts revealed that the New Zealand government had considerable unfunded net liabilities—in plain English, it was broke.

Welfare payments were targeted to enhance personal self-reliance, especially of single unemployed people and the provision of welfare services was, where possible, handed to competing private producers. Payments to the unemployed were no longer calculated as a percentage of the latest wage or salary but were fixed to ensure a minimum income necessary for survival (Richardson, 1995). The combination of welfare targeting and the flatter income-tax regime did not overcome—and in some instances exacerbated—high marginal taxes at transition to work (St. John 1993; see also Boston 1992).

Although controversial, the policy was guided by a comprehensive, consistent, coherent and transparent strategy. The government's trading enterprises have shed 30,000 employees since 1987, the (non-trading) core administration a further 4,000. From 1990/91 to 1994/95, real government consumption spending has shrunk every year by an average 0.5 percent annually. The share of government spending in gross national expenditure has been reduced, and public debts are being repaid, leading to the upgrading of credit ratings. By 1993/94, the operating balance of the government showed a surplus, which has since grown in size. The net liability position (the "Crown Balance") has been steadily cut back, partly by repaying debts from the proceeds of privatization and outlays on debt services have plummeted. As of the 1996 budget, the slimmed-down government could longer be considered insolvent by accountants who apply general business principles. For the first time, the government had a net worth of NZ$3.2 billion, a figure that is confidently expected to rise despite a mild recession. The sound fiscal situation enabled the government to cut income-tax rates, pay down public debt further and increase health and education outlays.

In an uncanny repetition of history, Ruth Richardson lost the finance portfolio after the 1993 election in which the electorate again returned the National Party, though with a marked reduction of its majority. It appears that the key movers of reform in New Zealand pay a political price and that prime ministers and cabinet majorities tend to lose the taste for reform after a first, concentrated effort. Since 1994, the reforms have ceased although many critics point to the need to continue social-welfare acts and to privatize residual production enterprises (Kasper 1996; James 1997).

In the 1993 election, the New Zealand electorate also voted on a referendum about the electoral system. It threw out the British "first-past-the post" system that tends to make for decisive majorities, in favour of a mixed system of party lists under which parties receive seats according to their proportion of the votes and direct representation. This vote was widely interpreted as a protest against the imposition of dramatic reforms by both major political parties and against the short-term burdens that the reforms had imposed on the population. Nonetheless, even the outspoken enemies of reform (amongst them the intellectual left, the old trade union establishment, and churchmen) did not propose to resurrect the previous socio-economic order. Their criticism is confined to specific elements and second-order aspects of the new institutional rules. The new electoral system, which makes for multiparty coalitions and political compromises, is such that further economic and social-welfare reforms are unlikely. The new system also makes it unlikely, however, that the reformed economic constitution of New Zealand will be undone.

First fruit of reform

Thanks to the two waves of deregulation in the decade 1984 to 1994, New Zealand has moved from being the most regulated to the least regulated economy in the OECD, and the public sector has been dramatically reshaped and scaled back. Government now concentrates on the rule of law and limits its "social justice mission" to providing a minimum safety net. Subsidies for exporters and farmers have been discontinued; interest rates and the exchange rate have been deregulated (figure 1). Tariff protection has been scaled back and is about to disappear. Manufacturing underwent dramatic structural adjustments and became oriented to the world market and competitive (Savage and Bollard 1990). The tax system was reformed, shifting from progressive income taxes to flatter and lower direct taxes combined with a comprehensive Goods and Services Tax (GST). Many state enterprises have been sold off; most others underwent dramatic performance-oriented management reforms, as did now corporatized government departments. Public sector finances have been made transparent.

The reforms of the period from 1984 to 1994 did not all proceed in a pre-determined sequence. Consequently, many relative prices—including the real wage, interest and exchange rates—were distorted during the transition. In particular, the quarantining of labour markets and welfare provision in the first round of reform ensured that labour costs rose relative to the prices of goods and that labour productivity was hampered, leading to a profit squeeze. The incentive for many workers to search for a new job was reduced. The removal of protection and tax concessions hit previously protected industries harder than others. On the other hand, the level of producer costs was reduced by reforms of the infrastructure—rail, ports, communications—and import liberalization, as well as a credible commitment to price stability during the second half of the reform sequence. For example, the cost of rail freight dropped by 48 percent in real terms (made possible by a reduction in the staff of New Zealand Rail from 21,000 to about 5,000 by 1995), and productivity has been raised by no less than 35 percent since New Zealand Rail's privatization in 1993. State enterprises frequently doubled their productivity and reduced their charges.

In the first wave of deregulation, the aggregate economic growth rate dropped, reflecting much "creative destruction" of previously privileged industry and jobs (figure 1). Industrial employment fell from 328,000 in 1986 to 243,000 in 1991, and the construction industry lost 40 percent of its workforce (Bollard 1992: 36–7). Because the Labour government had inserted a contradictory element into the reform strategy by re-introducing compulsory unionism and because labour markets were perceived to be exempted from reform pressures, wage and salary payments rose by 18 percent in 1986 alone (figure 1), quickly eroding the competitive advantage from devaluation and driving up inflation. With a lag, employment growth plummeted, and unemployment rose during the second half of the 1980s. The asset market crash of 1987 complicated matters.

In the wake of the first wave of reform and the shrinkage of industry jobs, labour productivity rose significantly faster than before. From 1984/85 to 1990/91, it grew by about 3 percent annually. Industry was forced to specialize in the face of cheaper imports; it was also forced to seek economies of scale by conquering export markets, most notably in Australia, which was joined to New Zealand under the Closer Economic Relationship (CER) agreement (appendix 2).

The second wave of reform (1991/92) was initiated against a background of negative growth and high unemployment but low inflation and a weak exchange rate (figure 1). By mid-1991, the New Zealand economy began to pull out of the various adjustment shocks, and a sense of optimism began to spread. By September 1993, real GDP had risen 10 percentage points (seasonally adjusted) above the cyclical trough of June 1991. From 1991, New Zealand bettered the OECD average increase in productivity (see table 1), job creation, growth and aggregate production.

Figure 1 Reforms and economic performance in New Zealand from 1980 to 1996

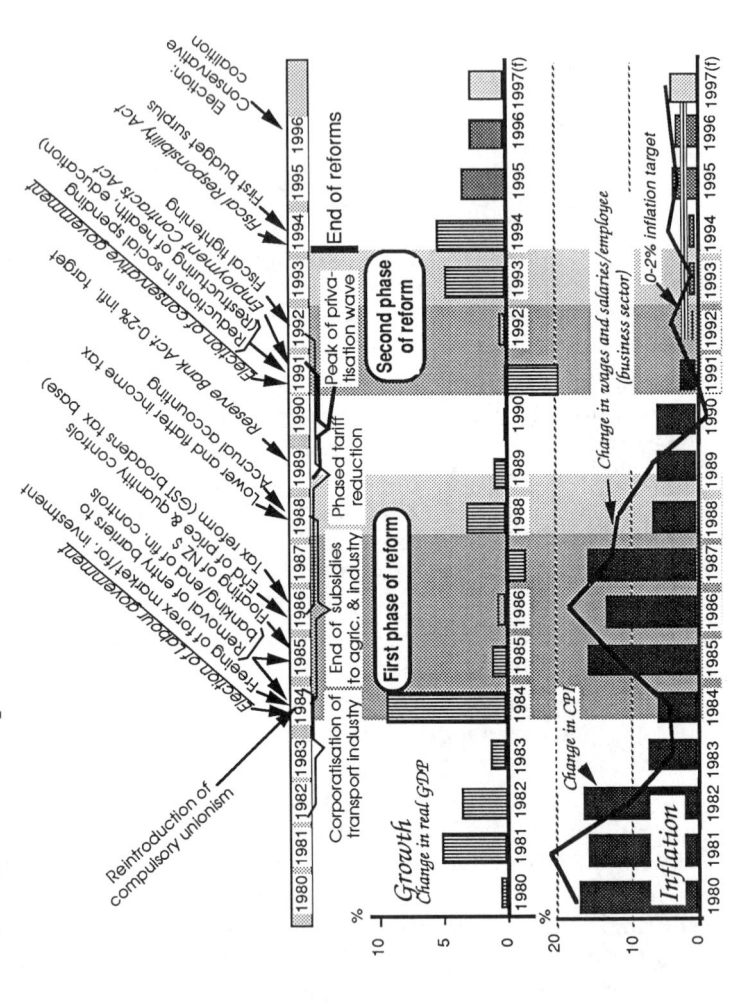

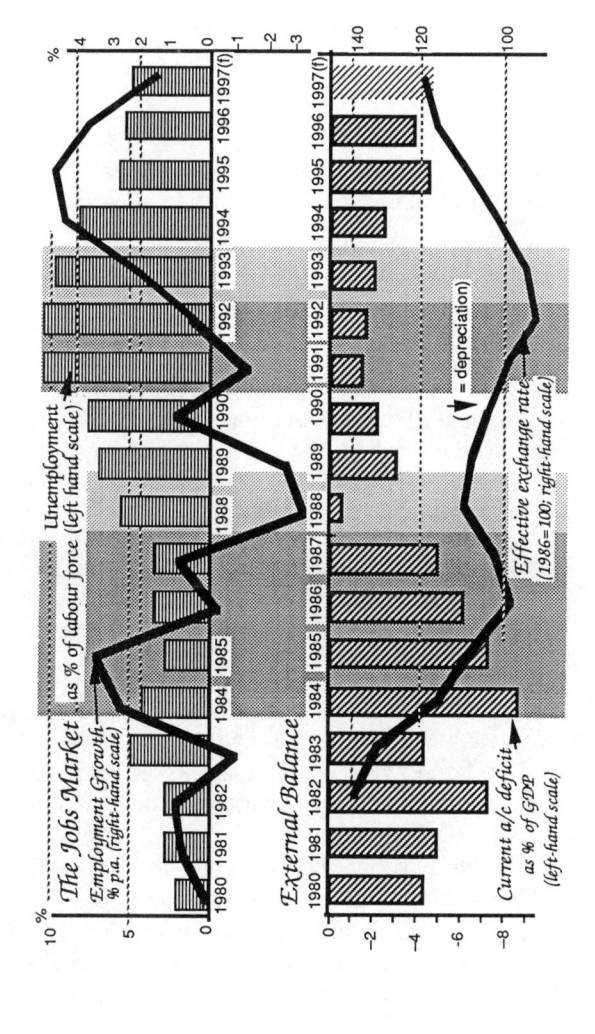

Source: OECD (*Outlook*, December 1996) and New Zealand Treasury

Major mocroeconomic effects of the reform

From the viewpoint of 1997, the major macroeconomic effects of the entire integrated reform package have been:

- The economy has overcome the shock of the first phase of reforms (1984–88) and now grows with low inflation, indicating a greatly enhanced elasticity of supply and greatly improved production structures. The mild recession in 1996 was triggered by energetic monetary tightening in response to price rises.

- The economy responded with unprecedented productivity increases to the up-turn of demand. Wages and salaries have risen moderately and without driving up labour-unit costs.

- Business investment runs high in response to greater institutional stability and higher profits, and direct foreign investment is attracted to New Zealand.

- National savings, which ran at a low rate during the first phase of reforms (1984 to 1988), increased though not sufficiently to finance all of the growth in business investment. The current account deficit has increased recently, but this is not a major concern, as is indicated by the considerable appreciation of the New Zealand dollar.

- Public spending has been pruned back and the budget is in surplus. This has not only allowed a repayment of public debts and increases in health and education spending but also some income tax cuts.

One of the most remarkable aspects of this recovery was that it began at a time of poor world demand during which New Zealanders captured a growing share of the world market. And whilst some of the performance can be attributed to the long cyclical upturn that took place from 1991 to 1995, it would not have been imaginable without the pervasive and energetic reforms (Hull 1996; Evans, Grimes, Wilkinson and Teese 1996). No one predicts a return to the slow-growth, high-inflation economy of the preceding two decades. Indeed, I would forecast medium-term growth to run at about 4 percent per annum.

Enhanced competitiveness

As of mid-1997, the economy has weathered a pause in growth after rapid growth from 1991 to 1994. Inflation remains low.

It is projected that the economy will keep growing for the remainder of the decade at a rate of 4 to 5 percent. Confidence is running high, as reflected in healthy business investment. Unemployment has dropped and the white, male unemployment rate stands at about 5 percent (see sec. 3 below). Interest rates are the same as in the United States (for 10-year bonds at about 7 percent). New Zealand's international competitiveness has improved dramatically. If, for example, one takes the data published annually by the World Economic Forum, one can see the beneficial effects of the reform agenda in the early 1990s.

(1) In 1989, New Zealand's international competitiveness index ranked a poor eighteenth amongst OECD countries (IMEDE/WEF 1989: 1), and twenty-second amongst the 33 countries covered (Kasper 1991: 39).

(2) By 1996, New Zealand had moved to ninth place out of 41 ranked countries (Schwab-Sachs 1996: 106–7), and the quality of government intervention in the economy received the top ranking amongst all 49 countries covered in the assessment.

(3) The 1996 Global Competitiveness Report described New Zealand as "the new star in competitiveness." Though not strictly comparable with the earlier reports, it rates New Zealand third among 49 countries on competitiveness (the United States comes fourth and Canada, eighth) and second on growth prospects (Schwab-Sachs 1996). Management and civil institutions are now rated as the best in the world! (Schwab-Sachs 1996: 106)

Such dramatic changes in the ranking for international competitiveness are rare.

The new "economic constitution"

With hindsight, the reforms may look like a predesigned, cohesive program. They were not. Nonetheless, the central elements of New Zealand's reform now fit together in a logical mosaic:

- a commitment to monetary and fiscal rectitude and stability, underpinned by credible, legislated commitments in the form of the Reserve Bank Act of 1989 and the Fiscal Responsibility Act of 1994

- a near-total withdrawal of direct state intervention in individual product and service markets, reinforced by the opening of the economy to international competition
- a liberalization of factor markets, first for capital, and after 1991 for labour (underpinned by the Employment Contracts Act of 1991) and a pruning-back of distortive welfare payments.

Once New Zealanders knew they were no longer able to hide behind protective tariff walls and no longer protected by wage-setting tribunals and the government's prop-ups of their living standards, they set about rethinking the fundamental question: what is the role of government in an open, affluent, post-industrial society. Political leaders recast all three of the basic functions of government that James Buchanan identified (1975).

(1) Government has a *function to protect* the institutions that facilitate human interaction and delineate and protect individual domains of freedom. This protective function was strengthened. The protection of money was devolved to an independent central bank and the delivery of the core business of government administration was corporatized, i.e., it was entrusted to non-tenured civil servants who are held accountable for fulfilling clearly defined, targetted goals.

(2) The *productive function of government* was thoroughly reviewed and, by and large, reduced to providing genuine public goods—goods and services, such as defence or the judiciary, where free riding is likely if the good or service is not financed through taxes. The large remainder of socialized production was first corporatized, then privatized to a considerable extent. In some other cases, such as the production of public health and education services, control was devolved to regional and local authorities but production is still in the public domain.

(3) The *redistributive function*, which had undermined the protective and productive functions, was totally re-evaluated. Interventions to "correct" market outcomes were almost completely abolished as part of the deregulation program. As a consequence, the many unintended side effects of redistributive, politicized interventionism disappeared and a previ-

ously dysfunctional market order became highly effective. Much redistribution by the tax-subsidy mechanism of the welfare state (transfer payments) was streamlined and targetted on the poor, with the aim to cut out "welfare churning" for the middle class and to give effect to market incentives, although many consider these reforms to be incomplete.

In addition to Buchanan's three functions, governments also have to raise funds and administer their resources (*fiscal-administrative function*). Here, too, reforms were thorough, simple and transparent. Taxation was shifted from progressive income to flat value-added taxation, and tax burdens were reduced. The budget process was made transparent, the budget balanced and parliament made accountable not only for current revenues and outlays, but, like any business, for assets and liabililties. Voters now get independently prepared balance sheets before elections.

Reforms of the labour market
History from 1890 to 1991

The prevailing traditional philosophy of governance in virtually all Western "mixed economies" has long asserted that labour markets are special and different from markets for other production factors and products in that the price (the wage) has great social impact.[3] It was concluded that the labour market could not be left to the vagaries of the market process and that labour should not be treated as a commodity. In many Western countries, governments, as well as organized labour and employer federations, consequently gained a strong, direct, influence on all aspects of work, often to the detriment of individual communication between employer and employee.

New Zealand not only shared this philosophical tradition; it often took a lead and subordinated efficiency considerations to demands for security and equality of outcomes. In 1894, after the new technology of ship-borne refrigeration had opened profitable new markets overseas for New Zealand meat and dairy producers, and after bitter strikes had erupted in the maritime industries over a share of the windfalls from the new trade, New Zealand's first Liberal government undertook to rule out strikes. The key influence was William Pember Reeves, a Fabian, who designed the Industrial Conciliation and Arbitration Act of 1894. It gave unions special legal privileges and political protections in exchange for their promise to give up the right to strike. The Act set up a conciliation and arbitration mechanism, administered by a specialist labour court (Hawke 1985). This had the effect of taking industrial relations and the workplace out of the common law.

From the outset, the trade-off between the right to strike on the one hand and official arbitration on the other was controversial amongst organized labour. The stronger unions—especially where high capital intensity gave them "hold-up leverage" (Williamson 1985) and where tariffs protected them from international competition—ignored the proscription of strikes. The judicial system allowed the unions to proceed opportunistically as they saw fit (Jones 1993a: 2). In 1916, the labour movement created its own political party, the New Zealand Labour Party. When it won control of the government in 1935, in the wake of the Great Depression, the Labour Party made unionism compulsory, ensuring the labour movement a secure income from membership.

In the post-war period and up to the 1980s, the unions enjoyed four legally sanctioned and governmentally enforced privileges beyond the legislated privileges given to unions anywhere in Europe.

(1) Union membership was compulsory for all those working in a defined craft area. If no other unions were laying claim to a type of work or occupation, a few people could form a union, register with the government's Registrar of Unions and be given monopoly rights to cover henceforth all workers in the registered occupation or craft. Workers had no choice of union unless they changed their occupation.

(2) Unions, once registered, had the monopoly to cover all work in "their" occupation or craft with all employers.

(3) Unions could notify a "representative sample" of employers of new claims and negotiate with those in the sample. Under the law, all employers of that specific type of occupation and craft were then covered by the agreed award. This was called "blanket coverage." In practice, it often meant that employers who had not bargained for wage or other conditions, indeed, who were not even aware of the fact that negotiations were going on, had to pay and comply after the conclusion of negotiations (Jones 1993a; Brook 1990).

"Blanket coverage" was supported by those businesses that wanted the comforting situation in which every competitor had the same wage-cost and that preferred the "cost-plus" framework of cosy closed markets.

(4) When disputes arose, employers and workers were subjected to compulsory arbitration in the government's Arbitration Court (later the Labour Court and now the Employment Court). Compulsory arbitration had the effect of replacing direct conflict resolution by legalistic and politicized confrontation, freezing historic wage relativities (thus creating rigid relations among wages) and removing specific technical, regional, or business circumstances almost completely from wage negotiations, because wages were fixed at the aggregate industry level. Complex circumstances specific to place and time relating to work practices, productivity, and special circumstances in individual workplaces were pushed aside for the convenience of centralized national wage awards.

The economic, often personal, relationship between employers and employees was transformed into legalist antagonism and bluffing, and conducted through spokesmen before a court—like a broken-down marriage that functions only through divorce lawyers. The industrial-relations system frequently gave priority to industrial relations peace to the detriment of economic necessities, cooperation in the workplace, innovation, and flexible adjustment. Shortages of specific labour and skills coexisted with labour surpluses, either in the form of underutilised staff or—especially after 1985—in the form of rising unemployment. Pay had little relationship to performance and the widespread perception amongst workers was that they were paid for their mere presence in the workplace.

The system survived for a long time because it was underpinned by official protection from competition in many products, services, and occupations, and by the nation's great resource wealth shared by relatively few people. As we saw in part 1, the entire economic system came under growing strain in the 1970s and 1980s.

In 1983, the National Party government led by Jim Bolger, the minister of Labour, abolished compulsory union membership. After the election of the Labour government in 1984, compulsory union membership was reintroduced to quarantine labour markets on the grounds of "social justice" from the dramatic reforms of capital and product markets and of the government.

As Douglas's reforms took hold, the inconsistency between the new set of rules and the institutions governing industrial relations became evident. In 1987, the Labour government passed a new Labour Relations Act that perpetuated many features of the corporatist old order but abolished the government's role as the enforcer of industrial awards, which was henceforth to be the task of employer or labour organizations. When industrial conflicts erupted, the government would remain on the sidelines. This created a new industrial relations climate that forced employers and unions to act more responsibly. The minister for Labour also began action to amalgamate the many, often small, crafts unions into unions of at least 1,000 members. In 1989, the Labour government, as part of its effort to reform the notoriously troubled and inefficient waterfront, cancelled officially endorsed wage and employment arrangements in the ports, leaving the waterfront to its own devices. In one port, employers and employees negotiated a reasonably workable agreement to improve work practices and productivity and allow the port to compete better with other ports. The habit of free, unsupervised industrial negotiation spread to other ports and proved itself practicable. Relations in the workplace improved in one of New Zealand's previously most disrupted sectors. This was to become the model for the labour market reforms of the early 1990s.

In the campaign for the 1990 election, the newly free-market-oriented National Party made the reform of the corporatist, regulated labour market its key point of distinction from the Labour platform. They put this forward amidst a growing awareness in newly deregulated industries that labour rigidities were the Achilles' heel of the New Zealand economy and the Employers' Federation, an integral part of the industrial relations establishment, spoke up for a gradual reform. But the entire economic order surrounding work had changed. The New Zealand Business Roundtable had argued consistently from 1986 onwards for quick, radical change: labour should, like any other good or service, be subject to freely negotiated contracts subject only to the general provisions of contract law (New Zealand Business Roundtable 1986; Brook 1990). They advocated steadfastly a clear first-best position, based on simple legislation, a few pages long, that would permit spontaneous variety in workplace arrangements and contrast with the prevailing, prescriptive tradition.

The Employment Contracts Act

In the years from 1988 to 1990 this latter approach gained the political endorsement of the National Party under the opposition leader, Jim Bolger, shadow finance minister, Ruth Richardson, and opposition industrial-relations spokesman, Bill Birch. The OECD and other international observers signalled that the reform program was being sabotaged by the refusal to free industrial relations (OECD 1989). The National Party won office in October 1990; it was well prepared on labour market reform. Its Employment Contracts Bill was before Parliament by Christmas and became law the following May; the process moved with a speed and energy reminiscent of the reform thrust of Roger Douglas in the mid-1980s.

The main aim of the proposed legislation was to enhance the adaptability of private enterprises so that they could compete more effectively in the global market place. Its key features were:

- the guarantee of the freedom of association, which includes the freedom not to associate; this meant the reintroduction of voluntary union membership, turning unions into strictly private associations without special legislated privileges (the Bill did not even mention the word "union")

- the freedom of contract over labour services and legal support to enforce commitments made; this implied a thorough reform of the rules governing bargaining processes and structures.

As is common in New Zealand with major legislation, the Employment Contracts Bill was made the subject of Select Committee hearings to collect and assess public reactions and to review the legislation. The Select Committee received hundreds of submissions, many from unions. At the same time, the government cut social welfare payments, a circumstance that led to public agitation and street rallies in which welfare recipients joined unions to protest against the reforms introduced by the new conservative government. The press and academics with a stake in the specialized field of industrial relations studies added their protests. Many employers were nervous and unsure. In this atmosphere, parliament edited the Bill with strong input from civil servants wedded to the old system (Jones 1992: 8). Yet, despite some weaknesses, the legislation emerged from the onslaught of pressure groups intact and was adopted into law on May 15, 1991. The key provisions of the Act (of 91 pages) were straightforward.

- Part I of the Act establishes freedom of association in plain language: "Employees have the freedom to choose whether or not to associate with other employees for advancing the employees' collective employment interests ... nothing ... shall confer on any person, by reason of that person's membership or non-membership of an employees' organization any preference ... no person shall exert undue influence ..."

- In Part II, employees are given freedom to bargain, with or without the assistance of freely chosen agents, to obtain judicially enforceable employment contracts of a stated duration.

- In Part III, allowance was made for "personal grievances" concerning contested dismissals and discrimination, harassment, and duress. In this respect, the Act retained some features of special labour law, and not the contract law, that the draught legislation had proposed to throw out: procedural defects in dismissal procedures retained some recognition in law, making firing for substantive causes more difficult but recognising that procedural defects can be set aside when substantive cause is proven. This was a major change from the past when it was very difficult to dismiss staff.

- Part IV of the Act states that "employment contracts create enforceable rights and obligations." It retains Tribunals[4] and the Employment Court to settle disputes, subject to review on points of law in the ordinary courts.

- Part V recognises the rights to strike and lock out, but only after the expiry of the employment contract and after decisions at the enterprise level (not industry level). The remainder of the Act deals with the setting up of Tribunals and the Employment Court and transitional and miscellaneous provisions. Previous awards were allowed to carry on until they were replaced by negotiated contracts.

The most important innovative features of the Employment Contracts Act were:

- Employment was in principle the concern of freely contracting individuals, not, as previously, of collective entities such as entire industries or enterprises. Where people agreed to associate, deals could be struck to cover entire enterprises or multi-enterprise groups (freedom of association).
- The law was did not prescribe the content of employment contracts, although wage rates were subject to minimum wage laws.
- The ECA abolished compulsion and union monopoly powers. No area of work could be claimed any more as "belonging" to a group or organization.
- The ECA made it illegal for unions to strike against multi-employer (i.e., industry-wide) collective arrangements; strike action has to be decided at the enterprise level.
- Recourse to arbitration is voluntary. The ECA, however, provides for special courts where conflicts remain (Employment Tribunals, the Employment Court) as well as appeals to the civil judicial system to enforce, interpret, and mediate employment contracts.[5]
- "Blanket coverage" is gone. All affected are now involved in negotiating new wages and work practices.
- The New Zealand taxpayer, who previously used to fund the transaction costs of award negotiations, is no longer responsible for the expenses of contract negotiation. Contract negotiations are now fairly straightforward and simple; this has cut overall transaction costs in operating the labour market.
- Government does not register unions or collect detailed information on contracts,[6] just as it does not collect much information on credit contracts or garage sales.
- Freedom, choice, responsibility, and flexibility in giving and taking have changed the attitudes of workers and managers.

Predictions and outcomes

The Employment Contracts Act ushered in a genuine revolution. A set of institutions that had evolved over about 100 years—reliance on organized interest groups, politicization, collective bargaining, compulsory arbitration—was replaced by a completely new labour market that relied upon depoliticized, decentralized market processes based on much older British traditions of freedom of contract and the rule of law. The Act completed the change-over in the various, mutually supportive suborders of the market to give New Zealanders a cohesive institutional framework of free markets that was conducive to individual initiative, self-reliance, flexible adjustment and competition. It was supplemented by a minimum safety net of public welfare provisions. One can conclude that workplaces in New Zealand are now operating under more of the flexible market and social welfare conditions that the 1994 OECD Jobs Study advocated as a solution to the employment problem widespread among the members of the OECD. New Zealand has avoided the OECD's idea of "active labour market policies" (OECD 1994).

It is not possible to analyse the results of the ECA by econometric analysis because the changes were comprehensive, affecting numerous structural and institutional conditions. One has to rely, therefore, on less stringent methods such as opinion surveys, case studies and episodic evidence. During the controversy over the Employment Contracts Bill in 1990 and early 1991, and following the legislation, many vocal opponents of the Bill made a number of predictions about the effects of the reform to mobilise resistance against it:

- Real wages would fall, creating "poor quality jobs" (New Zealand Council of Trade Unions 1991).

- "Anarchy" and "uncivilised behaviour" would break out (Council of Trade Unions leader, Ken Douglas); strikes and confrontation would become prevalent.

- "Gangster unionism" would become widespread (Prof. R. Harbridge, *Dominion* April 4, 1991).

- National awards would be impossible, and employers would not be able to calculate their costs and high unemployment would become entrenched (*Dominion Sunday Times* May 19, 1991).

- Workplace democracy and participation would be suppressed (Prof. M. Wilson, *Radio New Zealand Sunday Supplement* February 24, 1991).

Some businesses went on the public record to express fears of discontinuity (Jones 1992), but the New Zealand Business Roundtable kept arguing the case for pervasive, principled reform. The Primate of the Catholic Church in New Zealand even called the legislation "sinful" (quoted by D. Myers in *Business Review Weekly*, May 8, 1992). The Labour Party committed itself to abolishing the ECA, if elected. When the ECA became law, the Council of Trade Unions set up a telephone "Sweatline," so that the predicted employer abuses could be reported and rectified. There were relatively few complaints, most of which the unions did not know how to address. The union initiative soon lapsed for lack of demand (*The Dominion* May 2, 1992).

With the benefit of hindsight, one can say that all the fears projected to mobilize the public in 1991 were groundless. The tactics of the government of trusting its overwhelming electoral mandate, and sticking to its strategy cost them some support at the following election in 1993, when the economy was suffering from a continuing recession and high unemployment. This led to a protest against further reforms in the form of a referendum to change the electoral system in ways that would make clear majorities less likely and multi-party coalitions more probable.

Given the recession during 1991/92 and the prevailing price stability, wages and salaries per employee in the business sector rose only slightly after the Employment Contracts Act became law (see figure 1). Where wages were increased, this was usually in exchange for cooperation in gaining productivity. The prediction of widespread strikes turned out to be wrong: strike activity fell. In the first ten months after the passage of the ECA, 90 percent fewer working days were lost than in the ten months from May 1990 to March 1991 (*New Zealand Herald* July 23, 1992). Work days lost in the private sector during the period from 1991 to 1996 were only 10 percent of those lost from 1985 to 1990.

The unions, who previously could feel sure of their privileged position, now had to prove their usefulness to their members, and often began to provide information and services. Some added value and gained membership, others lost members and had to dismiss union officials. Overall, union membership fell from 675,000 in 1990 to 345,000 in mid-1995 (*The Australian Financial Review* June 5, 1995: 14).The Engineers Union, which had in the past often set the pace for other unions, saw a drop in membership from 60,000 members in 1980 to 36,000 in 1992 (*The*

Australian Financial Review July 3, 1992). Since then, the union has converted itself into a service provider to its "employee clients," carrying out, for example, management training for members. The case of all 2,000 workers leaving their union in the Comalco aluminium smelter was rare (Jones 1994). On the whole – and in line with an OECD-wide trend – overall union membership dropped to 30 percent of the workforce in 1994 (Maloney 1994a). Maloney found that "industry growth rates in both employment and aggregate hours of work ... were higher in industries experiencing large reduction in unionisation" (1994a: 340). In the absence of reliable statistics, other labour-market observers estimate that union membership is markedly lower, possibly approaching the 16 to 17 percent mark in the United States (Alan Jones, private communication, June 1995).

The number of unions dropped quickly from 80 before the passage of the ECA to 66 by the end of 1992 though many unions maintained an influential position, particularly in capital-intensive industries where they could exert influence by shutting down expensive capital stock and in the public sector (Hince and Harbridge 1994: 4). Other unions reshaped themselves into innovative service providers and many have restructured, and are now in a more competitive mode.

Contrary to what some observers predicted, the drop in union coverage (and strike activity) has not reduced real wages or led to gross inequities and injustices in the workplace.

The Employers' Federation has also had to adjust. Whereas it used to negotiate numerous awards for the employers in an industry, so that wages at various firms rose by the same rate in each wage round, the central employer body now has nothing to do with wage negotiations, though it provides labour market information to paying members. Its regional organizations are offering to act as bargaining agents for employers, but many firms now act on their own behalf or employ independent bargaining agents. Few other industry organizations have found it necessary to act as collective coordinators of employer bargaining and, as a result, wage negotiation has been "decollectivised" on both the supply and the demand side.

Surveys and case studies

Opinion surveys have been used to record the immediate effects of the ECA on employees and businesses, partly because existing statistics were not designed to record such fundamental systems change.

(1) A survey of 190 employment contracts by the Department of Labour in 1992 showed that most new contracts were enterprise-based (not industry-wide), that unions acted as bargaining agents in about 45 percent of cases, that 5 percent of wages decreased, 23 percent did not change and 65 percent increased, and that work hours became more flexible.[7]

(2) A detailed survey of employers in March 1993 showed that the impact of the ECA was to improve greatly the flexibility of operations and the productivity of labour, to raise staff training and to reduce the costs of hiring and firing (see table 2).

Table 2 Survey (March 1993) of business leaders on the impact of the Employment Contracts Act

Factor	Lower	Same	Higher	n.a.*	Net Balance†
Wage rates (ordinary time)	12	63	21	4	9
Employment rate	11	69	16	4	5
Growth of labour productivity	1	47	45	6	47
Over-time work	20	55	14	11	−7
Part-time work	6	51	26	17	24
Cost of hiring additional labour	28	54	3	15	−29
Cost of shedding labour	19	55	4	22	−19
Level of staff training	1	59	30	10	32
Flexibility of operations	1	31	63	6	66
Quality of management	1	55	37	8	39

(Percent of replies saying that, without the ECA, the factor would be.)

* n.a. = not available
† Net Balance = percentage of "Lower" replies minus percentage of "Higher" replies as a percent of total replies other than "n.a."
Source: New Zealand Institute of Economic Research, cited in Marshall 1994: 3.

(3) A subsequent survey of 1,000 employees and 500 company directors, conducted for the Department of Labour in September 1993, 15 months after the legislation, revealed that employees

with new contracts were more likely to approve of the new system than workers still on awards; 42 percent reported take-home wage or salary increases, 39 percent no change in incomes, and 19 percent reported a decrease in wage or salary (Department of Labour, New Zealand 1994). Ordinary work times now varied much more in length and/or in starting and ending times than they did under the old system. Fifty percent of enterprises attributed productivity increases to the ECA, and about half of the senior managers agreed with the statement that the old award system had blocked productivity improvements. Employers felt much more favourably about the ECA than employees, 73 percent of whom perceived a drop in job security. There was an interesting contrast between (a) a general question asking about employees' overall opinion of the ECA, to which 36 percent responded with approval, but 43 percent with disapproval, and (b) a specific question whether people were satisfied with the terms and conditions of their employment: 73 percent approved and only 15 were dissatisfied. Personal satisfaction had obviously not influenced general political opinion.

(4) A related Heylen opinion poll (September 1993) found that 46 percent of private enterprises attributed productivity improvements to the ECA, with one in five saying it was an important source of productivity growth. Forty percent of public-sector enterprises also indicated that productivity enhancements in the preceding year were in some way caused by the ECA (Marshall 1994: 3).

High satisfaction with the new system

In February 1996, 5 years after the promulgation of the Employment Contracts Act, MRL Research Group, an opinion-polling organization, conducted a comprehensive survey of what workers thought about the consequences of the ECA (reported in *National Business Review*, February 16, 1996: 22–23). The results of the survey document a growing acceptance of labour-market liberalization and remarkably high rates of satisfaction with working life:

- 41 percent of workers surveyed favoured the new system and only 24 percent disapproved
- 54 percent agreed that the new labour-market order enabled New Zealand's firms to compete better and 52 per-

cent saw a direct relationship between more flexible work practices and competitiveness

- 46 percent thought that the ECA had led to productivity improvements and 54 percent that it had had a positive effect upon the economy
- 76 percent of those surveyed said that they were satisfied or very satisfied with their work conditons, 78 percent said the same about their employers, 85 percent, about the content of their work, and 76 percent, about their job security.

It is remarkable that 77 percent of all workers now want to negotiate only directly with their employers and only 21 percent want third parties, such as unions and agents, to be involved.

The survey confirms that employees and managers have adjusted successfully to the free labour contract conditions. While opinions about the economy-wide effects of the ECA are still mixed, people experience great personal satisfaction in their own work sphere. It will probably take longer-lasting positive personal experiences until people make adjustments to their political opinions and ideologies.

No OECD country has witnessed a steeper decline in strike activity than New Zealand and words like "industrial relations," "strike," "lock-out," "boycott," and "picket line" have disappeared from the headlines. Indeed, wage contracts are now as unremarkable as contracts for the purchase of houses.

Two case studies

The general impression from opinion surveys is supported and supplemented by a careful case study of a plasterboard firm with two plants that followed different paths to contract negotiation, but arrived at similar positive results (see appendix 3, A Tale of Two Cities: A Microview of the Workplace Revolution). Positive outcomes have been reported by many other companies, too. Thus, the aluminium company Comalco reported a drop of 17 percent in crude labour costs and a decrease in production time of 31 percent in its aluminium smelter (after they implemented their first employment contract), and the chemical industry offered increases in wage rates between 2.5 percent and 8 percent in its first contract negotiations in exchange for new work practices (Jones 1993b: 12).

In practice, both employers and employees adopted the contract system fairly smoothly. By February 1993, few jobs were left under the old awards system, although 23.7 percent of the private sector workforce replicated their award conditions in their contracts. One third of all contracts had been negotiated individually by employees, 43.2 percent worked under collective enterprise contracts, and 9 percent had signed new multienterprise contracts (Household Labour Survey of Statistics New Zealand, April 1993). Most strikes were ended by direct negotiation and without recourse to outside intermediaries.

Attitudinal consequences and rule changes

Opinion survey, case studies, newspaper reports and episodic evidence support conclusions that one would predict on the basis of simple economic theory about how the ECA works.

(1) Employees and employers were given an easily comprehended, simple law that cast the work relationship into the familiar framework of common law contracts. It did away with an untransparent, complex system of regulations that had left much to the arbitrary rule of men and tribunals. The new system was normally perceived as more just. It strengthened the rule of law in the work place and, even small employers and individual workers, who had previously been confronted with anonymous, collective industrial relations, now enjoyed the protection of the law and were free to negotiate and shape their own work relationships. Collectivist and compulsory industrial relations gave way to contracts between people and free associations.

(2) Managers gained a new capacity to manage the human resources in their companies. They can now offer wage incentives for more productive work practices and innovations. Communication between workers and managers is now direct and more intensive, while workers have gained much more say about how they want the workplace to be organised. Both workers and managers made active use of these new freedoms from collective regulation of the workplace and varied work practices to suit the specific circumstances of time and place.

(3) It has become easier to dismiss staff who are inefficient or act against the employer's interests. Before the ECA, New Zealand workers who were dismissed, say, for absenteeism or

drunkenness, could go before the Mediation Service or the Labour Court to claim that proper procedures had not been followed during their dismissal. Since most managers were not trained in legal procedures and since the Mediation Service and Labour Court tended to search for lapses in documentation and procedure, it was *de facto* very difficult to fire staff. Consequently, it was less attractive to create new positions, and many managers had stopped trying effectively to manage the labour force. Under the draft legislation, procedural shortcomings would not have constituted grounds for overturning dismissal but the final version of the ECA retained procedural grounds and laid the foundation for the Employment Court to create rules that will again make dismissals costly and complicated.

(4) Unions have no automatic rights as negotiators. For every contract, they have to be authorized by each member before they can act. Therefore, they have to compete with other bargaining agents, some of whom are former union officials who set up private bargaining businesses, and with individual workers who negotiate their own deals. After three years under the new regime, a sample of contracts showed that union representation is still the most common form of bargaining: some 85 percent of employees used union representatives to negotiate on their behalf (Harbridge and Honeybone 1994: 25). Other evidence indicates that this estimate may be on the high side. Whatever the share, workers gained control over their lives, and the union officials they now choose act on their behalf, and act as instructed by the workers. In one case soon after the passage of the ECA, a building-materials firm proposed separate contracts covering geographically dispersed quarries. The union, used to nationwide coverage, demanded one uniform industry contract. Yet, the workers instructed the union to accept the several contracts that their company wanted, contracts that contained regional variations (Jones 1991: 17). There are numerous similar instances that show that employees willingly took control of their own job conditions.

(5) In many firms, negotiated changes in work practices have allowed a much better utilization of the capital stock. As already mentioned, New Zealand had become accustomed to wasting capital, not least because of the rigidities of the old labour system. Employment contracts, and the across-the-board liberaliza-

tion of economic life, now allowed firms to work multiple shifts and to ensure that work schedules did not interrupt the steady use of the capital stock. The predictable response of business to the higher capital productivity allowed by the ECA has been a steep rise in investment.

(6) Under the old system, the wage was often paid for mere presence in the workplace, and not for performance or quality. New Zealand's workers used to maximize their incomes by working much overtime; in many industries, hours on the job were long. Under the new system, performance counts towards the size of pay packets, and multiple shifts have often reduced effective work hours. Performance measurement under new employment contracts has often posed challenges to management and affected the work attitudes of all involved. The gains were most readily reaped where a participative style of management was practiced and where teams explored the opportunities of the newly found freedom by communicating.

(7) Wage rates became more differentiated, with many movements in relative pay rates and regional diversity in pay scales, a circumstance that attracts investments to backward rural areas and the poorer South Island. The biggest changes in relative wages occurred in the first two years under the new system. Since then work relativities have been fairly stable (Harbridge and Honeybone 1994).

(8) Wage calculation was often simplified: a plethora of specific "penalty rates," for, e.g., weekend work, noisy conditions or weather, was integrated into uniform, more transparent, pay scales. The simplification of wage calculation saved firms and workers considerable transaction costs. High "penalties" for overtime (double rate or more) became less frequent, while productivity clauses have become quite frequent. By 1994, 15 percent of all contracts contained such clauses, and flexible work hours have increased to 38 percent of contracts (Harbridge and Honeybone 1994: 10).

(9) Initially, the aggregate real wage level moved little due to the recession and a high degree of price stability, but basic wage rates rose, on average, by about 1 percentage point in 1992/93 and in 1993/94 (Harbridge and Honeybone 1994: 4).

(10) The contracts system has led to the emergence of differential pay for skills. The old centralised system had given fairly equal rates of pay to all, so that highly skilled toolmakers often found it preferable to work as taxi drivers or waterfront workers. Under the contracts system, people with skills have an incentive to market scarce skills, and there is evidence that needed skills are now indeed deployed where they have the highest productivity. Conversely, low-skilled people are increasingly facing low wage increases. This is not surprising because the New Zealand labour market is being internationalised and low-skilled New Zealanders are competing more directly with bountiful Asian labour supplies.

(11) In the first three years under the ECA, the private sector tended to record higher wage increases than community and public services (Harbridge and Honeybone 1994: 6).

(12) A possibly unexpected result has been the disappearance in many workplaces of the historic distinction between blue-collar and white-collar workers. Team spirit has taken over from class distinction. The legacy of long-passed industrial conflicts in a faraway island, Britain, has been shed and a sense of cooperation and partnership is evolving in the better-run firms.

(13) The traditional, politicized, national industrial-relations "circus" with conspicuous annual "wage rounds" has given way to contracts in numerous labour markets that do not merit much public attention. What had often been personalized conflicts between interest groups about some perceived fundamentals has now been diffused in numerous decentralized contract negotiations, which resolve possible conflicts according to the specific circumstances of place and time. Industrial-relations problems and strikes, a frequent item in New Zealand media coverage before, have virtually disappeared from the headlines and, in a way, industrial relations has nearly disappeared from the public attention.

As a result of the ECA, workplace arrangements are more performance oriented and respond flexibly to changed circumstances, but overall patterns of work, pay, and other contract conditions have not changed greatly. Few workers or firms were disoriented by the changeover, and information about market rates of pay was obviously readily available.

Arguably the most important gain for many New Zealanders was not material. The new contract relationship befits a modern society of self-assured, free, educated citizens. Many New Zealanders discovered that they could talk to each other directly and solve problems. The work relationship has become more satisfying for many, as opinion polls show, and management has become much more participative. All this has given new meaning and fulfilment to a very important part of many peoples' lives, namely their workplaces.

The complaint to the International Labour Organization

As public opinion began to turn more in favour of the new employment law, the New Zealand Council of Trade Unions mounted an attack in February 1993 on certain aspects of the ECA before the International Labour Organization (ILO). It tried to overturn by international covenant what New Zealand's elected parliament had put in place. The Council complained that the New Zealand government had violated the freedom of association, claiming that the ECA's removal of recognition of unions violated the Freedom of Association Convention 1948, and the Right-to-Organize and Collective Bargaining Convention 1949. The government rejected the ILO's interim conclusions pointing out that the "Employment Contracts Act is an important element of the government's strategy for economic growth, increased employment and building strong communities and a cohesive society" (New Zealand Government 1994: 29).

The ILO did not uphold most of its preliminary findings in its final report and the New Zealand government, which had in any case not ratified these conventions (International Labour Organization 1994: 40), affirmed from the outset that it would not amend the Act and thus ensured public confidence in the stability of the new institutions. In early 1994, after exhaustive investigations, the ILO Committee (case no. 1698) found no major objections against the ECA but "affirmed established principles of collective bargaining" and hoped that there would be tripartite discussions among industry, organized labour, and government. It also reiterated that "workers and their organizations should be able to call for industrial action in support of multi-employer collective employment contracts, which is currently made expressly illegal under section 63(e) of the [Employment Contracts] Act." The ILO offered its advisory services to the

New Zealand government (International Labour Organisation 1994: 85-86). The government of New Zealand and the ILO agreed to disagree on the basic philosophical issue of individual freedom versus corporatist collectivism. The government's rejection of the collective social arrangements preferred by the ILO is a logical extension of the individualist philosophies that have guided the labour-market reforms.

Residual market imperfections

Although it is widely recognized that the ECA placed the entire work sphere on a dramatically different institutional foundation, the reforms have been called "an incomplete revolution" (Brook 1991). There has been some criticism from employers of various remnants of the traditional system.

(1) The New Zealand Business Roundtable has been critical of the continued existence of a legally mandated minimum wage (Stigler 1946; see also Cumming 1988; Gorman 1993; Minford 1993), not least on the grounds that this makes labour-market entry harder than necessary for less productive workers (ACIL Economics and Policy 1994; Sloan 1994; see also Brosnan-Rea 1991; Hartley 1992). The best available evidence, differentiated for teenagers and adults, shows that the minimum wage has some effect on job creation: careful econometric analysis suggests that a 10 percent rise in the minimum wage would reduce employment of all young adults (20 to 24 years of age) by between 1.4 percent and 1.8 percent, and of young adults without school or post-school qualifications by as much as 3.4 to 3.8 percent. The employment rate for young adults would be increased by a minimum wage reduction (Maloney 1994b).

(2) Observers on the employers' side have been critical of the continued existence of the Employment Court and its practice of finding frequently in favour of employees. For example, the fact that employers failed to follow proper procedures leading to dismissals, even if there are substantive grounds for dismissal, still often leads to rulings that reinstate dismissed workers; in other words old conventions are perpetuated although they may be at odds with the spirit of the ECA (New Zealand Business Roundtable/New Zealand Employers Federation 1992; Sloan 1994, Howard 1995). There have been calls for the abolition of this special industrial-relations court, so that jurisdiction over

employment contracts can be transferred to civil courts with wider experience in general commercial affairs (Jones 1993b: 8). The ECA extended personal grievance coverage to employees who were not members of unions, including white-collar employees, and opened the door for more legal wrangles and a shift to procedural criteria. However, standard legal safeguards and common law coverage appear to be asserting themselves gradually (Howard, 1995). The (general) Court of Appeal upheld fewer than half of the Labour/Employment Court's decisions brought before it between 1987 and 1993 (23 out of a total of 48 cases). Nonetheless, the costs of running the country's employment system would probably be reduced if all employment contract matters were simply subjected to the common law and handed over to non-specialised, general courts.

(3) Social welfare provisions, although tightened and revised (St. John 1993; Sloan 1994), are still perceived by some observers as weakening the material incentive to search for work. As mentioned, the combination of a welfare safety net and a fairly flat income tax creates high marginal tax rates at the transition to work. Hence it can serve as a deterrent to seeking employment. It was a matter for concern that many people have transferred from receiving unemployment payments to sickness, accident, or other social security payments but as unemployment rates dropped this trend became weaker.

(4) The most enduring objections to the ECA come from the labour movement, both organized labour and its political wing, the Labour Party, which is committed to doing away with key provisions of the Act. The reasons for their objections are obvious: loss of fee-paying membership and loss of monopoly control. They rely on popular support from those segments of the electorate that are less interested in economic efficiency and more in equity and non-material objectives. However, opinion polls regularly indicate that the Labour Party now has few adherents.

A government-appointed taskforce to look into measures to combat high unemployment reported late in 1994 (Prime Ministerial Taskforce 1994). Its report contained an elaborate collection of numerous detailed proposals but it found little positive response, partly, one presumes, because New Zealand has moved from detailed administrative "can-doism" to reliance on a framework of fundamental rules within which spontaneous market forces are left to produce desirable results. That approach was already leading to substantial drops in unemployment by the time the report was published.

Policy lessons for other countries?

Economic results to date

In the first half of 1991, the recession that had begun in 1989 came to an end in New Zealand. Output grew by 15 percent in the three years leading to 1995, as much as it had during the entire decade from 1974 to 1984, a period that New Zealanders used to regard as the good old days. Since early 1991, the upturn in demand and output has been steady and has been accompanied by moderate rises in real earnings: the average annual rate from the passage of the ECA to the end of 1994 is 0.4 percent. The shape of the upturn contrasts with earlier cyclical turnarounds, when improved demand promptly triggered across-the-board wage increases. Thus, the upswing in 1984/85, when the Labour government had begun the reform program but re-regulated labour markets, led quickly to a very rapid increase in wages followed by rising inflation and unemployment (compare figure 1).

The profile of the upturn from 1991 to 1994 was markedly different. Despite upward wage adjustments in the wake of the ECA (figure 2), the upturn led to robust job creation and a spectacular drop in unemployment. The recovery, especially in manufacturing and export activities, created numerous new employment opportunities. Between the passage of the ECA and the middle of 1995, over 150,000 new jobs were created, the equivalent of the entire workforce of Christchurch or Wellington (and 10.3 percent of the number of jobs at the bottom of the recession). In March 1995, there were 5 percent more jobs than a year earlier and the government was predicting a further 135,000 new jobs by 1998 (Myers 1995: 2); and net job creation continued throughout the cyclical growth pause of 1995/96. In 1995, the number of jobs grew by 3.5%.

In the wake of the ECA, the workforce shows many indications of training to improve skills. The rise in the employment of people with tertiary qualifications has far exceeded total job growth, and the share of skill-intensive activities in total output is rising fast. This reflects the growing division of labour between New Zealand and the new industrial countries of East Asia where low-skilled labour is comparatively cheap. As a consequence of the internationalization of the New Zealand labour market and the wage flexibility under the new regime, rewards for skill have been rising. The New Zealand workforce has reacted constructively to the market signals: people with skills, who used to work in jobs where these skills were not demanded, now move to jobs where their skills earn extra income and many young workers now acquire and use post-school qualifications (1994: 43 percent of 20- to 24-year-olds, up from only 12 percent in 1966). Among the young, there are now few without any qualifications, the exception being many Maoris and Pacific Islanders.

The outcomes of the labour market reforms were greatly influenced by the growing openness of the economy and the competition on product markets, which amounts to competition for New Zealand labour. This was expressed clearly in an interview by Rex Jones, the leader of the Engineering Union, when he said: "New Zealand workers and employers together are taking on the export markets of the world" (*The Australian Financial Review*, June 5, 1995: 14). The New Zealand workforce is becoming internationally more competitive. The "World Competitiveness Reports" show an improvement in the international competitiveness of the "People Factor": whereas New Zealand's "Human Resources" were rated twenty-second out of 33 old and new industrial countries in 1989 (Kasper 1991: 39), they attained thirteenth rank out of 41 countries in 1994 (IMD-WEF 1994: 44). It would be hard not to attribute most of this enhancement to the improved institutional framework surrounding labour markets. By 1993, New Zealand had a 25 percent to 50 percent wage to cost advantage over Australia (Jones 1993a: 12); and wharfage costs were 20 percent to 25 percent below those in Australian ports. Increasing numbers of plants relocate from Hong Kong and Australia, where costs are high, to New Zealand. Apart from natural-resource advantages, flexible work practices that allow multi-shift use of the capital stock and low wage rates are cited as reasons for this locational innovation.

The enhanced responsiveness of liberalized labour markets has had a considerable impact on unemployment:

(1) From a high of nearly 11 percent in September 1991, the aggregate rate of unemployment has fallen consistently (to 6.1 percent in March 1996; figure 2). The unemployment rate of male *Pakehas* (New Zealanders of European extraction) stood at 4.3 percent in March 1996.

(2) Many long unemployed are being drawn back into employment. The reemployment of people with lesser job skills may have affected the rate of change in average weekly earnings during 1993 (figure 2) but it nevertheless ensured a welcome reduction in hard-core unemployment. In March 1995, the number of the long-term jobless was no less than 36.5 percent fewer than a year earlier. The trend continued.

(3) The upturn in the jobs market has also begun to affect the Maori and Pacific Islanders, typically groups with high unemployment, high welfare dependency, and serious social problems. In March 1996, the Maori unemployment rate was 19 percent (down from 27.3 percent five years earlier).

(4) Unemployment among youths is higher than the aggregate but is falling in line with overall unemployment. Many employment contracts with young people offer modest wages, but this wage flexibility allows young people to get their feet on the lowest rung of the jobs ladder and to gain on-the-job training.

(5) There are first reports of skill shortages and the number of unfilled vacancies has increased slightly.

Assessing the record

It is clear that the completion of the reform agenda by the ECA has played a substantial role in attaining output and employment growth and achieving improvements in real earnings. It is also obvious that the sequence of the New Zealand reforms—deregulation of capital and product markets before the freeing up of labour markets, macroeconomic stabilisation and public expenditure control (see section 1)—has imposed high burdens on the workforce that an ill-advised Labour government had hoped to protect. Academics and observers in international organizations (OECD 1991) would probably have designed a different sequence of reforms but political constraints made it inevitable that the reform be carried out "back to front." Matters of labour and social welfare have probably the most widespread appeal in electoral democracies, so that it is almost impossible to make these areas the frontrunners of comprehensive institutional reform, even if that would be a desirable sequence of policy reforms. Only when all the surrounding props for the old labour-market suborder had been removed and the costs of the traditional suborder had become evident, was labour reform politically feasible.

Figure 2 Growth and labour markets from 1990 to 1996

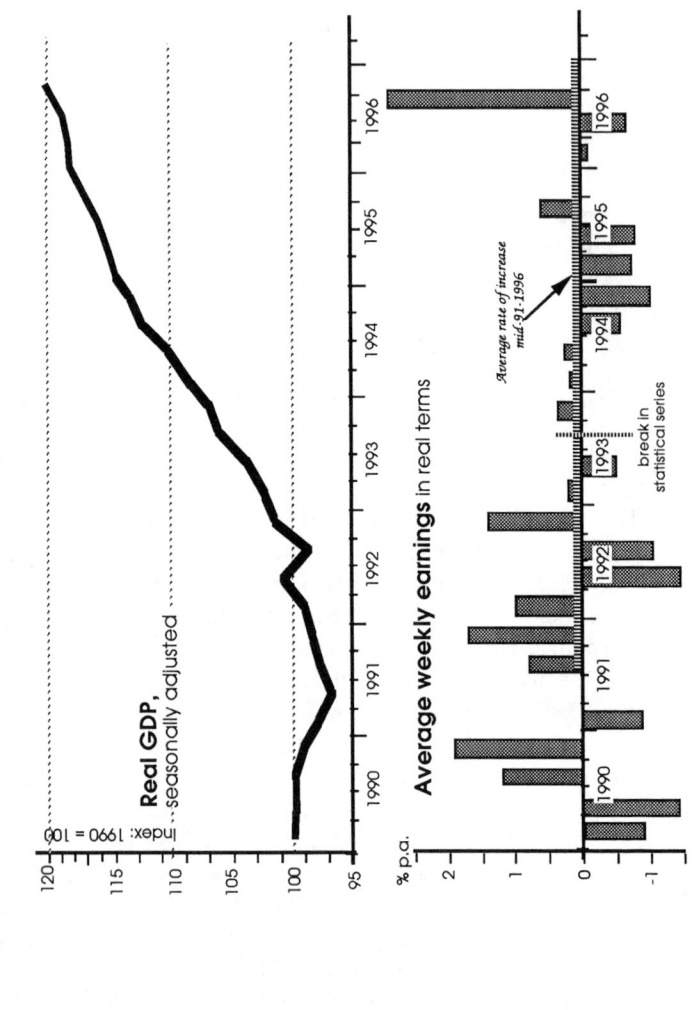

188

Employment

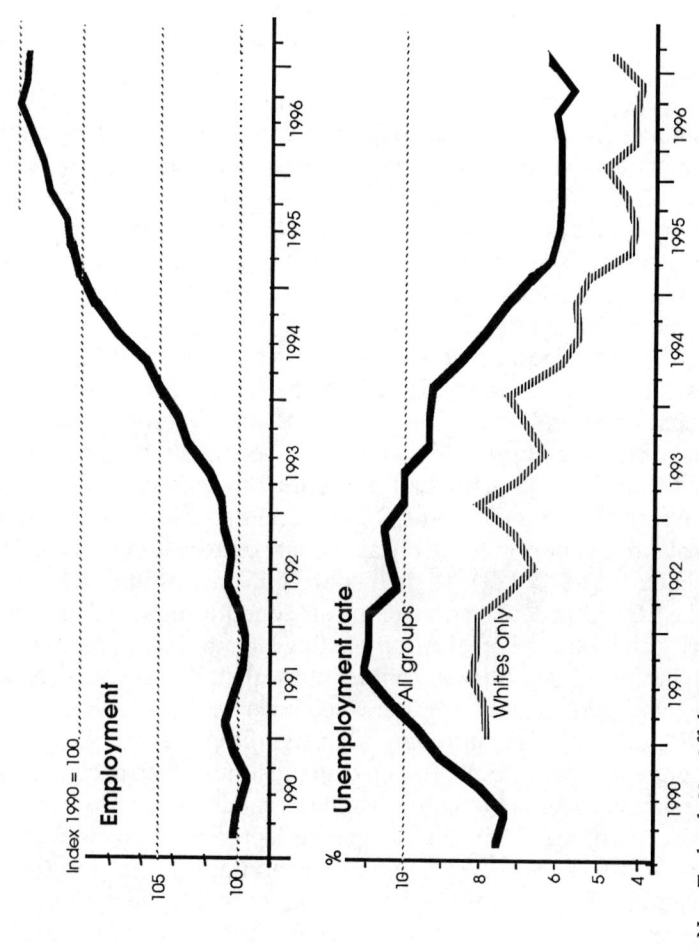

Index 1990 = 100

Unemployment rate

All groups

Whites only

Sources: Statistics New Zealand, *Hot Off the Press*, passim.

It has been widely debated whether the improvement in labour markets and joblessness should be attributed to the cyclical upswing or to the reform of the institutional order through the ECA. The most careful econometric analysis has been conducted by Tim Maloney (1994a, c). Using industry-level quarterly data from the second quarter of 1986 to the fourth quarter of 1993, he found that "at least one percentage point of [the] employment growth [of 4.4 percent growth since the ECA] can be attributed to this legislation" (Maloney 1994c: 20). But he speculates that the ECA was partly responsible for the cyclical upturn, so that more of the employment growth could arguably be credited to the Act. Maloney's data base does not cover the continued upturn during 1994 and 1995, when internal labour and productivity reserves in plants would have been exhausted and the continued demand expansion still led to more job creation. It is possible that an update would point to a more substantial impact on job creation and unemployment by the institutional and legal changes. Maloney (1994c) also found that average real wages fell by 0.5 percent from the third quarter of 1991 to the fourth quarter of 1993, which he entirely attributes to the Act. Yet, renewed growth in wage incomes during 1994 and 1995 (see figure 2) might alter that conclusion (Bollard, Lattimore, and Silverstone 1996).

Another econometric study of the recent behaviour of the New Zealand economy touched on labour-market reactions to the ECA (Hall 1996: 110–111). It cited sources in making the case that "the ECA has been a key factor in subsequently improved productivity and lessened pressure on existing labour costs and the costs of hiring. If so, then it could follow that the costs of New Zealand's disinflation process would have been somewhat lower if the ECA had been introduced at a significantly earlier date." To explore this point, Hall presented an illustrative macroeconometric simulation that brought forward the competitive impact of the ECA up to early 1986. He assumed a 5 percent improvement of labour productivity over 2.5 years and an initial wage drop (relative to the substantial baseline increases) of 2.5 percent for two successive quarters, which remained in place for two years; thereafter he assumed a gradual return to baseline wage levels. The assumed combination of a permanent productivity gain and temporary wage reduction would—according to hall's estimates—have raised real output substantially over the following decade. Hall further found that "[a]s a result [of the simulation], employment gains were substantial and sustained ... Unemployment outcomes would also have been relatively better" had the ECA been passed earlier. The experiment points to a substantial beneficial effect by the ECA on employment and growth.

Another, less rigorous, way of arriving at a quantitative estimate of the effects of the ECA five years after its introduction is to compare New Zealand's recovery with that of Australia:

(1) Both countries embarked on comprehensive microeconomic reforms in the 1980s but with one important difference: whereas New Zealand completed its reform in the early 1990s, Australia quarantined the labour market and, to a large extent, the government and welfare sector, from the reform.[8] Differences in aggregate performance may therefore be attributed to New Zealand's reform program.

(2) Both countries have similar histories and economic structures, largely concurrent business cycles, and, as old industrial countries in the frontline of competition with East Asia, a similar competitive exposure.

(3) Economic growth reached its lowest point in both countries in the first half of 1991 and both have enjoyed a long steady recovery since. The slope of New Zealand's recovery has, however, been significantly steeper (figure 3).

(4) The centralised wage-fixing system of Australia, subject to an "Accord" between the central union body and the federal government to control wages (a soft kind of incomes policy), yielded higher average wage-earnings (notably, early in the upturn) than did the decentralised New Zealand contract system. The average real wage from 1990 to early 1995 rose by a 0.8 percent per annum in Australia, but by only 0.4 percent per annum in the liberalized New Zealand labour markets.

(5) Australia's wage-fixing system is connected with impressive differences in job creation and reduction of unemployment (figure 3). The Australian system responded with a long employment lag: non-government employment began to pick up only nine quarters after the turn-around in output. Since the bottom of the recession and the ECA, New Zealand's economy has generated 10 percent more jobs,[9] the Australian economy none. Indeed, 15 quarters into the cyclical upswing, there were still 1.2 percent fewer civilian jobs in Australia than there had been in the recession year 1990. By contrast, the "Kiwi job creation machine" is now second to none.

Figure 3 Labour market performance: comparison with Australia

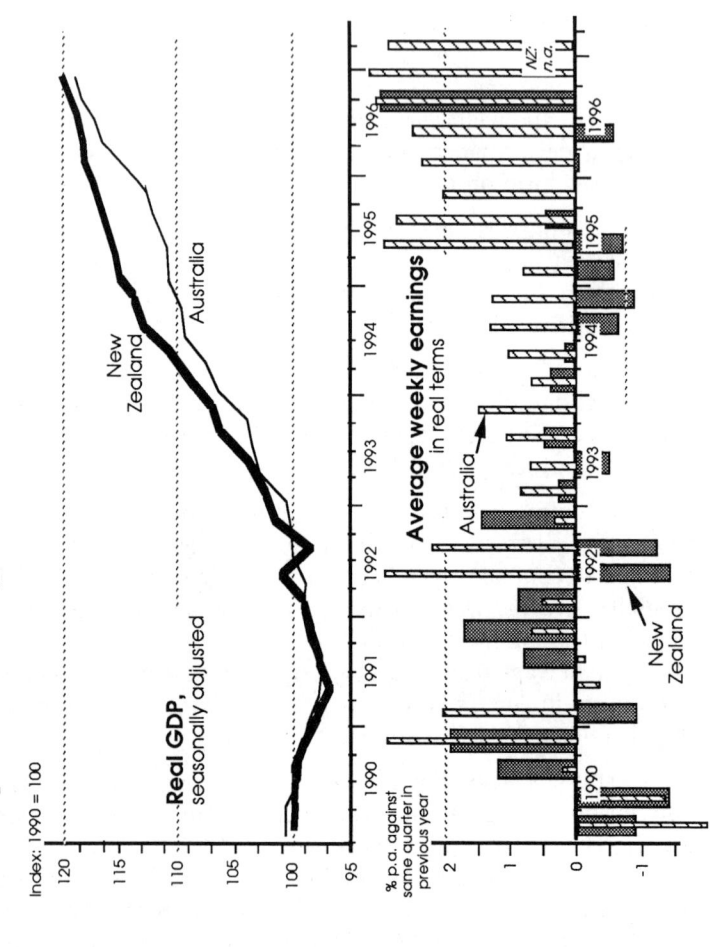

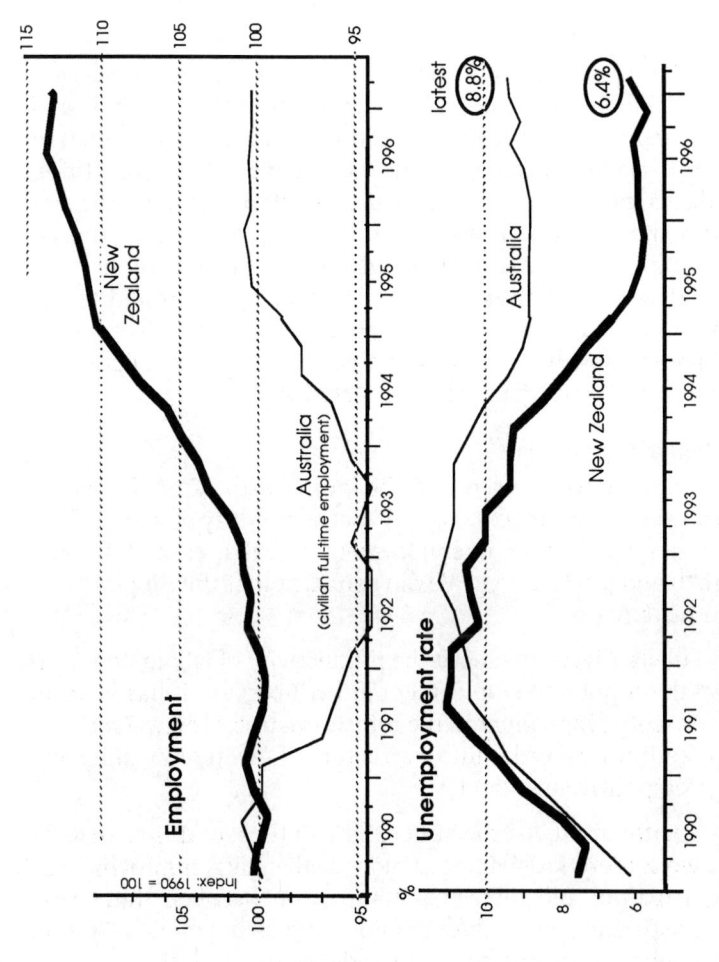

Source: Statistics New Zealand; Australian Bureau of Statistics

(6) From the start of the recovery, New Zealand's unemployment rate dropped: as of June 1996 it was 6.1 percent. In Australia, with largely unreformed labour market institutions similar to New Zealand's former system, unemployment rates fell later and by less (2.9 percentage points from the peak in umemployment to the latest available period, against New Zealand's 4.7 percentage points).

This comparison offers fairly convincing evidence that decentralized labour markets yield more employment, growth and wage income than a regulated, centrally coordinated industrial order. It also puts the lie to the view that market competition produces inequitable outcomes and therefore has to be corrected somehow by collective interventions. On the contrary, free labour markets accepted an "unemployment discount" in the form of moderate wage rises and thereby spread jobs around to the less competitive workers. Compared to Australians, New Zealanders now have more equitable access to work opportunities (on the comparison, see also Kerr 1995).

Summary evaluation

The evidence to date seems to be in line with expectations derived from *a priori* theory, namely that a freer play of market forces clears markets of unemployment imbalances and favours growth and job creation. We can conclude that the Employment Contracts Act has

(1) substantively enhanced the productivity of labour and capital, output and employment growth because it has been an essential ingredient in the transformation of New Zealand's institutional order into a structure of greater flexibility and competitiveness, and

(2) greatly improved the atmosphere in the workplace, making work more satisfying and more challenging, improving participation and direct communication between those who are partners in productive effort, and giving more people an equitable opportunity to provide for themselves.

Arguments that predicted a drop in real wages have not come true, despite high unemployment and poor demand when the ECA came in force. Nor have widespread workplace conflicts erupted, as some predicted. Intransigent critics of the Act argued that it was "a law which is only good for a recession," but the long recovery from 1991 to 1996 has shown that it is essential for sustainable low-inflation growth. The Employment Contracts Act, a success from the viewpoint of efficiency growth, job creation, and equity of opportunity, fits in with New Zealand's overall economic order. It has, therefore, become effective as attitudes, expectations, the style of management, and work practices have been adapted to the new institutional framework.

The only drawback is that it has aroused opposition from previously deeply entrenched influential groups. The organized labour movement has not given up the fight for at least a partial return to the *status quo ante*, which it had enjoyed for nearly a century. The general public, however, as well as employees and employers have become used to the new ground rules. The two parties that argued for the repeal of the Employment Contracts Act in the election campaign of 1996 both lost seats and the new government coalition is committed not only to retaining but also to tightening the labour-contract system (Bradford 1997).

Perspectives for the future

Most observers predict fairly high growth rates for the remainder of this decade and anticipate low inflation and high employment. Few would undo the central features of the reforms that have led, during the long cyclical upturn from 1991 to 1995 and beyond, to a rise in real national product of nearly 20 percent, the creation of over 200,000 new non-governmental jobs (20 percent above the 1991 recession level) and an average rate of inflation of 1.6 percent per annum.

Given entrenched political opposition to some features of the ECA, however, and the possibility that the general political opinion about the ECA may not be influenced fully by the personal workplace experience of most workers, one has to contemplate at least two scenarios for the future:

(1) It is possible that the political system may overturn the ECA and reintroduce contradictions into the current economic order. This would undermine the medium-term benefits of the "onerous decade of reform" that started in 1984, but would, over time and after frictions in the job and other markets, probably lead to labour behaviour compatible with the maxims of national and international product market competition. No political group

will ever be able to re-erect the plethora of controls needed to prop up a centralist industrial-relations system, replicating the thoroughly "negotiated economy" that once existed. Consequently, the competitive forces of open product and capital markets will pull labour-market institutions and workplace attitudes eventually in line. But this may come after long time lags and at considerable cost in terms of jobs, as experience has shown in other countries which followed a zig-zag course of economic reform (Papageorgiu, Choski and Michaely 1990).

(2) The alternative is that the free market order will be allowed to settle down and generate prosperity and freedom for all, so that widespread and durable electoral support for free markets all around grows sufficiently to make a re-regulation of labour markets impossible. Then, the political parties committed to labour-market collectivity would be defeated repeatedly at the polls and would eventually abandon the political commitment to undoing individual contracts under the sheer weight of long-term success. Such an ideological conversion occurred, for example, when the West German Social Democrats recognised the durable success of the Erhard reforms in their "Godesberg Program" of 1957, and recently the British Labour Party acknowledged the durable success of Thatcher's privatization policy by jettisoning nationalization from their party program.

It is not clear which scenario will be played through in the next century—whether the political or the economic imperative will gain the upper hand. The battle for the compatibility of economic, political, and social orders in New Zealand has not yet been completely won. It is the battle for the hearts and minds of the electorate that takes place in all electoral democracies between the obvious solutions of populist collectivism and the less obvious strategy of cultivating the spontaneous forces of genuine competition. The New Zealand story will therefore be of continuing interest.

Appendix 1
Basic background data for New Zealand

Land surface: 268,676 km^2

North-south extension over both islands: approx. 1,500 km

Population (mid-1995): 3.5 million

Growth rate, last 30 years: 0.93% per annum

Labour force (mid-1995): 1.7 million

GDP per-capita (1995): US$14,550 (62% of US per-capita GDP, if purchase-power parities are applied)

Growth of per-capita GDP (1970–96): 2.1% per annum

Exports (1995): 32% of GDP

Foreign debt (1995): 75% of GDP

Public debt (1995–96): 32% of GDP

Inflation (CPI, 1991–96): 2.1% per annum

Tax rate on mid-range income: 21%

Appendix 2
Chronology of major reforms from 1982 to 1997

1982–84	• corporatization of the publicly owned transport industry
1983	• start of Closer Economic Relationship (CER) with Australia, to open both economies to free trade in goods and services
1983–89	• phasing out of all import licensing requirements
July 1984	• reformist, economically rationalist, Labour government elected

198 Unions and Right-to-Work Laws

1984	• devaluation of the NZ$ by 20%
	• freeing-up of the foreign exchange market and international capital flows
1984	• controls on domestic credit abolished
	• removal of interest rate controls
1984	• end to general price and wage freeze
1984	• re-introduction of compulsory unionism (closed shops)
1984	• termination of government guarantees of minimum prices for agricultural products.
1984-88	• abolition of major wage and price controls
	• abolition of several compulsory domestic agricultural marketing boards (boards with monopolies to export retained)
1984	• government withdraws from direct involvement in wage negotiations
1984 on	• corporatization of government departments
	• shift to public service provision on a commercial basis (i.e., full-cost recovery)
	• output measurement in public sector
	• government procurement opened to private competitors
	• local autonomy in hospitals and education
	• core of government moves to accrual accounting to show net asset effects of policies
1984-89	• all government-regulated monopolies are exposed to outside competition (contestability)
1985	• deregulation of banking (end of quantity restrictions)
	• removal of entry barriers into banking
1985	• freely floating exchange-rate
1985	• simplification of corporate tax structure
1985	• all subsidies to agriculture and industry are being phased out

1985–88	• house rents and energy prices are deregulated
1986	• foundation of the New Zealand Business Roundtable, which is to become a key forum for ideas on economic and social reforms
1986	• tax reforms begin with introduction of comprehensive uniform, one-stage General Goods and Services Tax (GST), now at 12.5% • most other indirect taxes abolished
1986	• Commerce Act liberalizes merger and take-over provisions, stressing dynamic efficiency and relying upon international competition to control business behaviour • it also puts trade practices on liberal basis
1986–91	• corporatization and restructuring of government-owned electricity industry
1986–92	• pre-announced, gradual, across-the-board reduction of import tariffs (exemptions for motor vehicles and textiles, garments and footwear)
1987	• Labour Party is re-elected • tensions between economic reformers and the political Left in the Party
1987	• income tax scale is lowered and made flatter • targeting of "poverty traps" in the tax-welfare system
1987	• deregulation of domestic airlines
1987–89	• telecommunications deregulated • privatization of the telecom sector foreshadowed
1987	• Labour Relations Act encourages decentralized bargaining and union amalgamation • compulsory unionism is reaffirmed.
1988	• Roger Douglas dismissed from post as finance minister.
1988–92	• privatization of gas, other energy holdings and New Zealand Telecom foreshadowed and initiated

1988–90	• all import quotas and import licensing (protection) phased out for most industries • residual tariff protection for motor cars, clothing, and footwear remains in the range from 25% to 35%
1988	• State Sector Act places public sector employment on a footing comparable to private sector employment • redesign of public accounts to accrual accounting
1988–89	• decentralisation of compulsory education system, based on elected boards of trustees
1989	• Public Finance Act changes management of government departments • output-based monitoring of performance • removal of all restrictions on shop trading hours
1989	• Reserve Bank Act makes Reserve Bank of New Zealand independent of government and stipulates a price-level target of 0% to 2%
1989	• corporatization of all ports
1989	• David Lange, the prime minister, resigns
1989–91	• peak of privatization wave (Post Office Savings Bank, Rural Bank, Bank of New Zealand, Air New Zealand, Telecom, insurance)
1989–93	• gradual liberalization of immigration • attraction of business migrants
1990	• deregulation of the taxi industry
1990	• all bilateral tariffs with Australia are rapidly eliminated under the Common Economic Relations (CER) agreement • unilateral, phased, tariff reductions vis-à-vis other countries are reaffirmed (effective rate of protection in 1989/90 was 19%, as against 37% in 1985/86) • tariffs announced to be 10% on most goods by 1996
1990	• establishment of a contestable pool of public funds for research and development replaces direct funding of research institutes

Oct. 1990	• election of the conservative-reformist National Party government initiates stringent fiscal policies and labour-market reforms • substantial expenditure cuts
1991	• comprehensive overhaul of the social welfare system with the object of replacing reliance on the state by self-reliance and market provision.
May 1991	• Employment Contracts Act adopted • labour markets liberalized completely (voluntary unionism, contestable unions of any size, freedom of arrangements for employer/employee bargaining at joint or individual level)
1991	• removal of sabotage in coastal shipping
1992	• corporatization of government research organisations
1993	• National Party government re-elected • referendum on voting system seen as voter protest against the reforms imposed on the public by political and business elites
1993	• sale of New Zealand Rail (sale will lead to a further productivity increase over 2 years of 35%)
1994	• reformist finance minister Ruth Richardson leaves Parliament
1994	• Fiscal Responsibility Act obliges government to be transparent in its accounts and to adhere to the same accounting standards used in private companies • the operating surplus has to take account of the debt-servicing costs • government posts the first budget surplus in 17 years
1994	• government sets in train moves to abolish all remaining tariffs (the highest tariffs are to be no more than 15% by 2000)
1994	• Roger Douglas, with the support of business, launches a radically reformist political party (ACT) with a platform to complete the reforms of taxation and economic institutions and the aim of adopting a zero income tax

1995
- government spending reduced to 35% of GDP (down from 41% in 1990/91)
- budget surplus (nearly 4% of GDP and projected to rise to 7.3% by 1997/98) achieves a positive net asset position for the government

1996
- budget surplus allows the government to legislate a gradual reduction of the median personal income tax rate from 33% to 21%
- government also able to repay public debts faster

1996
- in an election under new "mixed member" electoral system, voters elect a National Party-led coalition committed to retaining the Employment Contracts Act; parties that promised to abrogate the ECA lose seats in parliament
- new coalition raises welfare spending, postpones income-tax cuts, and raises the minimum wage

1997
- the Labour minister announces a recasting of the ECA to strengthen the parallels with common contract law

Appendix 3
A tale of two cities: a microview of the workplace revolution

Statistical and other summary evidence is frequently less able to explain the genuine economic and social causes of productivity growth than case studies. Following is material from a carefully documented case study of changes in the workplace in the early 1990s in two plants belonging to the Fletcher Challenge group (McMorland, Hunter, and Woodcock 1993). The case study sheds light on the effects of the ECA in two plants—one in Christchurch, the other in Auckland—producing plasterboards and related building materials. It illustrates the profound change in the rules and institutional settings, as well as in the process, responsibilities and outcomes of industrial work.

The company, Winstone Wallboards Limited (WWL), was long-established and, like all New Zealand manufacturing, heavily union-dominated and subject to strict union demarcation of different jobs. It also enjoyed a monopoly in the domestic market. In the manufacturing shake-out of the 1980s, WWL had closed its plant in Wellington and what had long been a family company was taken over by Fletcher Challenge, a major conglomerate.

The workers were loyal to WWL, but their loyalty did not extend to a commitment to good work practices and high productivity. Workers and foremen paid little attention to training, quality control, and safety since the pressure of market competition was absent (McMorland, Hunter, and Woodcock 1993: 9). Workers operated long shifts to claim overtime pay and had no incentive to increase output.

Around the time the ECA became law in May 1991, both plants were due for a new wage agreement. In Christchurch, an energetic former production manager with the company took over the task of managing direct contacts with the workforce and established authority by dismissing a non-cooperative foreman and communicating directly with the workers. The workers understood that their plant might be closed and that cheap plasterboard would be coming in from Thailand. When the law changed, it was agreed to extend the wage structure from the old award for a year to gain a breathing space. There was much nervousness on both sides about the new challenge but management saw this as a chance to raise productivity and do away with deeply entrenched, counterproductive work practices. It was also decided at an early stage to opt for a plantwide contract, not individual contracts.

The workers soon decided that they would not entrust the contract negotiation to their old union, the Carpenters' Union. Nor did they take up a competitive bid for the negotiating task from the Engineers Union (McMorland, Hunter, and Woodcock 1993: 16), partly because they had resented compulsory union membership, and partly because they resented the demarcation of work imposed by the unions. A consultative committee was elected by the workers to negotiate a new wage contract that was subject, however, to a final vote by all workers. The production workers cleverly kept open their option of retaining a union as a bargaining agent. In the end, the negotiation established a basis wage, standards for skills and a "Gainsharing Plan" under which productivity improvements would be shared within teams of workers.

This contract was accepted by the workers, who immediately showed a direct interest in productivity. Since they were paid for output and no longer for their mere presence in the workplace, they did not maximize hours of labour input but concentrated on efficient performance of their jobs. All soon had the feeling that they were involved in a win-win process (18). The quantity of output went up, the speed of the production line was increased (41 metres of output per minute in 1991, 43 metres in 1992, 49 metres, a 15 percent increase over the previous year in 1993, and a further increase of 6 percent in 1994 (McMorland, Hunter, and Woodcock 1993: 34). The quality of output also improved, so that the firm switched to selling only grade A plasterboard. Workers were rotated among the jobs in the plant, adding interest to their work, workers with multiple skills became the norm, and the need for supervision decreased. A new contract in July 1993 was settled within one day.

In the Auckland plant, the process of change differed, as the workers opted for union negotiators, but also elected a representative consultative committee. There was considerable confusion and conflict, which the workers resented, between two unions in the negotiation. Managers did not do much to communicate; indeed management switched to a three-shift operation, depriving many workers of overtime income. Negotiations were at an impasse. However, the example of the success at Christchurch informed the negotiations and the basic format of the Christchurch enterprise contract was eventually replicated. When, after the negotiations, workers realized that they would increase their incomes, staff morale and productivity rose. Once a virtuous circle of productivity gain and higher wages was in place, the Auckland plant overtook Christchurch in productivity and product quality.

Acknowledgments

The essay was originally written at the invitation of Professor Horst Siebert, the President of the Institute of World Economics at Kiel, Germany. The research was sponsored by the Bertelsmann Foundation, the Heinz Nixdorf Foundation and the Ludwig-

Erhard-Foundation as part of a major research project, "The Social Market Economy—Challenges and Conceptual Response," which deals with the rejuvenation of the "social market economy," amongst other things, by reevaluating the role of government in labour markets and social welfare. The project is motivated by a concern that the institutional order that underpins the market economy and the rule of law have been eroded in Western democracies and that this has contributed to a spreading disillusionment with elected government as well as a loss of economic dynamism and the appearance of high unemployment.

After original publication in Germany (*Liberating Labour: The New Zealand Employment Contracts Act* [Kiel: Institute for World Economics, 1995]), an updated, slightly revised, version was published in Australia and New Zealand by the Centre for Independent Studies (*Free to Work: The Liberalisation of New Zealand's Labour Markets* [Sydney/Wellington: Centre for Independent Studies, 1996]). Andrew Norton of the Centre did some valuable editing work. This is a further update of that publication. The kind permission of the Bertelsmann Foundation to republish is gratefully acknowledged, and I wish to thank Mr Fazil Mihlar of The Fraser Institute for editorial assistance.

In preparing this study, I greatly appreciated the practical and friendly help I was given when in New Zealand. I had to draw heavily on the published and the unpublished work of others, who gave generously of their time and knowledge. Since this paper deals with structural reforms that have, as yet, not had the time to work themselves out fully, I have greatly benefited from the professional judgments and forecasts of experts in the field. In particular, I acknowledge the help of Her Excellency Ms Rosemary Banks, Deputy High Commissioner, NZ High Commission, Canberra, Australia; Ms Julie Fry, The Treasury (NZ), Wellington, New Zealand; Dr Jim Hagan, Manager, The Treasury (NZ), Wellington, New Zealand; Dr Viv Hall, Victoria University, Wellington, New Zealand; Professor Kevin Hince, Director, Industrial Relations Centre, Victoria University, Wellington, New Zealand; Mr Alan Jones, Fletcher Challenge Ltd., Auckland, New Zealand; Dr Peter Kenyon, Institute of Applied Economic and Social Research, Melbourne University, Melbourne, Australia; Mr Roger Kerr, New Zealand Business Roundtable, Wellington, New Zealand; Dr Tim Maloney, Economics Department, Auckland University, Auckland, New Zealand; Mr Steve Marshall, Chief Executive, NZ Employers'

Federation Inc., Wellington, New Zealand; Mr John Pask, Business Analyst, NZ Employers' Federation Inc., Wellington, New Zealand; Mr Greg Williamson, Saunders Unsworth, Wellington, New Zealand. Some were good enough to read through an earlier draft of this report and point out oversights, inaccuracies and errors of interpretation by this outsider. Possible errors and misreadings of the evidence remain, of course, exclusively my responsibility. Last, not least, I wish to thank the staff of The Fraser Institute for their interest and expedient assistance.

This chapter provides an analytical progress report on a remarkable but as yet incomplete experiment. One of the main messages of this study is that labour-market reform can only work to best effect within a framework of comprehensive economic reform and it begins, therefore, with a sketch of the overall reform program. It is not exhaustive, however, either as a study of the New Zealand economy or as a legal commentary on the new legislation and the reader whose curiosity goes beyond what is attempted here is referred to the References at the end.

Notes

1 This section has benefited from an unpublished survey paper by Keiran Murray (1994) and the monograph by Alan Bollard.
2 Australia and New Zealand have always had an integrated labour market with unrestricted mobility across the Tasman Sea (no restrictions on settlement or work for citizens of either country in the other), but product markets were separated by tariffs and quotas since New Zealand refused to join the proposed Australasian Federation of 1901. Only with the implementation of the Closer Economic Relationship (CER) free trade agreement in the late 1980s have product markets become as integrated as labour markets.
3 In this respect, the old industrial countries of the West differ fundamentally from the new industrial economies of east Asia, where governments have by and large abstained from "social justice interventions" in labour market, taxation, and social arrrangements. It is probably no coincidence that New Zealand, a front-line state in the competition with Asia, is one of the first mature Western societies to re-examine the fundamental belief underpinning the concept of the Western "mixed economy" or "social market economy" that goverments should intervene on equity grounds to correct market outcomes.

4 The Employment Tribunals continue the former Mediation and Conciliation Service. They are tax-financed, providing mediation assistance and adjudicating on differences in the interpretation of contract clauses. Tribunal decisions may be appealed in the Employment Court.
5 The Employment Tribunals and the Employment Court, which are staffed by the same officials who ran the old system, have at times tried to deviate from the spirit of the new contracting philosophy. Civil courts and competitive pressures in product markets are some protection against a relapse into the self-centred, special industrial relations rules of the past, but the Employment Court has repeatedly interpreted the ECA in ways that rely more on the collective memory of an arbitration system and less on the common-law spirit of the ECA.
6 Efforts to gain a collective statistical picture of the many diffuse labour markets are made by the Industrial Relations Centre at Victoria University, Wellington (e.g., Harbridge, Honeybone, and Kiely 1994; Hince and Harbridge 1994) and occasional surveys by the Department of Labour (1994). The secretary of Labour asks to be informed of collective contracts covering 20 or more employees for statistical purposes but, since there are no sanctions, some employers treat employment contracts as private and do not report
7 This evidence in not quite reconcilable with the results of surveys done by the Industrial Relations Centre at Victoria University on behalf of, and financed by, trade unions (Harbridge 1993).
8 The most obvious differences between the two countries are population (New Zealand, 3.5 millions; Australia, 17.7 millions) and living standards (at purchase-power parity, in 1993 New Zealand had a percapita income of US$15,390; Australia, of US$18,490). Source: World Bank World Tables 1995.
9 Some knowledgable observers believe that employment statistics under-report employment growth since the introduction of the ECA (Maloney 1994a: 340).

References

ACIL Economics and Policy (1994). *What Future for New Zealand's Minimum Wage Law?* Mimeograph. Canberra, AU: ACIL.

Bascand, P., and S. Frawley (1991). Possible Consequences of the Employment Contracts Act for People with Disabilities. *New Zealand Journal of Industrial Relations* 16, 4: 309–15.

Bollard, A. (1992). *New Zealand 1984–1991.* San Francisco, CA: International Centre for Economic Growth Press.

Bollard, A., and R. Buckle, eds. (1987). *Economic Liberalisation in New Zealand*. Wellington, NZ: Allen & Unwin.

Bollard, A., and D. Mayes (1991) *Corporatisation and Privatisation in New Zealand*. Working Paper 91/16, New Zealand Institute of Economic Research, Wellington.

Bollard, A., R. Lattimore, and B. Silverstone, eds. (1996). *A Study of Economic Reform: The Case of New Zealand*. Amsterdam: North Holland.

Boston, J. (1992). Redesigning New Zealand's Welfare State. In J. Boston and P. Dalziel (eds.), *The Decent Society? Essays in Response to National's Economic and Social Policies* (Auckland, NZ: Oxford University Press): 1–18.

Boxall, P. (1991). New Zealand's Employment Contracts Act 1991: An Analysis of Background, Provisions and Implications. *Australian Bulletin of Labour* 17, 4: 284–309.

Boxall, P., ed. (1995). *The Challenge of Human Resource Management*, Auckland, NZ: Longman Paul

Bradford, M. (1997). What Happens Next? Keynote address by the minister of Labour to the Annual Industrial Relations Conference, Wellington (March 3). Mimeograph. Wellington: Department of Labour.

Brook, P. (1989). Reform of the Labour Market. In S. Walker (ed.), *Rogernomics: Reshaping New Zealand's Economy* (Auckland, NZ: New Zealand Centre for Independent Studies): 183–207.

——— (1990). *Freedom at Work: The Case for Reforming Labour Law in New Zealand*. Auckland, NZ: Oxford University Press.

——— (1991). New Zealand's Employment Contracts Act: An Incomplete Revolution. *Policy* 7, 3 (Spring): 6–11.

Brosnan, P., and D. Rea (1991). An Adequate Minimum Code: A Basis for Freedom, Justice and Efficiency in the Labour Market. *New Zealand Journal of Industrial Relations* 16, 3: 143–58.

Brown, C., C. Gilroy, and A. Kohen (1982). The Effect of the Minimum Wage on Employment and Unemployment. *Journal of Economic Literature* 20 (June): 487–528.

Buchanan, J. (1975) *The Limits of Liberty: Between Ananarchy and Leviathan*. Chicago: Chicago University Press.

Crocombe, G.T., M.J. Enright, and M.E. Porter (1991). *Upgrading New Zealand's Competitive Advantage*. Auckland, NZ: Oxford University Press.

Cumming, J.M. (1988) A Theoretical and Empirical Analysis of Minimum Wage Legislation and Its Impact on Low Pay: A New Zealand Perspective. MA thesis, University of Auckland.

Deane, R. (1991) *Reflections on Privatisation*. Sydney, AU: Centre for Independent Studies.

Deeks, J., R. Parker, and R. Ryan (1994). *Labour and Employment Relations in New Zealand*. Auckland, NZ: Longman Paul.

Department of Labour, New Zealand (1994). *Contract: The Report on Current Industrial Relations in New Zealand* (vol. 8). Wellington, NZ: Department of Labour.

Douglas, R. (1982). *Toward Prosperity*. Auckland, NZ: D. Bateman.

——— (1990). Ten Principles of Successful Structural Reform. *Policy* 6, 1 (Autumn): 2–6.

Easton, B., ed. (1989). *The Making of Rogernomics*. Auckland, NZ: Auckland University Press.

Enderwick, P. (1992). Workplace Reform and International Competitiveness: The Case of New Zealand. *New Zealand Journal of Industrial Relations* 17, 2: 185–206.

Epstein, R.A. (1992). *Forbidden Grounds: The Case Against Employment Discrimination Laws*. Cambridge, MA: Harvard University Press.

Evans, L., A Grimes, B. Wilkinson, B. Teece (1996). Economic Reform in New Zealand, 1984–95: The Pursuit of Efficiency. *Journal of Economic Literature* 34, 4 (December): 1856–1902.

Garvey, G. (1994). *The Market for Employment*. Sydney, AU: Centre for Independent Studies.

Geare, A.J. (1989) New Directions in New Zealand Labour Legislation. *International Labour Review* 128, 2: 213–28.

Gibbs, A. (1990) Obstacles to Progress in New Zealand. *Policy* 6, 4 (Summer): 13–17.

Gorman, L. (1993). Minimum Wages. In D.R. Henderson (ed.), *The Fortune Encyclopedia of Economics* (New York: Warner Books): 499–503.

Gould, J. (1985). *The Muldoon Years: An Essay on New Zealand's Recent Economic Growth*. Auckland, NZ: Hodder and Stoughton.

Hall, V.B. (1996). Economic Growth. In A. Bollard, R. Lattimore, and B. Silverstone (eds.), *A Study of Economic Reform: The Case of New Zealand* (Amsterdam: North Holland): 97–117.

Hansen, E., and D. Margaritis (1993). Financial Liberalisation and Monetary Policy in New Zealand. *The Australian Economic Review* 4: 28–36.

Harbridge, R. (1991). Collective Bargaining in New Zealand: Impact of the Employment Contracts Bill. *Australian Bulletin of Labour* 17, 4: 310–24.

———, ed. (1993). *Employment Contracts: New Zealand*. Wellington, NZ: Victoria University Press.

Harbridge, R., and A. Honeybone (1994). The Employment Contracts Act and Collective Bargaining Patterns: A Review of the 1993/94 Year. In R. Harbridge, A. Honeybone, and P. Kiely, *Employment Contracts: Bargaining Trends and Employment Law Update: 1993/94* (Wellington, NZ: Industrial Relations Centre): 1–8.

Harding, D., P. Kenyon, R. Blandy, and V. Hall (1994). Unemployment in the Short and Long Run. Report prepared for the New Zealand Treasury. Melbourne, AU: Institute for Economic and Social Research.

Hartley, P. (1992). The Effects of Minimum Wage Laws on Labour Markets. In H.R. Nicholls Society, *The New Province of Law and Order* (Melbourne, AU: H.R. Nicholls Society): 32–50.

Hawke, G.R. (1985) *The Making of New Zealand: An Economic History*. Cambridge: Cambridge University Press.

Hince, K., and R. Harbridge (1994) The Employment Contracts Act: An Interim Assessment. Mimeograph. Wellington, NZ: Industrial Relations Centre, Victoria University.

Howard, C. (1995). *Interpretation of the Employment Contracts Act*. Wellington, NZ: New Zealand Business Roundtable and New Zealand Employers Federation.

IMEDE-World Economic Forum (1989). *The World Competitiveness Report 1989*. Geneva-Lausanne: IMEDE-WEF.

International Management Development-World Economic Forum (1994). *The World Competitiveness Report 1994*. Geneva-Lausanne: IMD-WEF.

International Labour Organisation (1994). Case No. 1698, Complaint against the Government of New Zealand presented by the New Zealand Council of Trade Unions (NZCTU). Geneva: ILO.

James, C. (1992) *New Territory: The Transformation of New Zealand 1984–92*. Wellington, NZ: Bridget Williams.

James, M. (1997). New Zealand's Reforms—the Next Stage: Michael James Interviews Sir Roger Douglas. *Institute for Public Affairs Review* 49, 3 (March): 7–8.

Jones, A. (1991). Transition: Labour Relations in New Zealand in the 1980s and 1990s. Mimeograph. Paper delivered to the H.R. Nicholls Society, Adelaide, 21 September.

——— (1992). What are We Afraid of? The Employment Contracts Act: A Personal View. Mimeograph.

——— (1993a). The New Zealand Experience. Mimeograph. Paper delivered at the Australian Industrial Commission Conference on Australian Industrial Relations, Sydney, 17 February.

——— (1993b). The Overturning of Employment Court Decisions. *The Dominion*, 12 August: 8.

——— (1994). New Zealand Labour Market. *Benefits and Compensation International* 24, 1 (July/August): 2–7.

Kasper, W. (1985). *The Destruction and Creation of Jobs*. Perth, AU: Australian Institute of Public Policy.

——— (1990). *Populate or Languish? Rethinking New Zealand's Immigration Policy*. Wellington, NZ: New Zealand Business Roundtable.

——— (1991). *Globalization, Locational Innovation and East Asian Development*. No. PB91-024. San Francisco, CA: Center for Pacific Basin Monetary and Economic Studies, Federal Reserve Bank of San Francisco.

―――― (1996). Responsibility and Reform: A Conversation with Ruth Richardson. *Policy* 12, 3: 25–31.
Kenyon, P. (1993). The New Zealand Experiment: Introduction. *The Australian Economic Review* 4: 5–9.
Kerr, R. (1994). Looking Back Together. Mimeograph. Speech at Tasman Institute, 22 November 1994. Wellington, NZ: New Zealand Business Roundtable.
Kerr, R. (1995). A Job Half Done, Economic Reform in Australia and New Zealand. Mimeograph. Address to the Australian Stock Exchange's Annual Dinner (26 June).
Layard, R., S. Nickell, and R. Jackman (1991). *Unemployment: Macroeconomic Performance and the Labour Market.* Oxford: Oxford University Press.
Maloney, T. (1993). Estimating the Effects of the Employment Contracts Act on Aggregate Employment and Average Wages in New Zealand. Mimeograph. Auckland, NZ: Department of Economics, University of Auckland.
―――― (1994a). Does the Adult Minimum Wage Affect Employment and Unemployment in New Zealand. Working Papers in Economics No. 137. Auckland, NZ: Department of Economics, University of Auckland.
―――― (1994b). Estimating the Effects of the Employment Contracts Act on Employment and Wages in New Zealand. *Australian Bulletin of Labour* 20, 4: 320–343.
―――― (1994c). Has New Zealand's Employment Contracts Act Increased Employment and Reduced Wages? Working Papers in Economics No. 135. Auckland, NZ: Department of Economics, University of Auckland.
Marshall, S. (1994). The Impact of the Employment Contracts Act. *Economic Alert* 5, 6: 1–4.
McMillan, J. (1994). Report on New Zealand: Kiwis Can Fly—Reforming New Zealand's Economy. *International Economic Insights* 5,1 (January/February): 39–41.
McMorland, I., B. Hunter, and B. Woodcock (1993). *Enterprising Change, Changes in Work Practices Following the Employment Contracts Act (1991) at Winstone Wallboards Limited.* Auckland, NZ: Fletcher Challenge.
Minford, P. (1993). Review Article: Has Labour Market Economics Achieved a Synthesis? *Economic Journal* 103, 419 (July): 1050–156.
Murray, K. (1994). Evolution of Economic and Social Policy Environment and Consequences for Employment and Unemployment: 1950–1994. Paper submitted to the Prime Ministerial Taskforce on Employment (Wellington). Mimeograph.
Myers, D. (1990). Reforming New Zealand's Labour Market. *Policy* 6,3 (Spring): 6–11.

Myers, D. (1995). *Moving into the Fast Lane.* Mimeograph. Address to the Auckland Chambers of Commerce. Wellington, NZ: New Zealand Business Roundtable.

New Zealand Business Roundtable (1986). *New Zealand Labour Market Reform.* Wellington, NZ: NZBR.

——— (1987). *Why New Zealand Needs a Flexible, Decentralised Labour Market.* Wellington, NZ: NZBR.

——— (1988). *Employment Equity: Issues of Competition and Regulation.* Wellington, NZ: NZBR.

——— (1990). *Choice in the Workplace: A Better Framework for Labour Law.* Wellington, NZ: NZBR.

——— (1991). *Building a Competitive Economy.* Wellington, NZ: NZBR.

——— (1992). *From Accession to Recovery.* Wellington, NZ: NZBR.

——— (1993). *Towards an Enterprise Culture.* Wellington, NZ: NZBR.

——— (1994). *The Next Decade of Change.* Wellington, NZ: NZBR.

New Zealand Business Roundtable and New Zealand Employers' Federation (1992). *A Study of the Labour/Employment Court.* Wellington, NZ: NZBR/NZEF.

New Zealand Council of Trade Unions (1991). *Labour Market Reform and Economic Recovery: Impact of the Employment Contracts Bill.* Mimeograph. Wellington, NZ: NZCTU.

New Zealand Government (1994). *New Zealand Government's Response to the Interim Conclusions of the Freedom of Associations Committee.* Mimeograph. Wellington, NZ: Department of Labour.

Organisation for Economic Cooperation and Development (1989). *Economic Survey of New Zealand 1988/89.* Paris: OECD.

——— (1991). *Economic Survey of New Zealand 1990/91.* Paris: OECD.

——— (1994). *The Job Report.* Paris: OECD.

Papageorgiu, D., A. Choski, and M. Michaely (1990). *Liberalising Foreign Trade in Developing Countries: The Lessons from Experience.* Washington, DC: The World Bank.

Prebble, M., and P. Rebstock (1992). *Incentives and Labour Supply: Modelling Taxes and Benefits.* Wellington, NZ: Institute of Policy Studies.

Prebble, R. (1996). *I've Been Thinking.* Auckland, NZ: Seaview Publishing.

Prime Ministerial Taskforce on Employment (1994). *Employment: The Issues.* 2 vols. Wellington, NZ: Prime Ministerial Taskforce on Employment.

Richardson, R. (1995). *Making a Difference.* Christchurch, NZ: Shoal Bay.

Savage, J., and A. Bollard, eds. (1990). *Turning it Around: Closure and Revitalisation of New Zealand Industry.* Auckland, NZ: Oxford University Press.

Schwab, K., and J.D. Sachs (1996). *The Global Competitiveness Report 1996.* Geneva: World Economic Forum.

Silverstone, B., and B. Daldy (1993). Recent Labour Market and Industrial Relations Experience in New Zealand. *The Australian Economic Review* 4: 17–22.

Sloan, J. (1994). Towards Full Employment in New Zealand. Mimeograph. Wellington, NZ: New Zealand Business Roundtable.

Stigler, G. (1946). The Economics of Minimum Wage Legislation. *American Economic Review* 36: 358–65.

St John, S. (1993). Tax and Welfare Reforms in New Zealand. *The Australian Economic Review* 4: 37–42.

Treasury of New Zealand (1990). Briefing the Incoming Government 1990. Wellington, NZ: The Treasury.

Trotter, R. (1989). Making Individuals Count. *Policy* 5, 4 (Summer): 54–58.

Walker, S., ed. (1989). *Rogernomics: Reshaping New Zealand's Economy*. Wellington, NZ: GP Books (for Centre for Independent Studies).

Williamson, O. (1985). *The Economic Institutions of Capitalism*. New York: Free Press.

Woodfield, A., and D. Smyth (1991). How to Reduce New Zealand's Unemployment. *Policy* (Spring): 11–13.

Critique of Alberta's Right-to-Work Study

FAZIL MIHLAR

In March 1995, motion 503 was introduced in the Alberta Legislature by the member of the legislative assembly for Peace River, Gary Friedel. This motion urged the provincial government to study the economic benefits of Right-to-Work legislation. The motion passed. The Joint Review Committee, Right-to-Work Study, was formed by the Alberta Economic Development Authority (AEDA) to examine the issue of Right-to-Work and its potential economic impact upon Alberta. The AEDA's Joint Review Committee released its study on November 30, 1995; it did not recommend the implementation of Right-to-Work laws in Alberta, concluding that Alberta already had a competitive economic regime (see Alberta Economic Development Authority [AEDA] 1995b: iii–v). However, while Alberta's economic regime is competitive when compared to other Canadian jurisdictions (see appendix A), it is *not* competitive when compared to American states. When one assesses the committee's report in the light of the available evidence, one can readily see why the AEDA's conclusions were misguided.

Alberta's labour regime

About 25 percent of Alberta's workforce is unionized. In the private sector, 13 percent of the employees belong to a union. In the public sector, 60 percent of the employees belong to unions subject either to provincial or to federal labour legislation. Approximately 25 percent of employees are public sector workers employed by provincial and municipal governments, school boards, health authorities, or firms in federally regulated industries like transportation, communications, and utilities. The Alberta Labour Relations Code (ALRC) applies to approximately 70 percent of all unionized employees in the private sector but not to provincial or federal government employees, farm or domestic workers, managers, labour relations staff, or anyone working in industries regulated by the federal government (AEDA 1995a).

Private sector unionism in Alberta is structured and regulated by the ALRC. Section 27 of the ALRC specifies that employers and unions are free to enter into an agreement whereby all employees are required to be union members. A union that gets a majority of workers' votes in a certification election becomes the exclusive bargaining agent for all of the workers in a bargaining unit. Thus, on matters that come under the scope of collective bargaining, individual workers are not allowed to represent themselves and each worker is forced to accept the representation services of the exclusive bargaining agent. Most labour agreements have a union security clause. Where the union security clause is absent, the plant is commonly referred to as an open shop. Where a union security clause is included, the plant can be either a closed shop, or a Rand-formula shop. In Alberta, according to a survey, 45 percent of unionized firms have closed-shop provisions and 48 percent have Rand-formula provisions (AEDA 1995a).

Under the ALRC, exclusive representation means that workers are not free, on an individual basis, to decide whether to be represented by a union, and also that there cannot be competing unions offering representation services to minorities. Union security contracts negotiated under the ALRC stipulate that individuals who are subsequently employed in a particular firm are not free to opt out of union membership or the payment of union dues. Therefore, union security contracts cannot be called voluntary-exchange contracts.

Analysis of the AEDA's conclusions

Conclusion 1 Alberta compares favourably with other Canadian provinces in economic terms. Alberta's employment growth has been four times faster than that of the other provinces in recent years (AEDA 1995b: iv).

Critique Comparing Alberta only with other Canadian provinces is inappropriate and misleading. As the Committee's report acknowledges, the United States is Alberta's largest trading partner. Thus, appropriate comparisons should include job creation statistics in neighbouring American states, since the comparison should be trade-weighted and not focused only on the performance of other Canadian provinces. The export sector is vital for Alberta's economic health, given that exports comprise 40 percent of the province's GDP (CIBC Wood Gundy 1995: 29). We should, therefore, compare Alberta to American jurisdictions, rather than to just other Canadian provinces.

As table 1 indicates, neighbouring American states with flexible labour regimes (i.e., Right-to-Work laws) have out-performed Alberta in terms of job creation during the last few years.

Table 1 Employment Growth (in percent) by selected industry sectors in Alberta and American states (1992 to 1994)

Sector	Alberta	Arizona	Idaho	Nevada	Utah
Construction	4.4	36.2	32.4	40.3	37.8
Manufacturing	6.1	11.2	9.8	28.7	8.8
Transportation and utilities	8.1	5.3	7.8	14.5	21.5
Finance, insurance, and real estate	3.5	17.1	12.0	17.5	23.6
Services	n/a	12.8	13.9	15.8	14.6
Total (all industries)	4.0	11.0	11.0	15.2	12.0

n/a: not available
Note: Arizona, Idaho, Nevada, and Utah have Right-to-Work laws (voluntary unions). Most importantly, these states disallow closed-shop unions.
Sources: Alberta Department of Education and Career Development, *Labour Force Statistics by Industry, Alberta*, 1995; U.S. Department of Labour, *Employment and Earnings*, Vol. 42, No.5, May 1995; and author's own calculations.

Right-to-Work states offer firms a business environment free of the many regulations imposed by labour unions that raise costs, while non-Right-to-Work states raise the cost of hiring more employees. As a result, businesses in Right-to-Work states have lower costs, allowing them to produce goods and services competitively and to employ more people. Contrary to the Committee's claim that Alberta has performed well with respect to job creation, the evidence shows that its performance is not nearly so good as that of its major trading partners.

The evidence shows that there has been a dramatic increase in manufacturing activity in Right-to-Work states. Between 1947 and 1992, manufacturing employment increased by 148 percent in Right-to-Work states. Over the same period, growth in manufacturing employment was almost zero in non-Right-to-Work states. If we look at manufacturing employment per 100 inhabitants, a similar pattern emerges. In 1947, Right-to-Work states had 6 manufacturing employees per 100 inhabitants and non-Right-to-Work states had 12 per 100, double that of Right-to-Work states. By 1992, both the Right-to-Work states and the non-Right-to-Work states had 7 manufacturing employees per 100 inhabitants. In 1992, manufacturing constituted 21 percent of total employment in the counties of non-Right-to-Work states within 25 miles of the border while, in the counties of the Right-to-Work states within 25 miles of the border, manufacturing employment accounted for 28.6 percent of total employment. Indeed, on average, manufacturing employment increases by one-third when we move from a non-Right-to-Work state to a Right-to-Work state (Holmes 1995: 1–3).

Table 2 shows the number of manufacturing jobs in Right-to-Work states as opposed to non-Right-to-Work states.

Table 2 Average number of manufacturing jobs (in thousands) between 1960 and 1993

	1960	1993	Change	% Change
Right-to-Work States	166.7	296.1	129.4	77.6
Non-Right-to-Work States	441.2	395.0	-46.8	-10.6

Source: Cited in Robert Anders, *The Economic Benefits of Voluntary Unionism: A Report for the Joint Review Committee, Right-To-Work Study of the Alberta Economic Development Authority*, Calgary, Alberta: Canadians Against Forced Unionism, August, 1995.

Right-to-Work states have attracted more investment, have higher economic growth rates and have created more jobs than non-Right-to-Work states (for a detailed examination of the evidence, see Mihlar 1995). The Committee, however, managed either to ignore the evidence or simply to dismiss it with statements such as "the rate of unemployment is unaffected by Right-to-Work legislation" (1995b: iv).

Conclusion 2 Experience in the United States would indicate that employment and business growth may be helped by Right-to-Work legislation, but "RTW legislation in and of itself does not create a competitive advantage nor would it cure a competitive disadvantage" (AEDA 1995b: 34).

Critique One-factor explanations in social sciences, especially in economic relationships, are tenuous at best. In most instances, several variables impinge upon outcomes like positive economic growth and higher levels of employment. These factors include: lower payroll taxes, lower income taxes, fewer regulations, a labour regime unencumbered by rigid rules and, finally, the perceived and real costs of doing business (Gwartney and Stroup 1993: 59–61).

The purpose of the labour code and related labour regulations should be to make Albertans, including labour, economically better-off by fostering a prosperous economy. Alberta policy-makers concerned about wealth and job creation need to recognize the basic factors that determine high levels of economic activity.

In the *Wealth of Nations*, Adam Smith pointed out that real riches come from the power of production and supply, not gold collected through the accumulation of a trade surplus (Smith 1776/1965). John Maynard Keynes also argued persuasively that investment is determined by the expectations and "animal spirits" of investors (Keynes 1964: 46–51, 147–64). The crucial source of initiative in any economic system is investment: economies do not grow of their own accord or by government fiat but rather as the result of the enterprise of men and women willing to take risks and transform ideas into products, and products into industry. Indeed, it is ambition and resolve that foster, enterprise and growth. An economic regime that has either a perceived or a real high relative cost of doing business will bring certain kinds of efforts to a halt (Gilder 1981: 170–89), since the expectations of investors determine growth in investment, the economy, and employment.

The imposition of regulatory measures upon the labour market that are more costly than those adopted by Alberta's trading partners, particularly the United States, will induce firms to find more "business-friendly" jurisdictions in which to locate their business operations. In addition, firms substitute capital for labour when the cost of labour is relatively high (Chamie 1995; Parker 1995).

New technologies, more open markets, and changing patterns of world trade are key features of the current global economy. They are reflected in the development of the North American Free Trade Agreement, the European Union, and similar trade liaisons in Australia, New Zealand and Asia. Alberta's small open economy is dependent upon trade and cannot insulate itself from these global changes. Alberta's industries face heavy competition from other jurisdictions both for investment capital and for human resources. In a global economy characterized by falling transportation and communications costs as well as by freer trade, capital is increasingly mobile. Firms will locate or re-locate to jurisdictions that impose a minimum of costly regulations, including constraints upon the labour market (see Gunderson 1992; Hunsley 1993).

The Committee's report does say, however, that Right-to-Work states are attracting new businesses. Indeed, it goes further and, having asked the question: what effect has Right-to-Work legislation had on employment and business growth in the United States, answers that the effect is wholly positive (AEDA 1995b: 21). According to the evidence on job growth, Right-to-Work laws, along with other factors such as lower tax rates, have created more jobs in the Right-to-Work states than have been created in the non-Right-to-Work states.

A recent study by Thomas J. Holmes of the Federal Reserve Bank of Minneapolis (1995) concludes that there is a discontinuous drop in manufacturing activity when crossing from a Right-to-Work state to a non-Right-to-Work state. The Holmes paper attempts to isolate the factors that cause economic growth and job creation. Holmes classifies a state as "pro-business" if it has a Right-to-Work law and as "anti-business" if the state does not have Right-to-Work laws. The basis for selecting Right-to-Work laws is that Right-to-Work laws provide flexibility to firms and weaken union power. States that have Right-to-Work laws also tend to adopt a variety of pro-business policies such as lower levels of taxation and fewer regulations.

Surveys indicate that states with Right-to-Work laws are more friendly towards business. The Fantus Company rankings (see table 3) were based on 15 factors including, the existence of Right-to-Work laws, corporate and income taxes, and unemployment insurance payments (see Weinstein and Firestine 1978). Indeed, among the top 20 states ranked as having the best climate for business, 19 of them are Right-to-Work states. Many other surveys such as those conducted by Area Development Magazine and the centre for Business and Economic Research of the University of Tennessee, also suggest that Right-to-Work laws are an important component of a pro-business climate (see Bennett 1994; National Institute for Labour Relations Research [NILRR] 1994b). Therefore, Right-to-Work laws, considered along with other factors serve as a good proxy for a pro-business legislative climate.

Table 3 Fantus legislative business climate rankings

Rankings	State	Does the state have Right-to-Work laws?
1	Texas	yes
2	Alabama	yes
3	Virginia	yes
4	South Dakota	yes
5	South Carolina	yes
6	North Carolina	yes
7	Florida	yes
8	Arkansas	yes
9	Indiana	no (had a RTW law until 1965)
10	Utah	yes
11	North Dakota	yes
12	Mississippi	yes
13	Georgia	yes
14	Iowa	yes
15	Tennessee	yes
16	Arizona	yes
17	Nebraska	yes
18	Colorado	yes
19	Missouri	yes
20	Kansas	yes

Source: Weinstein and Firestine (1978): 137.

Conclusion 3 "There is, however, a broader issue of Alberta's overall competitive advantage, especially as it relates to the U.S. The fact that Alberta does indeed enjoy some international competitive advantages is [not] particularly well known" (AEDA 1995b: v).

Critique Alberta does appear to possess a competitive advantage from having the lowest overall tax burden in the country. Nevertheless, although Alberta performs well relative to other Canadian provinces, it does not perform well when compared to competing jurisdictions in the United States. Alberta's per-capita taxes are CDN$634 higher than the average of the neighbouring ten states, including California, Oregon, Wyoming, Utah, and Idaho (see table 4; Alberta Tax Reform Commission 1994). Using tax rates as one measure of competitiveness, Alberta does not appear to have a competitive tax regime when compared with its trading partners.

Table 4   Provincial and state tax rates for Alberta and selected American states (1994-95)

Taxes	Alberta	Washington	Oregon	Nevada	Wyoming
Income tax (range; %)	8–14.5	no tax	5–9	no tax	no tax
Corporation tax (%)	15.5	no tax	6.6	no tax	no tax
Sales tax (%)	no tax	6.5	no tax	6.5	4
Gasoline (¢/gal.)	9¢	23¢	24¢	24¢	9¢

Sources: Stephen Moore and Dean Stansel, "A Fiscal Policy Report Card on America's Governors: 1994," Washington: Cato Institute, 1994; and CIBC Wood Gundy, "1996 Provincial Profiles," Toronto: CIBC Wood Gundy, 1995.

Conclusion #4   Right-to-Work legislation has no effect on the incidence of strikes and lockouts (ADEA 1995b: 27).

Critique   This conclusion is disproven by evidence from the United Kingdom and New Zealand. Right-to-Work laws did help reduce the level and scope of strikes and lockouts in these countries. The United Kingdom under Prime Minister Margaret Thatcher initiated a series of reforms (voluntary unions) that resulted in the lowest level of strike activity since 1893 (for a detailed examination, see Hanson 1991). As table 4 illustrates, in 1979, a high of 30 million working days were lost due to strikes in the United Kingdom. By 1994, however, only 278,000 working days were lost due to strikes. By 1994, the total number of work stoppages on average had fallen from 2,000 per year to 205. The number of working days lost per 1,000 employees fell from 265 in 1975 to only 13 by 1994 (Bird and Davies 1995: 280).

Table 4 Strike activity and work stoppages in the United Kingdom from 1979 to 1994

Year	Working days lost (000s)	Working days lost per 1,000 employees	Workers involved (000s)	Stoppages
1979	29,474	1,273	4,608	2,125
1980	11,964	521	834	1,348
1981	4,266	195	1,513	1,344
1982	5,313	248	2,103	1,538
1983	3,754	178	574	1,364
1984	27,135	1,278	1,464	1,221
1985	6,402	299	791	903
1986	1,920	90	720	1,074
1987	3,546	164	887	1,016
1988	3,702	166	790	781
1989	4,128	182	727	701
1990	1,903	83	298	630
1991	761	34	176	369
1992	528	24	148	253
1993	649	30	385	211
1994	278	13	107	205

Source: Bird and Davies 1995.

In the case of New Zealand, the following table clearly illustrates that, by 1993, strike activity had reached its lowest level since 1921.

Table 5 Work stoppages in New Zealand for selected years between 1921 and 1993

Year	Total stoppages	Workers involved	Working days lost
1921	77	10,433	119,208
1926	59	6,264	47,811
1931	24	5,356	48,486
1936	43	7,354	16,980
1941	89	15,261	26,237
1946	96	15,696	30,393
1951	109	36,878	1,157,390
1956	50	13,579	23,870
1961	71	16,626	38,185
1966	145	33,132	99,095
1971	313	86,009	162,563
1976	487	201,085	488,441
1981	291	135,006	388,086
1986	215	100,633	1,329,054
1991	71	51,962	99,032
1992	54	26,803	113,742
1993	58	21,303	23,770

Source: New Zealand Official Yearbook 1995: 339.

The evidence suggests that Right-to-Work laws reduce strike activity, contrary to the conclusions reached by the Committee.

Conclusion 5 The evidence suggests that unions raise rather than reduce productivity (AEDA 1995b: 25).

Critique This conclusion is contrary to the empirical evidence provided by studies such as that of Professor Richard Long (1993) that shows that unionized firms tend to be less productive than non-unionized firms. Long studied 510 Canadian firms during the period from 1980 to 1985, and found that the median growth rate of non-union firms during this period was 27 percent in the manufacturing sector and 13.5 percent in the non-manufacturing sector. The median growth rate in unionized firms in the same sectors was zero. Long also made adjustments to his analysis to account for the fact unionized firms tend to be larger than non-unionized firms and engaged in declining industries. Even after these adjustments, his conclusions were that unionized firms grew 3.7 percent slower in manufacturing and 3.9 percent slower in the non-manufacturing sector (Long 1993: 691–703).

Closed-shop unions and high levels of unionization lead to labour-market rigidity and lower levels of productivity. Indeed, there is some evidence that, on average, unionized firms earn lower returns, have lower market value and earnings and are less productive than non-union firms operating in comparable industries (see Becker and Olson 1986; Maki and Meredith 1986; Hirsh 1991; Boal and Pencavel 1994). Moreover, rigid labour contracts drawn up under closed-shop conditions impede an employer's ability to adapt the mix of capital and labour in response to changing market conditions. Foreign and local investors find it more profitable to invest in jurisdictions more friendly to business and, although it is difficult to quantify the opportunity costs (foregone investment) and loss of jobs associated with rigid labour-market regulations, the costs are real. Foregone investment represents lost employment and lost wealth creation opportunities.

A recent study by the McKinsey Global Institute concluded that the main reason for high unemployment among some of the countries in the Organization for Economic Cooperation and Development continues to be government restrictions upon the labour market (cited in Reason Foundation 1995: 9). Interventions that restrict the labour market almost always have the unintended effects of reducing labour-market flexibility and impeding the labour-market adjustment process. The Organization for Economic Cooperation and Development (OECD) *Jobs Study* released last year concluded that government regulations affecting labour markets have been the primary source of labour market rigidity, reduced competitiveness, and slower rates of employment growth over the past two decades (OECD 1994). In short, labour market regulations that introduce more rigidity into the marketplace tend to reduce productivity.

Conclusion 6 In reference to the evidence presented on Idaho's strong economic performance, the Committee concluded on the basis of an intervention from the AFL/CIO that Idaho's economic resurgence was "part of the regional economic boom in the pacific Northwest states" (AFL/CIO 1994). The conclusion of the Committee was that Right-to-Work legislation was not directly responsible for Idaho's economic resurgence (AEDA 1995b: 20).

Critique Idaho has had a boom in economic activity that is reflected by high rates of personal income growth, low levels of unemployment, and a dramatic increase in business starts (NILRR 1994a). The reality is that, although the pacific Northwest states have been experiencing an economic boom, there appears to be a clear dividing line between the Right-to-Work states such as Nevada, Idaho, Utah and Wyoming—which saw their manufacturing job growth rise by 32.9 percent, 32.8 percent, 20.1 percent and 18.8 percent, respectively—and those states of the pacific Northwest that did not have Right-to-Work laws. In the latter states, Washington, Montana, Oregon and Colorado, manufacturing job growth rose 11.8 percent, 8.0 percent, 7.2 percent and 1.6 percent, respectively. Between 1986 and 1993, the Right-to-Work states saw an average manufacturing job growth rate of 26 percent while non-Right-to-Work states experienced an average growth rate of 7.0 percent (Wall Street Journal 1995). It is quite evident that the economic boom has had a disproportionately larger impact on Right-to-Work states than on non-Right-to-Work states. Once again, the conclusion reached by the Committee is erroneous.

Conclusion 7 Based on a study done by KPMG Management Consulting (1995) for the United States Trade and Investment division of the (Canadian) department of Foreign Affairs and International Trade, the Committee concluded that it costs less to do business in Canada than the United States (AEDA 1995b: 22–24).

Critique: KPMG's study analyzed 15 cities, 7 in the United States and 8 in Canada. It looked at several location-sensitive cost factors, including labour costs, electricity costs, federal and local taxes. KPMG used CDN$1.41 as the exchange rate, which of course puts Canada at a competitive advantage though they claim that the comparison would hold true if an exchange rate of CDN$1.22 had been used. The use of KPMG's study to conclude that it costs less to do business in Canadian cities as opposed to American cities is misleading, however, since the study included only two cities from Right-to-Work states in its sample of 7 American cities. Using this particular study for comparative purposes, therefore, is meaningless.

Conclusion

Positive economic benefits have accrued to jurisdictions that have implemented Right-to-Work laws and Right-to-Work legislation is an important element in creating an attractive business climate. A fundamental reform of labour laws in Alberta would make existing producers more competitive in domestic and export markets, and would stimulate the investment and job creation that would benefit all Albertans. If Alberta were to adopt Right-to-Work laws, it could become a magnet for job-creating investment from other parts of the world and it would be better able to compete with its major trading partners in the United States.

Labour-market flexibility is an important factor in the equation for economic prosperity. Currently, Alberta's labour code inhibits flexibility in labour markets, reduces incentives for increasing productivity, and increases the costs of production. The labour market needs to be reformed and flexibility in wages and in conditions of employment need to be introduced. By thus improving the efficiency of labour markets, impetus will be given to increased economic activity and wealth creation. In the final analysis, the Committee's decision and, by extension, the government of Alberta's decision will hinder Alberta's growth and all Albertans will feel its negative impacts.

Appendix A
Major tax rates (1995)

	AB	BC	SK	MB	ON	PQ	NB	NS	PE	NF
Personal Income Tax (%)										
Basic Rate	45.5	52.5	50.0	52.0	58.0	n/a	64.0	59.5	59.5	69.0
Top Marginal Rate (federal and provincial, incl. surtaxes)	46.1	54.2	51.9	50.4	53.2	52.9	51.4	50.3	50.3	51.3
Corporate Income Tax (%)										
Small Business Rate	6.0	10.0	8.0	9.0	9.5	5.75	7.0	5.0	7.5	5.0
Preferred Rate for Large Corporations	14.5				13.5	8.9			7.5	5.0
Top Rate	15.5	16.5	17.0	17.0	15.5	16.25	17.0	16.0	15.0	14.0
Sales Tax										
Retail Sales (%)	0.0	7.0	9.0	7.0	8.0	6.5	11.0	11.0	10.0	12.0
Cigarettes (¢/cig.)	7.0	11.0	8.0	8.0	1.7	2.2	3.3	3.3	5.7	10.3
Unleaded Gas (¢/L)	9.0	11.0	15.0	11.5	14.7	15.2	10.7	13.5	12.0	16.5

Source: CIBC Wood Gundy, 1996 Provincial Profiles, September, 1995, p. 10.

References

AFL-CIO (1994). *A Tale of Two Nations: What's Wrong with Right-to-Work.* Washington, DC: American Federation of Labor-Congress of Industrial Organizations.

Alberta Economic Development Authority (1995a). *Background Paper.* Joint Review Committee, Right-to-Work Study (June).

——— (1995b). *Final Report.* Joint Review Committee: Right-to-Work Study (November 30).

Alberta Tax Reform Commission (1994). *A Report to Albertans*, February.

Bennett, James (1994). *A Higher Standard of Living in Right-to-Work States*. Springfield, VA: National Institute for Labour Relations Research.

Chamie, Nicholas (1995). *Why the Jobless Recovery: Youth Abandon Labour Market*. Ottawa: Conference Board of Canada.

Becker, Brian, and Craig Olson (1986). Unionization and Shareholder Interest. *Industrial and Labour Relations Review* 42: 246–61.

Bird, Cerek, and Jackie Davies (1995). *Employment Gazette*. London: Statistical Services Division, Employment Division, July.

Boal, William, and John Pencavel (1994). The Effects of Labour Unions on Employment, Wages, and Days of Operation: Coal Mining in West Virginia. *The Quarterly Journal of Economics* 109, 1 (February): 241–66.

CIBC Wood Gundy (1995). *1996 Provincial Profiles*. September.

Gilder, George (1981). *Wealth and Poverty*. New York: Basic Books.

Gunderson, Morley (1992). Efficient Instruments for Labour Market Regulation. Kingston, Ontario: Queen's University School of Public Policy Studies, 1992.

Gwartney, James, and Richard Stroup (1993). *What Everyone Should Know about Economics and Prosperity*. Vancouver, BC: The Fraser Institute.

Hanson, Charles (1991). *Taming the Trade Unions*. London: Adam Smith Institute.

Hirsh, Barry (1991). Union Coverage and Profitability among U.S. Firms. *Review of Economics and Statistics* 73 (February): 69–77.

Holmes, Thomas (1995). The Effects of State Policies on the Location of Industry: Evidence from State Borders. Staff Report 205, Minneapolis: Federal Reserve Bank of Minneapolis, December, 1995.

Hunsley, Terrance (1993). *Social Policy in the Global Economy*, Kingston, ON: Queen's University School of Public Policy Studies.

Keynes, John Maynard (1964). *The General Theory of Employment, Interest, and Money*. New York: Harcourt, Brace and World.

KPMG Management Consulting (1995). A Comparison of Business Costs in Canada and the United States. Ottawa: Canada, Department of Foreign Affairs and International Trade.

Long, Richard J. (1993). The Effect of Unionization on Employment Growth of Canadian Companies. *Industrial and Labour Relations Review* 46,4 (July): 691–703.

Maki, D., and L.N. Meredith (1986). The Effects of Unions on Profitability: Canadian Evidence. *Relations Industrielles* 41: 55–67.

Mihlar, Fazil (1995). The Economic Benefits of Right-to-Work Legislation: A Submission to the Joint Review Committee on Right-to-Work Study, The Alberta Economic Development Authority. Vancouver: The Fraser Institute, August, 1995.

National Institute for Labour Relations Research (1994a). *Case Study: Idaho Economic Development and Right to Work.*

——— (1994b). *Jobs Up in Right to Work States.*

Organisation for Economic Cooperation and Development (1994). *OECD Jobs Study: Part 1.* Paris: OECD.

Parker, Ron (1995). Aspects of Economic Restructuring in Canada: 1989-1994. *Bank of Canada Review.* Ottawa: Bank of Canada, Summer.

Reason Foundation (1995). Creative Difficulties: Why Some Countries Have More Jobs. *Reason Magazine.* California: Reason Foundation, March.

Smith, Adam (1776/1965). *The Wealth of Nations.* Edwin Cannar (ed.). New York: Random House.

Union Dues (1995). *The Wall Street Journal* (February 21).

Weinstein, Bernard, and Robert Firestine (1978). *Regional Growth and Decline in the United States.* New York: Praeger Publishers.